Youth, Sex, and Government

Eruptions
New Thinking across the Disciplines

Erica McWilliam
General Editor

Vol. 3

PETER LANG
New York • Washington, D.C./Baltimore • Boston • Bern
Frankfurt am Main • Berlin • Brussels • Vienna • Oxford

Gordon Tait

Youth, Sex, and Government

PETER LANG
New York • Washington, D.C./Baltimore • Boston • Bern
Frankfurt am Main • Berlin • Brussels • Vienna • Oxford

Library of Congress Cataloging-in-Publication Data

Tait, Gordon.
Youth, sex, and government / Gordon Tait.
p. cm. — (Eruptions; vol. 3)
Includes bibliographical references and index.
1. Youth—Social conditions. 2. Youth—Sexual behavior.
3. Subculture. I. Title. II. Series.
HQ796.T318   305.235—dc21   98-50413
ISBN 0-8204-4049-3
ISSN 1091-8590

Die Deutsche Bibliothek-CIP-Einheitsaufnahme

Tait, Gordon:
Youth, sex, and government / Gordon Tait.
−New York; Washington, D.C./Baltimore; Boston; Bern;
Frankfurt am Main; Berlin; Brussels; Vienna; Oxford: Lang.
(Eruptions; Vol. 3)
ISBN 0-8204-4049-3

Cover design by Rachael Hearn

© 2000 Peter Lang Publishing, Inc., New York

All rights reserved.
Reprint or reproduction, even partially, in all forms such as microfilm,
xerography, microfiche, microcard, and offset strictly prohibited.

For Belinda, Ella and Buddy

TABLE OF CONTENTS

Acknowledgements	ix
Introduction	1
A New Approach to Youth Research	
Chapter 1	
Beyond Subcultures	13
Subculture Theory: The Dominant Paradigm	15
Criticizing the CCCS Youth Orthodoxy	22
A Marxist Understanding of Power and Ideology	26
Foucault, Truth, and Power	30
Reassessing Hegemony	35
Detotalizing Social History: Some Further Implications	39
Adjusting the Focus on Subcultures	45
From "Youth Homelessness" to "Streetkids"	49
Conclusion	53
Chapter 2	
Youth, Sex, and Government	55
Governmentality	59
Sexuality and the Emergence of Childhood	73
Youth, Sex, and Governmentality	86
Youth, Sex, and the Limits of Government	95
Conclusion	99
Chapter 3	
Governing the "At-Risk" Youth	101
The Rhetoric of Risk and the Problem of Youth	105
Risk and Government	113
The Dissolution of the Subject	116

Increasing the Scope of Government	118
From Practitioner to Administrator	120
An Alternative Interpretation of the Finn Report	122
Conclusion	130

Chapter 4
Sexing the Self   133

The Person, the Individual, and the Self	135
Youth and Self-government	140
Manuals in Self-management	146
Magazines, Sex, and Identity Management	149
Modes of Persuasion	152
Practices of the Self	160
Youth, Sex, and Maturity	166
Conclusion	168

Chapter 5
Governing the Body, Governing the Self   171

Fasting and the Self	172
Cultivating a Self: The Dietetics of Antiquity	174
Historicizing Fasting	179
Women, Piety, and Fasting	180
Setting Limits to Anorexia Nervosa	184
Government and the Invention of Anorexia Nervosa	186
Government, Health, and Diet	188
Medicine, Nosology, Hysteria	191
Shaping Anorexia Nervosa as a Disease Entity	194
Conclusion	199

Conclusion
Youth, Government, and Culture   201

Bibliography   219

Index   241

ACKNOWLEDGMENTS

I would like to express my gratitude to the following for their assistance in the production of this book: Tony Bennett, David Saunders, Ian Hunter, Denise Meredyth, Debbie Huber, Jim McKay, Belinda Carpenter, and the staff in the School of Cultural and Language Studies in Education, at the Queensland University of Technology.

INTRODUCTION

A New Approach to Youth Research

> Pushed by hormones that create exceptional tensions, at the same time facing general adult prohibitions and their own ignorance about how to go about whatever it is that they will evolve to do, a supportive youth subculture provides a variety of social definitions that allow young people to grope their way through many steps, misunderstandings and mistakes that lead to adult sexual life...By its very nature, then, such a subculture provides definitions of 'appropriate' behaviour for both boys and girls. Much of this, of course, is hidden from adults. (Polk, 1993:101)

The reasoning that underpins this quotation is familiar in a number of ways: a degree of biological determinism (pushed by hormones), a hydraulic understanding of sexuality (create exceptional tensions), a binary opposition of youth/adult (facing general adult prohibitions and their own ignorance), a teleological approach to youth (whatever it is that they will evolve to do), and so on. However, the most familiar element within this quotation is the use of a conceptual model that has dominated youth research for much of the last twenty years—subculture theory.

Subculture theory (or *resistance theory* as it has also been called), whether or not applied to the nexus between youth and sex, occupies an important and pervasive position within the field of youth research. Although it seemingly had its heyday in the late 1970s and early 1980s when it first appeared from within the Centre for Contemporary Cultural Studies (CCCS) in Birmingham, England, its domain assumptions concerning the relationship between youth, power, and culture still inform the majority of youth research. This appears to be the case, whether or not that research actually employs subculture theory directly. For example, texts such as Earnest Cashmore's (1984) *No Future: Youth and Society*, and Johanna Wynn and Rob White's (1997) *Rethinking Youth* are not instances of subculture research—and yet they still employ the same youth-as-resistance logic characteristic of the CCCS orthodoxy.

In addition to this, however, a considerable amount of youth research also continues to employ subculture theory directly. In 1993, White edited a book, *Youth Subcultures,* which brings together over twenty contemporary pieces of work on youth cultures. The book addresses and utilizes subculture theory in numerous ways, from theoretical issues pertaining to youth, to investigations into nineteenth-century, ethnic, and female youth subcultures. To stress the breadth and importance of the subject matter, White states that the targets for these analyses vary from "students to the unemployed, from young men to young women, from the homeless to graffiti artists," and that the issue of youth subcultures is approached from a wide variety of disciplinary perspectives, such as psychology, education, sociology, and criminology (White, 1993:Vlll). Certainly, within the book, the term *youth subculture* is employed in a variety of ways—at times almost interchangeably with *youth culture* and *youth experiences.* There is also the suggestion that a knowledge of youth subcultures is one of the most appropriate ways of gaining access to the real life and experiences of contemporary youth, and that acquiring the theoretical tools needed to study youth subcultures provides all the analytical resources required to approach the broader field of youth in general.

Unquestionably, subculture theory has provided the working vocabulary for a large proportion of youth research. Articles in White's book include Mark McFadden's "Youth Subcultures and Resistance" and Linley Walker's "Girls, Schooling and Subcultures of Resistance." Both of these articles examine what is still probably the central theme of "resistance to dominant culture." The emphasis on resistance reflects an underlying social control model of power. This model, which *a priori* understands the exercise of power as being coercive, will be problematized throughout this book. However, resistance is not the only motif that subculture theory has bequeathed to the wider field. Youth research also seems preoccupied with the way in which youth "expresses itself." Style is generally viewed as a form of coded communication, intelligible to initiates, but foreign and even menacing to the wider society. All in all, the subcultural youth represents a troubled stage of life, powerless, neither adult nor child, its many problems a measure of society's dysfunctionality. Most research into youth, whether subcultural or otherwise, has consequently produced results that confirm these initial assumptions.

This book will argue that recent developments in cultural studies have provided the theoretical resources to approach youth in a different way—one that largely avoids these previous characterizations. It is maintained that the work of Michel Foucault, Marcel Mauss, and Nikolas Rose has made it possible to remove youth from its previous theoretical location, and reinstate it upon more constructive terrain. First, the totalizing, stage-of-life approach to youth is replaced with a more focused method of research, one which does not regard youth to be a fact in itself but, rather, an artifact produced at the intersection of specific problematizations, particularly those concerning sex. Second, the style of the self-expressive youth can be reinterpreted as a *habitus*. This is a term taken from Pierre Bourdieu (1977), which refers to a set of historically acquired dispositions. A habitus is formed, in part, via the many techniques of self-government associated with the governmental construction of certain kinds of person. Thus, style is not the way in which the self is expressed, but part of the way in which it is formed. Finally, youth can be removed from the familiar social control model and reconceptualized within an understanding of power as productive, one that does not always appear to focus on youth as victim, but instead largely focuses upon the formation of "youthful" capacities and aptitudes within finite governmental programs. This also permits an avoidance of the characterization of sex evident within the quotation from Kenneth Polk at the beginning of this introduction—that of a society that represses inherent youthful sexuality. This familiar depiction is replaced by an examination of the management of sex. That is, how the sexual conduct of persons, such as youth, is governmentally organized.

In the sense that it is intended here, *the management of sex* is not understood as being restricted to the regulation of sex acts or practices engaged in by young people. Furthermore, it does not simply refer to an analysis of some of the wider imperatives associated with the control of youthful sexuality. After all, as will be discussed in chapter 2, the notion of "sexuality" is an historical construct that developed, in part, out of the governmental distribution of Christian confessional practices, and is itself a notion which covers only part of what is meant by the management of sex. Rather, the scope of this phrase is intended to be much broader, covering the totality of ways in which specific forms of conduct, practices of self-shaping, aspirations and attitudes are directed according to a series of (not necessarily related) regulatory programs—in particular, those pertinent to the category of youth.

For example, whereas formal, school-based sex education has sought to manage the sexual conduct of young people, this is by no means the only site where such government occurs. In chapter 4, the specific role played by young women's magazines in the management of sex is examined. In this section, it is concluded that although these magazines do offer direct guidance in the suitability of particular forms of social/sexual conduct, they also offer advice on the specificities of sexual technique and response. Furthermore, they act as manuals of self-formation within a range of other domains of sexed conduct, such as those involving advice on bodily adornment, information on changes in gendered dress codes, and the shaping of desires and aspirations.

The management of sex also refers to the formation, differentiation, and regulation of specific sexed identities, which occurs, in part, through the accumulation of various practices of self-formation, the aggregation of which forms the basis for the construction of a given persona. Thus, the persona of "teenage girl" would be assembled from raw material composed not only of an array of aspirations, codes of conduct, and forms of self-adornment, but also from a range of bodily practices. For example, in chapter 5 the focus falls upon the dietary practices that have periodically differentiated the habitus of girls from that of boys. In this particular instance, it is argued that for a number of historical reasons, young women have sought to manage themselves as young women by adopting specific ascetic eating practices.

Finally, the management of sex also refers to those mediated governmental programs that target the reformation of particular sexed practices, attitudes, and aspirations, and that address these ends indirectly. That is, the conduct of young people is often organized and administered through programs which are neither immediate nor personal (such as sex education or young women's magazines), but which rather seek to regulate the spaces within which young persons are formed. This occurs, for example, through programs that target the conduct of youth through sites such as the school, the courts, welfare agencies, and the family. As will be demonstrated in chapter 3, certain governmental programs have attempted to modify the vocational aspiration of girls (to suit changed market conditions), and thereby organize the boundaries of acceptable femininity indirectly by recognizing and enlisting the power of parental influence.

Thus, within *Youth, Sex, and Government,* sex is not simply a static social category, one that functions by either dichotomizing the population, or by operating in tandem with its cultural by-product, gender. Neither is sex simply a bodily function—a set of erotic and reproductive responses that can be explained within the broader conceptual framework of sexuality. Instead, this book employs the term *sex* to mean a complex and heterogeneous element of governmentality, an element whose meaning is contingent upon context, and which is the subject of many different regulatory practices.

The book is set out as follows. Chapter 1, *Beyond Subcultures,* commences with the observation that since the mid–1970s, youth research has been dominated by the neo-Marxist logic of subculture theory—exemplified by Stuart Hall and Tony Jefferson's (1976) *Resistance through Rituals* and Dick Hebdige's (1979) *Subculture.* This paradigm explains the formation of youth subcultures as an attempt by postwar British youth to resolve magically the social problems and contradictions created by their material conditions. As refracted versions of the parent culture, subcultures are depicted as conducting a counterhegemonic struggle against the social order. This struggle results in the production of various subcultural styles that constitute a form of discourse. The development of subculture theory constituted a significant theoretical advance, not only in terms of youth research (which was still employing the *delinquency* framework popularized by the Chicago School of the 1920s and 1930s), but also in terms of resolving some of the difficulties associated with existing Marxist theories of ideology.

Recent developments in cultural studies, however, have questioned some of the theoretical underpinnings of subculture theory. This chapter details some reservations over the traditional Marxist understanding of power. These reservations, in turn, undercut the concepts of ideology and hegemony, whose role in subculture theory has been pivotal. Furthermore, the advent of a more historically specific approach to social analysis problematizes two further important elements of subculture theory—the concept of consciousness and even that of culture itself. In light of these criticisms, a theory based upon class/generational consciousness and counterhegemonic struggle against the dominant ideological order is found wanting.

Additional problems for subculture theory are also discussed. First, it employs the broader category of youth (from which specific subcultures are drawn) unproblematically. In doing so, it has a tendency to homogenize what can often be quite distinct historical or social phenomena. Second, there is a normalizing component to the categories that subculture theory produces. That is, once constructed, specific subcultural characters act, in many ways, as modern versions of the juvenile delinquent and the maladjusted schoolchild. This is not a problem in itself, but is at odds with the liberatory aspirations of subculture research. Finally, subculture theory relies upon a number of binary oppositions, such as domination/subordination, resistance/conformity, and expression/regulation. Such dualisms both conceal the complexity of any given field of debate and, as one side of the binary is always privileged over the other, predetermine likely conclusions (Derrida, 1979:1981).

All in all, then, it will be suggested that youth subcultures, along with various other governmental objects and methodologies, are simply categories that chart the space between the normal and the delinquent. Furthermore, it will also be argued in chapter 1 that it is not only subculture research into youth that exhibits these characteristics (and hence flaws). For example, research into the young and homeless also tends to employ a totalizing and normalizing understanding of youth. It is contended that the character, the homeless youth, is actually an artifact produced by different knowledges and mechanisms of information gathering. It is an amalgam of data from numerous problematizations (that is, sites or issues that have generated governmental concern and intervention). The homeless youth is assembled with data gained from the health and welfare agencies, the schools, the criminal justice system, the Australian Bureau of Statistics, voluntary organizations, family services and so forth, and involves many kinds of expertise specifying this person as their object.

Chapter 2, *Youth, Sex, and Governmentality*, argues that the category of youth itself can be understood as an example of the governmental formation of a specific status. This chapter continues a task begun in chapter 1, in that it argues for the model of power based upon the concept of social control to be replaced by one based upon the notion of governmentality. To this end, the central tenets of governmentality itself are explained: how it augments previous forms of rule based upon sovereignty and discipline; how it largely dissolves the familiar state/civil society dichotomy by employing the medium of expertise to govern at a distance; and how specific analyses of the local effects of governmentality can be conducted utilizing the relationship between governmental programs, political rationalities, and governmental technologies.

Because this book is focusing particularly upon youth and sex, the question of sexuality also needs to be addressed. Instead of adopting the dominant essentialist, psy-based position, which locates it as a fundamental drive, chapter 2 examines how sexuality developed from the elaboration of Christian confessional practices, and came to be distributed through the machinery of this new form of government. Using the work of Foucault, it is argued that whereas formerly sexual relations had given rise to a *deployment of alliance*, this was to be augmented/superseded by the *deployment of sexuality*. Sexuality thereby became an ideal apparatus through which a broad range of governmental aspirations could be realized, primarily because it formed an ideal governmental nexus between the domains of the body and the population.

Having described the central theoretical machinery of government and sexuality, it is then appropriate to apply these ideas to the category of youth, which is accomplished first by showing a time when the category did not exist. From there, it can be demonstrated how and when the category of youth began to emerge. This occurred in a number of ways: it emerged as a by-product of the growth of a society characterized by governmentality (producing youth by the governmental processes of individuation/ normalization and the regulation of relations of time), and it emerged out of earlier governmental objects, (such as the child and the adolescent). Most importantly, it emerged at the intersection of numerous social concerns and programs—including those concerning sex.

Chapter 3, *Governing the "At-Risk" Youth,* operates as a case study for some of the ideas outlined in chapter 2. The at-risk youth is described in terms of the governmental construction of a specific category of person. First, it can be demonstrated that the category of the at-risk youth currently underpins a good deal of youth policy. Primarily, the category centers around a range of programs associated with the need for governmental intervention. The at-risk youth appears at the intersection of a variety of programs, such as vocational guidance, youth welfare, family management, and so on. In some ways, the at-risk youth simply replaces older characterizations used in the policing of the young. However, it will be argued that the preventative policies associated with risk permit a broader distribution of preventative action. That is, a greater number of young people can be brought into the field of regulatory strategies. Also, prevention is no longer primarily based upon personal expertise, but rather upon the gathering and collation of statistical knowledge which identifies risks within given populations.

Within a number of recent western educational policy documents (the main one examined here is the Finn Report—an Australian inquiry into credentialing, education, and vocational competency), certain categories of youth are considered to be more at-risk than others of not making the transition to adulthood successfully. Young women (as a type of at-risk youth) are deemed to require explicit intervention in order to increase their chances of obtaining certain types of employment, a requirement brought about by the misplaced vocational aspirations of their parents. It will also be pointed out that by employing a graded and highly specific set of risk categories and responses, the Report puts in place yet another element of an effective network of governmental intelligibility covering the young. Finally, it is argued that educational policy documents such as the Finn Report are significant in the administrative and cultural shaping of the category of youth. This is especially so in the case of the Finn Report, as it attempts to transform the period of transition from the time of school dependence to that of workplace independence, often seen as the time of life that actually demarcates youth as a category.

It is important to note that such governmental programs are only one-half of the matter. That is, there is a complex relationship between these governmental programs, and the ways in which individuals actually form themselves as youths. Chapter 4, *Sexing the Self*, employs the notion of *practices of the self* to better explain this process. It is by specific techniques of self-government, by instilling certain practices of the self within particular target groups, that government operates effectively. Taking as its target the population, and operating through domains such as the school and the family, diverse programs—acting largely at a distance—govern by managing the habits of the population. Significantly, the strategy of managing the habits of the population is investigated in terms of a governmental tendency to enlist the population in reforming itself. Likewise, the sexual practices of youth are the target of this form of intervention.

In order to make these claims, however, it is first necessary to problematize the traditional understanding of the self. Using the work of Mauss, it is argued that the subject is a historically contingent way of bearing personal attributes, in that they are related to an inner principle, or *self*. Specific subject positions are created, such as those associated with youth, through using various techniques of self-formation. Therefore, within programs such as those pertinent to the management of sex, specific technologies of the self structure the practices by which individuals pattern their own conduct. This establishes a particular kind of habitus, in this case, a youthful habitus. By this logic, youth can be understood as the doing of specific types of work on the self.

The final section of chapter 4 examines the manner in which a youthful self is fashioned. By utilizing Foucault's model of the four aspects of the relationship to one's self, it is possible to examine some of the ways in which youth both manages its sex and has its sex managed. This includes, for example, examining how a target population—youth—is persuaded to adhere to acceptable codes of sexual conduct. It also includes a consideration of the specific practices by which one is able to "transform oneself into the ethical subject of one's behaviour" (Foucault, 1987:27). These practices include mental and physical techniques, such as self-interrogation, incitements to confession, and regulation of the body through diet and exercise—all of which are components in the shaping of a youthful habitus. The focus will fall upon gaining an understanding of young women's magazines, a focus not based upon the familiar model of repression and patriarchal domination, but rather upon practical manuals which enrol young women to do specific kinds of work on themselves. In doing so, it is argued that they form an effective link between the governmental imperatives aimed at constructing particular personas (such as, for example, the sexually responsible young woman), and the actual practices whereby these imperatives are operationalized. These manuals do not prevent young women from learning to project a unique self, they constitute a significant source of practices and techniques through which particular types of self are shaped.

Chapter 5, *Governing the Body, Governing the Self* continues the analysis of self-government as it investigates the severe fasting practices most commonly found among young women. Currently, these practices are almost exclusively rationalized in terms of the condition anorexia nervosa. The objective validity of this condition is accepted fairly unquestioningly by the majority of the literature. Furthermore, this literature is built upon three domain assumptions, all of which will be challenged in this chapter.

The first is that the origins of anorexia nervosa can be traced to the struggles/contradictions between the authentic, inner self and the expectations of the wider culture, an explanatory mechanism that will have already been rejected earlier in the book. By examining the fasting practices of certain castes in ancient Greece, it will be contended that dietary asceticism constituted an important part of the means by which an acceptable *self* was constructed. The dietary restrictions that confirmed a life "lived rightly," were seen not only as being good advice on health, but also part of an important moral code. Since the self is not an inner essence, but is, rather, the consequence of the development of a particular habitus, then sex—and age-specific practices (such as severe fasting) act as mechanisms of social differentiation. Furthermore, having once been established as a model for human conduct, ascetic fasting then periodically resurfaced, as it has among some contemporary young women (although attached to very different belief systems).

The second assumption within anorexia nervosa research is that it is a new phenomenon, a set of practices that are, in some way, caused by contemporary definitions of femininity. In addition, this dietary response is best explained in terms of either conformity with, or resistance to, those definitions. The historical evidence, however, would suggest that severe fasting practices were also broadly distributed among pious Christian women from the thirteenth to the fifteenth centuries, where fasting was regarded as an important component of a female holiness that took food as its central theme. Within this context, severe fasting was not a response to existing images of femininity (either for or against); rather, it was part of a set of practices that were intended to shape the self in *imitatio Christi*. This conclusion supports the original contention that such fasting is part of the formation of a particular habitus (in this case, one focused around the notion of piety), not a transhistoric struggle with the inner self.

The final assumption evidenced within anorexia nervosa research is a triumphalist understanding of its discovery and explanation. Considered as an objective fact that exists in nature, science eventually deciphered severe fasting practices, interpreting them as a psychological problem common to adolescent girls. However, a more historicized approach leads to a different set of conclusions. By the eighteenth century, there was increasing governmental regulation of the population, which included a concern over health and diet. Furthermore, scientific knowledges were rapidly forming the basis for new canons of judgment. Consequently, women's ascetic dietary practices were re-interpreted in terms of a pathological illness that eventually emerged, after several boundary struggles, as the modern disease entity anorexia nervosa. This is not to suggest that anorexia nervosa is, therefore, a falsehood—simply that when new canons of judgment are employed, new realities come into being.

The book concludes by reiterating that the central intention has not been to suggest that the majority of existing youth research is of no value. Far from it. A great deal of interesting, relevant, and transformative work has been done in the field. This book, however, will offer an approach to the study of youth that has two central advantages over previous models.

First, by employing the notion of governmentality, this book provides a theoretical framework that can account for the historical specificity of formations of youth. Rather than regarding youth as an inevitable and transitory state of life, it will be demonstrated that the category of youth has emerged out of existing concerns over governmental objects such as the child, the juvenile delinquent, and the adolescent. Moreover, rather than depicting youth as a social group that is overly vulnerable to the global, coercive, and uncaring effects of state power, it will be argued that a more productive approach involves addressing the manner in which youth is shaped and administered, through the medium of expertise, within semi-autonomous domains such as the family and the school. It is within such domains that the category of youth is targeted, regulated, and reformed.

Second, by employing the notion of practices of the self, this book provides a theoretical framework that can account for the piecemeal construction of the youthful self. That is, it can explain and illustrate the manner in which formations of youth are recruited into different programs and practices of self-reformation. Just as the category of youth is best analyzed as a set of specific governmental artifacts (which should be addressed case by case), so, too, the youthful self is shaped by the application of various practices, produced in diverse contexts, and operating via an interrelated vocabulary of incitements.

The chapter concludes by returning to the subject that began the book, asking the question: If subcultures are not counterhegemonic responses to the dominant order, then how might they be understood and investigated by researchers, not only within youth studies, but also within the broader fields of cultural theory and cultural policy studies? The answer to these questions, in part using a worked example of the Gothics, provides the template for future research into the nature of the relationship between youth, government, and culture.

CHAPTER 1

Beyond Subcultures

This chapter argues that since the mid-1970s, academic research into youth, both in Australia and elsewhere, has been dominated by the subculture theory associated with the Centre for Contemporary Cultural Studies (CCCS) in Birmingham, England. This theoretical model contends that youth subcultures are formed as counterhegemonic attempts to resolve magically the social contradictions created by their material conditions. The most significant component of this resolution is the notion of "style as discourse," whereby members of youth subcultures communicate their ritual resistance to the wider community through characteristic codes of dress and conduct. It is proposed here that such an approach has a number of inherent problems. The first set of difficulties involves its understanding of power and its reliance upon notions such as hegemony, consciousness, and culture. The second set of problems is associated with its totalizing use of the notion of youth, the normalizing nature of the subcultural categories it produces, and the reliance upon conventional dichotomies, such as domination/ subordination and resistance/conformity. It will be argued that youth subcultures are simply social categories that chart the space between the normal and the delinquent. It will also be argued that other youth research—such as much of the work on homelessness—while perhaps not adopting subculture theory directly, shares many of its presuppositions, and, hence, its flaws. Consequently, this chapter will propose a theoretical model that does not accept youth as a self-evident signifier, or stage of life. Rather, it will focus upon the specific governmental programs that seek to administer a constructed population: youth.

An article entitled "The times they still are a' changing," by Carey Denholm, Tim Horniblow, and Rosemary Smalley (1992) delineates a number of contemporary youth subcultures—such as Bogans, Nerds, Skeggs, Jocks, and Gothics. It groups their styles of dress, musical tastes, language, and forms of behavior, and suggests that it is important for youth workers/teachers to be up-to-date in their knowledge of these kinds of social categories. In a similar style of study, Linda Forrester (1993) describes the characteristics of four subcultures—the Skaters, the Street Machiners, the Graffiti Artists, and the Street Dancers—arguing that these forms of youth expression represent a reaction against the dominant aesthetic cultural forms. In opposition to the "hegemonic bloc," young people "win space" for themselves. That is, subcultures are deemed to provide members with "agency" and a voice within a culture which otherwise leaves them "bewildered and isolated" (Forrester, 1993:111).

The theoretical framework employed in these two articles on youth is a standard one. Indeed, since the mid-1970s, seemingly the most plausible and pervasive method of attempting to understand ensuing waves of visible "problem youth," has been associated with the subculture theory of the Centre for Contemporary Cultural Studies in Birmingham, England (CCCS). Beginning with Phil Cohen's (1972) seminal "Subcultural Conflict and Working-Class Community," research employing this theoretical model burgeoned as the decade progressed. Cohen's paper was followed by work such as John Clarke's (1975) "The Skinheads and the Magical Recovery of Working-Class Community," Stuart Hall and Tony Jefferson's (1976) *Resistance through Rituals*, Geoff Mungham and Geoff Pearson's (1976) *Working-Class Youth Culture*, Paul Willis's (1977; 1978) *Learning to Labour* and *Profane Culture*, Ernest Cashmore's (1979) *Rastaman*, Dick Hebdige's (1979) *Subculture: The Meaning of Style*, to name but a few.

This style of research is by no means limited to the United Kingdom. There now exists a wealth of North American sociological and educational work that employs subculture theory (Brake, 1985; King, 1988; Hamm and Chambliss, 1994; Locher, 1995; Arnett, 1996; Young and Craig, 1997). Likewise, subculture theory has been an influential research paradigm in Australia and New Zealand (Braithwaite and Barker, 1978; Pearson, 1979; Kessler, Ashenden, Connell and Dowsett, 1982; Stratton, 1985; Wilson and Arnold, 1986; Walker, 1988; White, 1993).

Even the most cursory scan of contemporary youth research exposes the domination of subculture theory. Consequently, recurrent moral panics over certain kinds of youth conduct have resulted in some degree of causation and interpretation being found within the well-grounded tenets of the tried-and-tested subculture paradigm. Just as Mods and Skinheads were once understood in prescribed ethnographic terms, so a new generation of young people has found itself distilled into subcultures.

Subculture Theory: The Dominant Paradigm

Through the logic of subculture theory, large numbers of young people are positioned within discrete categories, seemingly with specific codes of behavior and ways of relating to the outside world. The conceptual framework that underpins this position, arguably best represented by texts such as Hall and Jefferson's (1976) *Resistance through Rituals* and Hebdige's (1979) *Subculture: The Meaning of Style*, consists of three main components: counterhegemonic struggle, generational consciousness, and style as discourse. These factors will be discussed in turn.

First, subculture theory employs a neo-Marxist explanation of the complex relationship that exists between dominant and subordinate social classes. The subordinate classes are seen as constantly striving for mechanisms by which to pierce their ideological oppression and thereby create spaces within which to realize themselves. These processes are then reflected at the level of culture:

> Just as different groups and classes are unequally ranked, in terms of their productive relations, wealth and power, so cultures are differentially ranked...The dominant culture represents itself as the culture. It tries to define and contain all other cultures within its exclusive range...Other cultural configurations will not only be subordinate to this dominant order; they will enter into struggle with it, seek to modify, negotiate, resist or even overthrow its reign—its hegemony. (Clarke, Hall, Jefferson, and Roberts, 1976:11–12)

Thus, youth subcultures are primarily located within the realm of counterhegemonic struggle. The writers of the CCCS argue that the twentieth century offers an illustration of the fluctuating success of bourgeois hegemony within the United Kingdom. They propose that the defeat of the labor movements of the 1920s led to the total domination of the working classes in the 1930s. This domination, however, was by no means hegemonic, as the social order was maintained more by direct coercion than by the successful recruitment of working-class consent, which, according to Gramsci, is the central prerequisite for the establishment of an effective bourgeois hegemony. After the watershed period of World War II and the ensuing social reconstruction, the 1950s saw the rise of popular ideologies centered around notions of increased affluence, consensus, and embourgeoisement. The working classes were deemed to have accepted their lot and joined the clamor to become middle class. Coercion was no longer required. By the late 1960s and 1970s, however, the promised affluence had failed to materialize, which caused a crisis for the hegemony of the ruling classes. While they still retained power, their authority was no longer unquestioningly accepted by the working classes (Clarke, Hall, Jefferson, and Roberts, 1976:17–25).

It was as a symptom of this collapse of hegemonic control that working-class youth found space for itself in the form of subcultures. These offered a means of ritualized resistance to the social order. Because they now acknowledged the relative permanence of their position at the bottom of the capitalist hierarchy, and as they lacked the means to effect any real change, the solution many chose was the "magical" resolution of their problems within youth subcultures (Clarke, Hall, Jefferson, and Roberts, 1976:30–33). In this manner, they conducted a counterhegemonic struggle (albeit indirectly), against the social order, dominant ideology, and the ruling classes. That is, while the formation of youth subcultures posed no real threat to existing power relations, they constituted a form of symbolic resistance that enabled their members to win cultural space for themselves.

The relationship between social class, symbolic resistance, and the winning of cultural space is exemplified in Tony Jefferson's (1976) analysis of the Teddy Boy subculture of the 1950s, entitled "Cultural Responses of the Teds." He argues that with its mock upper-class uniform of drape coats, crepe-soled shoes, and bootlace ties, and its violent reputation, the Teddy Boy subculture was a coded working-class response to declining status and encroachments upon its territory. This encroachment involved both that actual loss of land to post-war developers, and also "the less tangible expropriation of the culture attached to the land, i.e., the kinship networks and the 'articulations of communal space'" (Jefferson, 1976:81). Thus, the Teddy Boy subculture was a form of symbolic resistance through which working-class male youth won back some of this lost cultural space.

For those researchers still utilizing youth subculture theory, the nexus between social class, cultural space, and resistance is still deemed to be axiomatic. In the article by Denholm, Horniblow, and Smalley (1992:18), there is made an explicit link between the various subcultures and unemployment, poverty, and homelessness. It also grades different subcultures on the degree to which they either conform, or do not conform, to social codes and expectations. While some are categorized as obedient and respectful, this is contrasted with other groupings who are bitterly opposed to those who represent authority (Denholm, Horniblow, and Smalley, 1992:20). Likewise, Forrester (1993:112) argues that one of the major objectives of subcultures is for disadvantaged youth to win space within the cultural environment.

It should be mentioned that the CCCS does not restrict its analysis simply to working-class youth subcultures. In *Resistance through Rituals*, Clarke, Hall, Jefferson, and Roberts (1976:60) make a clear distinction between working-class and middle-class groups. In contrast to the working-class subcultures, such as the Skinheads and Teddy Boys, the middle-class response has generally been in the form of countercultures, as in the case of the Hippies. These are more diffuse, less group-centered, and more individualized than their working-class equivalents. It is also suggested that middle-class cultures are more overtly "ideological or political," in that they "articulate their opposition to dominant values" in a more overt way (Clarke, Hall, Jefferson, and Roberts, 1976:61). Irrespective of these (and other) differences, middle-class youth cultures are still deemed to remain within the realm of counterhegemonic struggle, and, hence, the same explanatory framework is deployed.

The CCCS, however, offers a more complex interpretation of youth subcultures than their being merely the ritualized manifestation of counterhegemonic struggle. The second tenet of subculture theory, the notion of generational consciousness, is also woven into the theoretical framework.

> We begin to see how forces, working right across a class, but differently experienced as between the generations, may form the basis for generating an outlook—a kind of consciousness—specific to age position: a generational consciousness. (Clarke, Hall, Jefferson, and Roberts, 1976: 51)

This second element is deemed to be just as important as, and, indeed, is regarded as inseparable from, class consciousness in the formation of youth subcultures. As Graham Murdock and Robin McCron (1976:24) note in "Youth and Class: The Career of Confusion," the writers of the CCCS became centrally concerned with "examining the relations between class and age and more particularly the way in which age acts as a mediation of class." The CCCS position argues that, from the 1950s onwards, youth as a group started to perceive itself to be intrinsically different from the parent generation. Consequently, youth became both a recognizable category and an available market. Although young people experienced their class position in a different manner from their parents, however, they still shared the same fundamental material conditions:

> Though the response was different according to age, position in the generational cycle and experience, the basic material and social situation which confronted them—the class problematic—was the same, for older men and women, for young workers and their families, and for working class teenagers. (Clarke, Hall, Jefferson, and Roberts, 1976:31–32)

Consequently, the life-styles of the subculture members must then be refracted or mediated versions of the parent culture. That is, while sharing the same essential material conditions, young people often come into contact with different sets of institutions than do their parents. Furthermore, the institutions that they do have in common are experienced differently. The writers of the CCCS suggest that this generational consciousness is best understood in relation to the life areas of education, work, and leisure. Each of these areas has a tendency to reinforce notions of the relative autonomy of youth as a category.

Phil Cohen (1972) uses the logic of a mediated parental culture to present an explanation for the actual advent of youth subcultures. His study of the East-End of London charts the fragmentation of the working class and the destruction of old family patterns, values, and habitats. He argues that the working classes became dichotomized with one part being elevated towards the status of lower middle-class (embourgeoisement) and the other descending toward the lumpen. According to this logic, the Mod stemmed from the upwardly mobile fragment of the working classes. They had smart clothes and haircuts, and every weekend magically became something that they were incapable of being during the week. Whereas the reality consisted of dull jobs with minimal prospects, the imaginary solution conjured up a world of excitement and affluence. In "The Meaning of Mod," Hebdige (1976:90) supports Cohen's position, contending that Mods were "existing in a ghost world of gangsterism, luxurious clubs and beautiful women, even if the reality only amounted to a draughty Parker anorak, a beaten up Vespa and fish and chips out of a greasy bag."

Conversely, according to Cohen's dichotomous model, the Skinhead (like the Teddy Boy of a decade before) originated from within the downwardly mobile section of the working classes, and consequently centered around the reification and accentuation of traditional working-class culture. In "The Skinheads and the Magical Recovery of Community," John Clarke (1975) also locates the origin of the Skinhead within lower working-class youth. He argues that, cut off from any possibility of upward social mobility, and in the broader context of worsening economic circumstances, some elements within lower working-class youth sought to magically re-create the sense of community lost since World War II by selectively appropriating and exaggerating elements of the parent culture, such as the notions of territoriality and machismo.

Again, the Denholm, Horniblow, and Smalley (1992:19) article also stresses the centrality of parents when attempting to explain subcultural differences. These writers even make the point that subcultural affiliation itself may indeed be dependent upon the "degree of autonomy" that the youths experience vis-a-vis their parents. The Forrester (1993:108) article is also grounded within Cohen's logic of a mediated version of parent cultures, albeit after expressing some reservations.

The final component of the CCCS position revolves around the notion of subcultural style. Each subculture has characteristic modes of behavior, values, and musical tastes, and each has its own vocabulary, not only of speech but, rather, of a discourse constructed from various cultural objects that are appropriated and endowed with new meaning. Working-class youth is viewed as extending the parental struggle with the dominant institutions, utilizing some responses, altering others, and creating some of its own (Clarke, Hall, Jefferson, and Roberts, 1976:52–57). As previously mentioned, it is argued that the Skinheads' notions of territoriality and machismo have their corollaries within the wider, working-class culture of their parents. Their choice of uniform is itself deemed to be an exaggerated adaptation of adult dress codes, thus functioning as a statement about being working class.

In *Subculture: The Meaning of Style*, Hebdige (1979) argues that different styles are forms of code by which subcultures communicate with the "straight" world. Objects are taken into the stylistic vocabulary and endowed with new and subversive meanings. Hebdige (1979:105) quotes Umberto Eco in calling this practice "semiotic guerilla warfare." Claude Levi-Strauss's concept of *bricolage* is also pivotal to Hebdige's understanding of style. Within bricolage, significant objects are moved from their original contexts and relocated. This relocation produces new meaning and, consequently new forms of discourse. According to Hebdige (1979:104), subcultural "bricoleurs," such as Mods (for example), took symbols such as the Union Jack and the motor scooter and subverted their "original, straight meanings":

> More subtly, the conventional insignia of the business world—the suit, collar and tie, short hair, etc.—were stripped of their original connotations—efficiency, ambition, compliance with authority—and transformed into 'empty' fetishes, objects to be desired, fondled and valued in their own right. (Hebdige, 1979:104–105)

For Denholm, Horniblow, and Smalley (1992), style is undoubtedly the most important axis of subculture theory. The vast majority of the article is taken up in the process of differentiating between the various groups, according to factors such as their appearance, language, music and key activities and behavior. These factors are almost identical to those identified in Hall and Jefferson's (1976) *Resistance through Rituals* and in Hebdige's (1979) *Subculture,* a decade and a half earlier. Indeed, Forrester (1993:111) borrows directly from Hebdige when she states that, "young people create their style through the process of bricolage, taking symbols and images with a certain meaning from a variety of sources and applying new meaning in the construction of style."

In summary then, the CCCS approach to studying youth is built upon the view that youth subcultures are formed as mediated versions of the wider working-class parent culture. Within this model, youth subcultures are deemed to be counterhegemonic groupings that constitute attempts by post-war youth to resolve magically the social problems and contradictions created by their material conditions. The most visible element of this resolution is the concept of *style as discourse*, whereby the various subcultures assemble a characteristic vocabulary of symbols (primarily involving dress, musical tastes, and codes of conduct) through which they seek to communicate with the wider community.

In comparison with existing frameworks for studying youth, the advent of subculture theory constituted a significant conceptual advance. Prior to its appearance, youth research had largely been dominated by the delinquency studies of the Chicago School, originally stemming from the 1920s and 1930s. Seminal work such as Clifford Shaw and Henry McKay's (1929) *Juvenile Delinquency and Urban Areas* and Fredrick Thrasher's (1927) *The Gang,* argued that youth problems had their genesis in social disorganization—deteriorating neighborhoods, shifting populations, and the mobility and disorganization of the slum (Thrasher, 1927:20). This style of delinquency-based youth research was later augmented and updated by studies such as Albert Cohen's (1955) *Delinquent Boys: The Culture of the Gang* and Richard Cloward and Lloyd Ohlin's (1960) *Delinquency and Opportunity: A Theory of Delinquent Gangs.* These latter texts predominantly emphasized status frustration in their explanations of delinquency. That is, delinquency has its origins in the disparity or strain between culturally induced aspirations and practical opportunities.

Retrospect suggests that this conceptual framework had numerous inherent problems. First, it was premised upon the popular belief within 1950s American sociology that their country was characterized by a basic consensus of values. As such, the strain that caused delinquency could be measured against a seemingly self-evident and widely accepted cultural scale. This underlying assumption, however, was soon challenged by research contending that:

> Regional and subcultural groups were characterised by different value systems rather than by an allegiance to some hypothesised set of unified values. If this was the case then it was futile trying to account for deviancy simply as behaviour that

did not conform to an assumed, but non-existent, cultural norm. (Muncie, 1984:53)

Second, the boundary between the delinquent and more mainstream youth was shown to be more tenuous than initially imagined. David Matza and Gresham Sykes (1961) demonstrated that not only did most delinquents drift in and out of delinquent behavior, but also that the majority of their values were identical to those espoused by the wider community. Finally, and most important, British research found little evidence of the status frustration that was so pivotal to the American literature (Downes, 1966). Consequently, any convincing explanation for atypical conduct among British youth would need to find an alternative conceptual framework.

In comparison with these existing delinquency models, the appearance in the mid-1970s of the subculture theory of the CCCS provided a sophisticated and convincing alternative approach to youth research. Not only did it offer a theoretical strategy for studying youth that did not stem from presuppositions concerning delinquency, but it also placed youth research at the center of cultural debate. It did so because the theoretical position adopted by the CCCS on youth subculture challenged several of the central precepts associated with existing Marxist theories of ideology. Although it will be argued in this chapter that, ultimately, underlying difficulties deriving from the Marxist problematic still remain, the work of the CCCS proved to be a significant and influential theoretical advance.

Criticizing the CCCS Youth Orthodoxy

As one of the central theoretical tools for addressing youth, the CCCS subculture orthodoxy has been the focus of considerable criticism as well as praise. Several of its more obvious theoretical flaws have already been well documented. For example, in a paper entitled *Defending Ski Jumpers: A Critique of Theories of Youth Subcultures*, Gary Clarke (1982:10) points out that the writers of the CCCS often glamorize the subcultures concerned. This is especially the case for Hebdige who frequently contrasts these groups with straights. While Clarke does not suggest that the spectacular minority should remain unstudied, he perceives a veiled inference that the majority of ordinary kids are too drab and passive to warrant investigation. Hebdige is not alone in his glamorization of youth subcultures. Similar criticisms (Walker, 1985:1986) have also been levelled at Paul Willis's (1977) classic *Learning to Labour*. Angela McRobbie (1980:39) places this in historical context by arguing that some academics, disappointed at the apparent failure of all forms of counterhegemonic resistance (such as student radicalism, trade unionism, the passivity of the working classes) looked desperately for other groups to carry the banner. In doing so, they found all the prerequisite characteristics in youth subcultures. Hence, Mods became quasi-revolutionaries, and Skinheads became the last line of resistance against post-war anomie. McRobbie (1980:47–49) also suggests that the CCCS position seems to propose that the only relevant variables in the subcultural equation are those of class and age, to the neglect of factors such as gender and race/ethnicity. Although this may have been an initial limitation, however, subsequent studies suggest it was not an inherent flaw of the method.

A further criticism involves the CCCS use of the notion of culture. The CCCS regard culture, in its widest terms, as being the practice that gives group life its meaning. Moreover, culture is the very way in which specific groups deal with the raw material of their social and material existence: "A social individual, born into a particular set of institutions and relations, is at the same moment born into a peculiar configuration of meanings, which give her access to and locate her within a 'culture'" (Clarke, Hall, Jefferson, and Roberts, 1976:11). The CCCS note that each social group manages its assigned institutions and relations in specific ways. Indeed, it is this very management that actually constitutes cultural reproduction and transmission. However, such a management only takes place within a predetermined field of possibilities and constraints (Clarke, Hall, Jefferson, and Roberts, 1976:11). This logic is borrowed directly from Marx, as evidenced in his often-quoted aphorism: "Men make their own history, but they do not make it just as they please; they do not make it under circumstances chosen by themselves, but under circumstances directly encountered, given and transmitted from the past" (Marx, 1951:225).

Fixed within a similar logic, youth subcultures can be regarded as a strategy, a coded response, whereby predominantly working-class young men also negotiate the material conditions of their collective existences. Subculture members are attempting to resolve (at an imaginary level) some of the contradictions they are unable to resolve at the concrete material level—and the manner of this resolution takes different forms. It follows then that the dissimilarities in meanings and responses of diverse (sub)cultural configurations are ultimately tied to differing material conditions. However, cultural configurations do not simply differ according to material conditions, they are ranked along the scale of cultural power (Clarke, Hall, Jefferson, and Roberts, 1976:11). This proposition is also borrowed directly from Marx who, in *The German Ideology*, contends that the class that controls the means of material production also produces the ruling ideas and the ruling culture (Marx, 1964:67). That is, because groups are understood and ranked with regard to their productive relations, these resulting cultures will also be ranked in relation to one another. Therefore, working-class culture is necessarily deemed to be subordinate, as it is the product of subordinate productive relations.

As Rosalind Coward (1977:81) points out in "Class, Culture and the Social Formation," this analysis is fundamentally hinged on the inseparable, homologous relationship between economic class and the ensuing production of culture. The authority of one culture over subordinate ones is most frequently achieved through consent (as opposed to direct coercion), which is explained by the CCCS through the Althusserian notion of state apparatuses becoming the basis for hegemonic ideology. Coward goes on to argue that for this view of subcultures to be supported, the CCCS position requires the following underlying presuppositions:

> The intentionality of the structure in dominance to reproduce itself; the assumption that the structure in dominance is preserved through ideology...the understanding of culture as different for different classes, a corollary of its definition as the objective expression of material interests; the political, ideological and "cultural" formations are conceived of as homologous with economic categories of class. (Coward, 1977:84)

Furthermore, Coward argues that by employing a model that ultimately regards the social formation as an expression of the division between capital and labor, an understanding of ideology is derived that is causally bound to economic interests. That is, the nexus between capital and labor is revealed in the form of economic classes that are then reflected in terms of culture and ideology. As she points out:

> The theory remains fundamentally committed to a conception of economic determination, with the economic understood, not as production and exchange relations, but as relations between monolithic classes, which are knowable through the object "consciousness." (Coward, 1977:90)

She is also arguing here that, despite what initially appears to be this relatively straightforward and unproblematic CCCS rendering of the "dependency of cultural activity upon a materialist account of the social formation," the CCCS position actually also relies heavily on an underlying idealism, in that it presupposes the existence of a free human consciousness endowed, *a priori*, with the capacity to realize meaning. Additionally, this idea is woven into an idealist version of history that is understood as progress—the "unfolding of some inner principle however, by which the working classes eventually free themselves from ideology (Coward, 1977:86).

Irrespective of the disparate nature of these criticisms, they share several domain assumptions which, generally speaking, demarcate them as being criticisms from within. That is, they detail problems regarding the specificities of the CCCS application of Marxism to youth issues, rather than challenge Marxist cultural theory itself. Even the Coward article, which illustrates some rudimentary problems with subculture theory, does not reject Marxism outright. Rather, it simply criticizes what it considers to be idealist and reductionist tendencies within contemporary Marxist work. In contrast with such criticisms from within, the remainder of this chapter will offer a more comprehensive and fundamental criticism of Marxism (and, hence, subculture theory)—one that problematizes some of the foundations upon which Marxism is actually built.

Despite this array of potential opening themes, probably the most useful place to start is with a disagreement over the Marxist notions of power and ideology. Consequently, the criticism will begin with an outline of the main tenets of the Marxist position on these two issues. First, it will be demonstrated that subculture theory depends upon a very specific understanding of power, and concomitantly, ideology. Thereafter will follow an outline of an alternative approach to these issues, which problematizes the power/ideology mechanism upon which subculture theory clearly depends. Finally, once this initial theoretical groundwork is laid, the CCCS's use of the notions of hegemony, consciousness, and culture will then be criticized more fully.

A Marxist Understanding of Power and Ideology

In the *History of Sexuality: An Introduction*, Michel Foucault (1976:87–89) characterizes and critiques what he refers to as the "juridico-discursive" theory of power, suggesting that it imbues not only Marxist thought but a great deal of social and political philosophy from the sixteenth century onward. While he suggests that such an understanding of the exercise of power might have been appropriate during the sixteenth century, from the eighteenth century onward, there evolved a new form of rule based around the notion of governmentality (the central focus of chapter 2). However, he argues, many forms of social analysis (including Marxism) still operate with this outmoded model of power; consequently, they misunderstand contemporary forms of rule.

The juridico-discursive model of power has six central characteristics. First, power is viewed as fundamentally coercive. As such, the exercise of power is normally regarded as being synonymous with repression, so that to be subject to this exercise is *a priori* undesirable. Power is imposed upon pregiven class subjects—in the case of Marxism, the working-classes. Second, power emanates from a single source, be it a sovereign or, in the case of Marxism, the ruling classes. It also operates to promote the interests of those classes. Power is, therefore, something that is possessed and coveted, like an object, which others will try to appropriate. Consequently, there is a powerful struggle to retain their power in the face of repeated challenges from the powerless. Third, power is a totalizing concept. It is regarded as global in its effects, operating throughout the entire social body. Indeed, in *The Communist Manifesto*, Marx and Engels (1955) argue that the entire history of mankind can be written in terms of the struggle for power between two antagonistic classes. Through this logic, phenomena as diverse as mass education, literature and the arts, the media, the law, international relations, agricultural policy, and so on, are all founded upon this same underlying assumption regarding the global and transhistoric exercise of power. Fourth, all power is understood as essentially the same, regardless of the manner in which it is exercised. It is not differentiated by its effects, location, or point of origin. The power that slave owners exercised over their slaves is deemed to be the same power that sovereigns exercise over their subjects, that the ruling class exercises over the working class, or even that teachers exercise over their pupils. Fifth, power is zero-sum. That is, power is considered to be a finite commodity—hence, a prerequisite for gaining power is that it must be taken from somewhere. As the working classes acquire more power through various forms of struggle, this, in turn, reduces the power of the dominant classes. Finally, the juridico-discursive model has generally anticipated a historical moment heralding the termination of the exercise of power. As Marx himself stated:

> When, in the course of development, class distinctions have disappeared and all production has been concentrated in the hands of a vast association of the whole nation, the public power will lose its political character. Political power, properly so called, is merely the organised power of one class for oppressing another. (Marx and Engels, 1955:29)

To summarize these *juridico-discursive* characteristics: power is a totalized, global generality that operates similarly across the entire social body. Such power is possessed by the ruling classes and is used to coerce and subjugate those of lower social ranking who, in turn, attempt to gain power for themselves at the expense of the ruling classes.

Whether or not Foucault's position on the shift from juridico-discursive to governmental forms of the exercise of power is adopted in its entirety, the main tenets of the juridico-discursive model and its view of power are clearly recognizable within the logic of youth subculture theory. The most significant aspect of this theory is that youth subcultures are a response to a hegemony imposed upon them from above. They are a display of resistance against the repressive power of the dominant order, just as working-class culture itself is a form of negotiated resistance to the exercise of ruling-class/state power. Indeed, dominant culture and youth subcultures "stand in opposition to one another, in relations of domination and subordination, along the scale of cultural power" (Clarke, Hall, Jefferson, and Roberts, 1976:11). Furthermore, by engaging in counterhegemonic struggle, youth subcultures are attempting to empower themselves at the expense of both the ruling-classes and working-class parental culture. In response, the ruling classes try to restrict damage to the success or legitimacy of their hegemony and, as such, prevent a loss of power. This is stated explicitly in *Resistance through Rituals*: "the struggle between classes over material and social life thus always assumes the forms of a continuous struggle over the distribution of cultural power" (Clarke, Hall, Jefferson, and Roberts, 1976:12). A final point of commonality between subculture theory and the juridico-discursive model of power involves the uniform nature of power. The writers of the CCCS do not distinguish between the power applied to different elements of the working classes. Nor do they distinguish between the various modalities of power exercised over youth subcultures by the media, the police, the schools, welfare agencies or business. Essentially these are all simply deemed to be manifestations of the same power that the ruling-class wields over subordinate classes, which constitute the generalized domain of class struggle. Hence, the social context of working-class youth subcultures, "working-class youth unemployment, educational disadvantage, compulsory miseducation, dead-end jobs, the routinization and specialization of labour, low pay and the loss of skills" (Clarke, Hall, Jefferson, and Roberts, 1976:47)—are all considered to be components of the same fundamental power relation.

Marxists, however, do not consider that such power is simply applied, directly and unproblematically, to the subordinate classes. Instead, the mediating notion of ideology is employed. In this manner, they are able to explain how the domination and contradictions inherent in capitalism remain largely unchallenged. Essentially, the traditional Marxist position argued that ideology acts to mask the sectional interests of those groups holding power. The consent of the subordinate classes is most effectively recruited when they accept and internalize the very beliefs that are implicated in the shaping of that subordination. These beliefs—ideologies—are actually a distortion of the truth. By internalizing these ideologies, the working classes are unable to perceive their true social circumstances, thereby living in a state of false consciousness.

It was as an attempt to think beyond this reductionist and totalizing conception of ideology that the CCCS employed the work of Louis Althusser in the construction of subculture theory. Althusser (1971) rejects the dominant Marxist position (taken primarily from *The German Ideology*) that ideology is the false representation of the real. Instead, he postulates the existence of an imaginary relation between human beings and their material conditions, which differs from their real relations to the conditions of their existence. That is, human subjects misrecognize the circumstances of their own formation as subjects. Consequently, the most fundamental forms of their experience are constituted through imaginary relations. In Althusser's (1971:155) influential "Ideology and Ideological State Apparatuses" from *Lenin and Philosophy and Other Essays*, he states that "What is represented in ideology is therefore not the system of the real relations which govern the existence of individuals, but the imaginary relation of those individuals to the real relations in which they live." The writers of the CCCS adopt this position directly, quoting Althusser's *For Marx*:

> In ideology, men do indeed express, not the real relation between them and their conditions of existence, but *the way* they live the relation between them and the conditions of their existence; this presupposes both a real and an *"imaginary", "lived"* relation. Ideology then, is...the (over determined) unity of the real relation and the imaginary relation...that expresses a will...a hope, or a nostalgia, rather than describing a reality. (Althusser in Clarke, Hall, Jefferson, and Roberts, 1976:48)

It is these assertions that provide the theoretical nucleus of subculture theory. By providing a strategy through which young people can negotiate the contradictions of their collective experiences, subcultures are deemed to possess a prominent ideological dimension. That is, subcultures "attempt to resolve by means of an 'imaginary relation'—i.e. ideologically—the real relations they cannot otherwise transcend" (Clarke, Hall, Jefferson, and Roberts, 1976:33). Hebdige (1976) supports this contention in the article "Reggae, Rastas and Rudies." He argues that Rastafarians (members of a black subculture characterized by reggae music, dreadlock hairstyles and the use of cannabis, who believe in an eventual return to their spiritual home in Ethiopia) magically resolve the problems associated with their exile by the adoption of a subcultural style based upon the romanticizing of their lost world in Africa, and the rejection and vilification of white culture (Hebdige, 1976:138). Similarly, the Rudies or Rude Boys (a predominantly black subculture of street hustlers, characterized by ska music, smart suits, and pork pie hats) can magically transcend their working-class circumstances by adopting, like the Mod, the trappings of a status beyond their reach in real life.

Having explained how the writers of the CCCS, using youth subcultures as a vehicle, sought to overcome the shortcomings of existing Marxist theories of ideology, it will now be contended that certain arguments within Foucault's work lead to a very different approach, one demonstrating that the underlying difficulties stemming from the Marxist problematic still remain. The next section examines this approach and argues that, if this analysis is accepted, there must be a concomitant reevaluation of subculture theory.

Foucault, Truth, and Power

First and foremost, Foucault (1980:117–119) argues that the traditional Marxist perception of power and ideology is inadequate for understanding contemporary forms of social organization. A more profitable analysis, he suggests, is one that focuses on the nexus between power and knowledge and the resulting notion of governmentality. In his writings, Foucault makes no attempt to weave his theories into a seamless, all-encompassing account of society. Instead, Foucault describes societies characterized by a fragmented and discontinuous series of transformations, supported and augmented by a multiplicity of different knowledges, practices, and truths. There is no global, "Foucaultian" worldview. His understanding of the social world is not based upon totalized theories within an unbroken, linear flow of history.

In relation to the pivotal Marxist notion of class struggle, Foucault argues that the binaries of domination/subordination and resistance/submission are inappropriate for understanding contemporary forms of government. Government should no longer be seen as synonymous with coercion, as power does not have its genesis in any specific location (whether that location be a person, in the case of a sovereign, or a group, such as the State or the ruling class), and, as such, is not mandatorily utilized in their interests. Furthermore, it is by no means applied directly to the subordinate classes, such as working-class youth subcultures. Instead, power:

> Comes from below; that is, there is no binary and all-encompassing opposition between rulers and ruled at the root of power relations, and serving as a general matrix—no such duality extending from the top down and reacting on more and more limited groups to the very depths of the social body. (Foucault, 1976:94)

Foucault does not believe that power operates as a coercive entity, forced upon a population from above; rather, it is exercised through the practices and technologies of government. As he explains: "individuals are the vehicles of power, not its point of application" (Foucault, 1976:94). Taking this argument one stage further, Foucault argues that power should not be regarded as repressive when it is actually productive. He notes that these technologies of government institute and arrange new ways of understanding and new codes of behavior. Power does not constrain and compel; primarily it brings things into being.

Furthermore, power is not seen to operate as a global and homogeneous influence across all the elements of social life. Power is not a singular relation: it is not placed, like a blanket, upon those to be subjugated. Rather, it acts in diverse ways in different locations. Foucault (1976:94) argues that "power is not something that is acquired, seized, or shared, something that one holds on to or allows to slip away; power is exercised from innumerable points, in the interplay of non-egalitarian and mobile relations." He argues that the most productive understanding can be gained by examining power at its extremities, at "those points where it becomes capillary." It should be analyzed as something that circulates throughout the techniques, practices, and routines of social institutions and which is applied to specific populations. In a further break from the Marxist model, Foucault does not share its optimism of a final end to the exercise of power, wherein the relations of exploitation are eventually overcome and, hence, the need for domination. Instead, he sees current forms of the exercise of power eventually being replaced by others. There is no future historical moment when the absolute truth of class relations is exposed, resulting in the final demise of ideology.

The relationship between power and truth is an important one for Foucault. He states that he is primarily interested in the manner in which different knowledges produce truth, and how those truths are then used in the process of government. In the interview "Truth and Power," Foucault expresses concern over ideology, the concept so prominent within Marxist, and hence subculture, theory. He states that he considers the notion difficult to use for the following reasons:

> The first is that...it is always in virtual opposition to something like the truth...The second inconvenience is that it refers, necessarily I believe, to something like a subject. Thirdly, ideology is in a secondary position in relation to something which must function as the infrastructure or economic or material determinant for it. (Foucault, 1980:118)

Each of these points can be addressed in turn, focusing in particular on their implications for subculture theory. First, Foucault maintains that the essential political question should not concern false consciousness or ideology, but the very notion of truth itself. Foucault adopts a Nietzschean viewpoint regarding truth, contending that it is something that cannot exist in absolute terms. Rather, he contends there are a variety of truths, constructed within definite contexts as the product of specific legitimated knowledges. Because truth is actually the product of legitimated knowledges, as those knowledges change, then so will truth (Foucault, 1980:131). Different societies produce different regimes of truth, and the production of these regimes is internal to the exercise of power and, thus, effective government. He proposes that truth is:

> A system of ordered procedures for the production, regulation, distribution, circulation and operation of statements. 'Truth' is linked in a circular relation with systems of power which produce and sustain it, and to the effects of power which it induces and which extend it. A 'regime' of truth. (Foucault, 1980:132)

Undoubtedly, this approach to the notion of truth problematizes the traditional Marxist understanding of ideology. In this analysis, the ideologies of the dominant classes, internalized by subordinate groups, prevent the recognition by the subordinate groups of the real conditions of their existence. Furthermore, as Mark Poster (1984) points out, without the concept of ideology and a ready explanation of how class consciousness slips away into false consciousness, Marxist theory would find it difficult to present a coherent account of the relative absence of class struggle in advanced societies. As previously mentioned, however, the writers of the CCCS employ the more sophisticated Althusserian model concerning ideology, wherein ideology is no longer regarded as a distorted representation of the real, but a representation of a lived, imaginary relation to the real conditions of existence. In this manner, they sought to avoid not only some of the totalizing and reductionist aspects of classical Marxist theory, but also recourse to the increasingly problematic notion of false consciousness, itself premised upon the possibility of absolute truth. In "Althusser and the Theory of Ideology," Paul Hirst argues that despite the ingeniousness of Althusser's contribution to Marxist thought, this theoretical maneuver is ultimately unsuccessful, as it still posits as the function of ideology the false representation that acts to perpetuate existing social relations.

> Despite his opposition to the notion of ideology as 'false consciousness' Althusser's conception of ideology involves *meconnaissance* as its main (and functional) effect...This recognition/misrecognition is known as such only from the effects of scientific knowledge. Nevertheless Althusser requires the *effects* of falsity (maintenance of the existing social order) in just the same way as classical theories. (Hirst, 1979:62–63)

The second point of opposition to the notion of ideology originates in Foucault's anti-humanism. He notes that, if the dominant classes are deemed to be the source of dominant ideology, this implies that ideology has its genesis within particular subjects. This is the case whether subject is understood in terms of the rational self-determining individual, or the Marxist collective subject. Such an unspoken reliance upon this autonomous subject provides one of the most crucial elements of subculture theory. That is, it acts as the rationale that underpins the expressivist assumptions associated with the notion of subcultural style. There is the clear and recurrent implication, from Cohen through Hebdige to Denholm, Horniblow, and Smalley, that subcultures are vehicles for personal and group expression. Furthermore, this expression has its origins within a self-determining human subject.

Despite the apparent familiarity and self-evidence of this argument, there are other ways of approaching the issue. For example, Poster (1984:86) argues that Foucault succeeds in side-stepping the necessity for locating the root of ideas within the subject altogether, by placing fundamental emphasis upon the notion of discourse. Foucault (1972:55) states that "discourse is not the majestic unfolding of a thinking, knowing, speaking subject, but, on the contrary, a totality, in which the dispersion of the subject, and his discontinuity with himself may be determined." This is not to suggest that the concept of the subject plays no part in Foucault's texts. Indeed, he even goes as far as to say that his objective has been to describe the various historical ways in which individuals are made into subjects (as opposed to being born as subjects). The subject in this case, however, is not a pregiven idealist entity upon which material forces and relations exert their influence. Instead, various subject positions are constituted within specific historical locations. Ian Hunter (1993a:244) extends this argument by proposing that the self-reflective, self-determining subject is, in fact, the contingent product of numerous identifiable practices. As such, it is neither given by nature nor guaranteed by history. That is:

> The means by which individuals come to conduct themselves as the subjects of their own thought and action—to achieve the inner relation to themselves as self-determining beings—are not themselves pre-given. They consist of definite ethical techniques and practices through which individuals are enabled to carry out "work of the self on the self"...the capacity for self-determining ethical conduct emerged from the dissemination of certain ethical institutions and practices, rather than from a timeless moral personality. (Hunter, 1993a:255–256)

Interestingly, Althusserian Marxists have also disposed of the philosophical, humanist subject, while retaining the notion of the subject in other ways. Hirst (1979:58) states that "Althusser treats the subject not as an essence but as an effect." Within this model, it is suggested that human consciousness is determined in numerous ideological ways. Furthermore, these various ways elude the grasp of that subject—and it is only through the intercession of an external force (that is, politics), that the subject can see the truth and, hence, realize the possibility of true self-determination. Hirst (1979:59), however, rightly points out that, irrespective of Althusser's problematization of the humanist subject, he still presupposes that the subject has a unitary identity, and that the subject effects that correspond to any given individual also equate with existing notions of consciousness. Mark Cousins and Athar Hussain (1986) augment Hirst's criticism of Althusser on this issue. They argue that any project based upon a quest to determine how the subject is formed begs the crucial aspect of the question. That is, there is already the presupposition that a general account of this process can be offered at all. In keeping with Foucault's steady refusal to totalize his theories and coupled with his perception of power, the necessary conclusion is that there is no general process of subjectification. Rather, this occurs in a multiplicity of ways and through numerous different mechanisms. Most importantly, the resulting subject positions do not cohere to form a unitary whole.

Finally, Foucault takes issue with the concept of ideology as he considers its validity rests on the traditional Marxist dichotomy of base/superstructure. Critics of Marxist theory have illustrated the recurrent underlying dependence upon in-the-final-analysis economism. Indeed, Coward's appraisal of the CCCS position on youth subcultures makes this very point: as previously stated, by ultimately regarding the social formation as an expression of the division between capital and labor, this leads to an understanding of ideology that is causally bound to economic interests. Foucault removes this problem by arguing that discourses do not need to be driven by material forces within society, such as by the economic base, as they are already powers in their own right.

In the light of these arguments, it can, therefore, be seen that Foucault not only rejects the general understanding of the notion of ideology, but also the ground upon which it is built. This leads Foucault to posit an alternative model centered around the construction of political technologies that act to ensure social cohesion and order. Whereas ideology is regarded as untruth, the misrepresentation of real knowledge after the exercise of power, this paradigm regards truth as the product of knowledges assembled through the process of social organization. As such, knowledge becomes a structural artifact, a product of new technologies, garnered from diverse locations that define the body as an object of power. Social regulation is, therefore, not primarily exercised on the working classes by repression or by distorting the way in which the real is perceived, but by the construction of a pervasive political rationality that produces capacities, aptitudes, and aspirations and that positions individuals as members of classes of person within a field of governmental intelligibility.

Reassessing Hegemony

By challenging the Marxist assumptions concerning ideology, and instead focusing on the relations of power and truth, it is possible to successfully relocate and redefine the Gramscian notion of hegemony, the most vital aspect of subculture theory. In *Resistance through Rituals*, the success or failure of the hegemonic rule over the working classes in the United

Kingdom is charted from the 1920s onward. In the specific case of subcultures, their emergence at a particular historical moment is deemed to be related to a widespread crisis within this hegemony.

This analysis is problematic, however. Because hegemony "provides the base line and the base-structures of legitimation for ruling-class power" (Clarke, Hall, Jefferson, and Roberts, 1976:39), hegemony must, therefore, be located within the same conceptual framework as the model of power that supports it. In other words, because the traditional Marxist approach regards power as a coercive totality, placed on those below from above, this results in an explanation of hegemony that confirms these domain assumptions.

> In relation to the hegemony of a ruling class, the working class is, by definition, a *subordinate* social and cultural formation. Capitalist production, Marx suggested, reproduces capital and labour in their ever antagonistic forms. The role of hegemony is to ensure that, in the social relations between the classes, each class is continually *reproduced* in its existing dominant or subordinate form. (Clarke, Hall, Jefferson, and Roberts, 1976:41)

Hegemony is also presented in a totalized and unified manner by the writers of the CCCS. According to this logic, hegemony is sustained by an alliance of ruling class fractions—a historic block. Moreover, hegemony occurs within the single political space that exists between the two mutually antagonistic parts of a historically dichotomized society. Hegemony is depicted as something that either is secured or is not—two monolithic classes, one being subjugated by giving its generalized consent to the other. Arguably then, it is the reductionist, totalizing understanding of power evidenced within Marxism that necessarily enables a parallel understanding of the mechanism by which that power is exercised—hegemony.

It should be pointed out, however, that there have been a number of concerted attempts to salvage this pivotal Marxist concept. In *Outside Literature*, Tony Bennett (1991) charts the relative lack of success of some of the most important of these ventures. As Bennett observes, Stuart Hall attempts to make the notion of hegemony more flexible, while staying upon the same theoretical and political terrain—that is, stressing the continuing centrality/fixity of material relations. Bennett suggests, however, that this is only accomplished, in the final analysis, by Hall undercutting his own arguments:

> Having identified "the determining lines of force of material relations" as a point of fixity in relation to which the positivity of the social can be constituted, he immediately undercuts this argument in contending that "we need to think material conditions in their determinate discursive form, not as a fixed absolute." Putting discourse on both sides of the equation in this way means that "material conditions," since they are discursive in form, cannot fulfil the role assigned to them of setting limits to discourse. (Bennett, 1991:256)

Hall is not alone in his attempts to loosen up the notion of hegemony. Ernesto Laclau and Chantal Mouffe also address this issue. In contrast to Hall, however, their central intention has been to move beyond Gramscian categories and stake out the new political terrain of a radical and plural democracy (Bennett, 1991:255). For example, in *Hegemony and Socialist Strategy*, Laclau and Mouffe (1985:191) argue against the existence of a singular political space, formed as a function of the traditional Marxist binary of capital and labor. It is, in part, the absence of this space that eliminates any possibility of a unified discourse of the left. Instead, the call is for an understanding of hegemony that foregrounds the role of discourse in the construction of diverse political antagonisms, antagonisms deemed to constitute the postmodern political terrain. As they point out, because these antagonisms constitute a "diversity, not a diversification," such points of rupture "cannot be led back to a single point from which they could all be embraced and explained by a single discourse" (Laclau and Mouffe, 1985:191).

However, irrespective of such changes in the way in which hegemony is understood, and to the context within which it is located, Bennett (1991:268) argues this heavily discursive re-reading of Gramsci still essentially operates from within the same fundamental logic. That is, it remains a politics of oppositional consciousness. Furthermore, it is a consciousness that is "indifferent to the specific properties of the particular institutional sites in which it is conducted"—an issue upon which writers like Foucault have a good deal to say.

In "The Politics of Truth and the Problem of Hegemony," Barry Smart (1986:162) discusses the role that Foucault's work can play in a reevaluation of the notion of hegemony, stating that, "Foucault's work prises open the problem of hegemony in so far as it de-centres the question of the state, introduces a non-reductionist conception of power, and displaces the concept of ideology." Smart uses Foucault's ideas to argue that, in order to remain viable at all, hegemony must be extracted from the Marxist problematic. He suggests that this important concept can no longer be understood in terms of the relationship between dichotomous classes, or in terms of force and coercion (or even consent), but rather as the manner in which techniques, routines, and procedures subtly permeate cultural practices, thereby facilitating social cohesion. This process of governmentalization is part of the shift of focus from the belief that power is located within, and exercised by, the ruling class/State, to an approach that concentrates instead upon the deployment of an array of techniques designed for the effective government of constructed populations. These techniques assist in the effective implementation of a grid of governance that regulates and determines the formation of the subject. Such a grid is not reducible to the dichotomy of force and consent, as it does not define a domain where they are practical or relevant criteria.

Smart argues, via Foucault, that hegemony is now best understood in terms of the profusion of mechanisms through which events are constituted and practices are developed. As previously stated, Foucault's central objective has been to create a history of the various ways in which individuals are made into subjects. Smart suggests that the corollary of this is an understanding of the mechanisms by which human beings govern themselves and others, where government is the "way in which the conduct of individuals or groups might be directed." It is this practice that corresponds to the exercise of hegemony. Smart (1986:160) argues that by concentrating upon the coupling of power and knowledge through which the human subject has been objectivized, and upon the techniques by which humans learn to recognize themselves, Foucault has attempted to expose the mechanisms from which the "strategic constitution of forms of hegemony may emerge." Smart goes on to summarize Foucault's value to any understanding of hegemony by contending that:

> Foucault, by virtue of his critical distance from the limits and limitations of the Marxist problematic has been able to transform the terms of the debate from a preoccupation with the ambiguous concept of "ideology" and its effects to a consideration of the relations of "truth" and "power" which are constitutive of hegemony. (Smart, 1986:161)

Although the manner in which Smart employs Foucault's work to problematize the notion of hegemony is exemplary, his continued use of the term itself can lead to confusion. After all, it brings with it significant and habituated theoretical connotations. Consequently, it seems more logical to abandon hegemony entirely, and speak, instead, of differentiated forms of social cohesion and regulation.

Detotalizing Social History: Some Further Implications

Having raised some doubts about the Marxist characterization of the relationship between power, ideology, and hegemony—crucial elements of the CCCS model—it is now possible to reevaluate the remaining axes of subculture theory. These axes include the notion of class/generational consciousness and even the concept of culture itself. The writers of the CCCS argue that subcultures are constructed at the juncture of two forms of consciousness: those related to social class and to age. These interact to form a new and specific way of seeing, understanding, and relating to the social world. For example, having been allocated membership of a certain social class, there is the explicit presumption that there goes with this affiliation a homogeneous worldview—known as class consciousness. As such, members of a particular social class are deemed likely to grasp their position in a similar manner. That is, those from the working classes perceive the world in a manner common to the working classes. In attempting to explain the formation of the class/generational consciousness, the core rationale for the existence of youth subcultures, it is claimed that:

> We begin to see how forces, working right across a class, but differentially experienced between generations, may have formed the basis for generating an outlook—a kind of consciousness—specific to age position..."Generational consciousness" thus has its roots in the real experiences of working-class youth as a whole. But it took a particularly intense form in the post-war sub-cultures. (Clarke, Hall, Jefferson, and Roberts, 1976:53–54)

Two central problems arise with this form of analysis. The first is the determinist nature of the position, that consciousness can be deemed to be the result of material conditions, as discussed by Coward earlier. In this manner, consciousness can simply be read off as the product of specific social structures (and, although this primarily refers to social class, similar observations can be made about the assumption that specific age categories also have distinctive worldviews). By this logic, class consciousness is constructed in terms of class relations, which are, in turn, a function of determinate relations of production. Therefore, as consciousness is deemed to give rise to certain forms of behavior and ways of understanding, these are then directly attributable to a given social location. Within the reasoning of subculture theory, material conditions (in combination with an age) result in a specific type of consciousness, such as that deemed to be possessed by Teddy Boys, Mods, and Skinheads. Coward also goes on to argue that the centrality of the notion of consciousness within subculture theory is an expression of several underlying idealist assumptions by the writers of the CCCS. *Culture* is regarded by the CCCS as the production of meaning by consciousnesses—the implication of this is that humans have the inherent capacity to invest material life with (economically determined) meaning. As previously mentioned, this idea is interwoven into an idealist version of history through which the working classes eventually free themselves from ideology (Coward, 1977:90).

The second problem with this position is that consciousness is depicted by the CCCS as a single entity, a unified capacity. Membership of a particular social class brings with it a consciousness, through which the world is to be perceived. Therefore, investigating the degree to which material conditions do or do not create a class consciousness, is to make the same fundamental mistake as was made by Althusser concerning the process of subjectification—that is, believing that it is possible to give a single account of this process at all. Foucault would argue that there is no singular process by which consciousness is constructed. Rather, if it is to have any validity at all as a concept, it must be regarded as being necessarily piecemeal, fragmentary, and incomplete. Therefore, it can never simply be determined by social class and age. To assign a specific worldview to subcultural membership is not only reductionist, but also based upon a fundamental misconception concerning consciousness itself.

An alternative approach to relying upon the problematic idea of consciousness involves employing the notion of interests instead. Indeed, in *Subculture: The Meaning of Style*, Hebdige (1979:13–15) attempts to refine the relationship between ideology and consciousness, in part by stressing the centrality of the unconscious rather than the conscious (which does not negate the criticisms raised above), but also by examining class interests. The central advantage of utilizing the idea of interests over that of consciousness is that interests are, by definition, multifarious. As such, it is unnecessary to locate them as part of a totalized worldview. Interests can be understood in terms of specific contexts and be related to finite courses of action. Hence, they can still be useful as a mechanism for interpreting social phenomena.

This is not to say that similar criticisms to those made of consciousness cannot be leveled at interests. After all, simply positing interests in the conceptual space previously occupied by consciousness (that is, replacing a common class consciousness with a common set of class interests, both produced as ideological dimensions of the social structure of class relations) is equally reductionist. Hebdige (1979:15) directly ties ideologies to class interests when he states that ideologies "tend to represent, in however obscure and contradictory a fashion, the interests of the *dominant* groups in society." In the article, "'Interests' in Political Analysis" (1986), Barry Hindess argues that interests cannot be understood simply as the transmission between social structure on the one hand and what groups do on the other. He notes that this assumption relies on the idea that social structures are somehow external to the actors concerned and that these actors will unproblematically reflect the interests attributed to them—an identical misconception to that evidenced in subculture theory's use of consciousness. Hindess goes on to suggest that to expect a specific set of interests from certain social groups is necessarily reductionist:

> If actors act on the basis of their decisions, and if those decisions involve complex internal processes, then we should not expect the connection between actors' social location and the interests they acknowledge to conform to any one general model. (Hindess, 1986:125)

Such criticisms of a totalizing approach to the notion of consciousness have their corollary in criticisms made of the final important axis of subculture theory—culture. In *Resistance through Rituals*, Clarke, Hall, Jefferson, and Roberts (1976:10) regard culture as a group's "peculiar and distinctive 'way of life.'" This is a familiar definition, and one which, in "Setting Limits to Culture," Ian Hunter (1988a) questions at length. Hunter's analysis is pertinent here in two ways:

First, he argues that a great deal of the work employing the notion of culture, both Marxist and otherwise, has been underpinned by dialectical reasoning. That is, this idea of culture is generally premised upon an assumption of the possibility of reconciling a number of "partial and instrumentally determined oppositions in the direction of totality" (Hunter, 1988a:106–107). Hunter argues that the work of Antonio Gramsci—whose ideas were instrumental in the shaping of subculture theory—relies upon such a dialectical understanding of culture. He notes that in *The Modern Prince and Other Writings*, Gramsci (1957) declares that the disappearance of internal social contradictions will eventually result in cultural unification of mankind—a unitary cultural system (Hunter, 1988a:106). Within this general logic, cultural development is regarded as being ultimately propelled by the dialectical struggle between "class consciousness and historical determination—or ideology and social forces" (Hunter, 1988a:114).

Having demonstrated its prevalence, Hunter takes issue with this dialectical understanding of culture. He argues that the image of a generalized formation of social structures, aptitudes, and practices should be replaced by a far more valid understanding of culture, which is based upon limited and specific cultural programs. Hunter contrasts his position with that of Raymond Williams, whom he regards as characterizing culture as a "general organon for all forms of human development." In *The Long Revolution,* Williams states:

> Certain basic ethical assumptions and certain major art forms, have proved similarly capable of being gathered into a general tradition which seems to represent...a line of common growth. It seems reasonable to speak of this tradition as a general human culture...(Williams in Hunter, 1988a:115)

Hunter argues that, far from being reasonable, the notion of culture must be conceived only in terms of specific normative and technical regimes. There is no global, totalized entity that can be defined as working-class culture, any more than there is its mental equivalent—working-class consciousness. Instead, culture should be understood as being discontinuously constructed through the various knowledges and practices that exist within a diversity of social institutions. This suggests that culture should be more appropriately located as: "a signpost pointing in the general direction of a patchwork of institutions in which human attributes are formed and which, having no necessary features in common, must be described and assessed from case to case" (Hunter, 1988a:115).

The second issue stemming from Hunter's work concerns the presupposition within the traditional model that the unified culture will give rise to the complete human being. He states that:

> Attempts to investigate the organisational specification and formation of cultural attributes are conducted in the shadow of the concept of culture...in the shadow of the model of a single general process of contradiction, mediation and overcoming at whose end lies the "fully developed" human being. (Hunter, 1988a:106)

After all, Hunter observes, a significant proportion of cultural attributes only have reality in that they were made into objects of knowledge (and, therefore, government) through the application of administrative and statistical calculation. Therefore, the attributes and capacities that youth is currently ascribed are actually the contingent outcome of specific historical circumstance and finite governmental programs, rather than a limited percentage of their full and natural complement. Hunter submits that the conventional wisdom concerning culture is, in fact, the result of the growth of previously restricted and elite caste practices of aesthetico-ethical self-cultivation. This idea of person-formation was central to the Romantic notion of culture as ultimately producing the complete and unified development of man and society. Arguably then, the Marxist position, in which the historical process eventually overcomes cultural divisions, can be seen as an extension of such Romantic aesthetic practices.

This is particularly evident when the CCCS discuss middle-class youth cultures. They discern within such countercultures, which, they believe, spring from the contradictions and divisions within the wider culture, a reconstructive potential, in that these countercultures anticipate or portend a utopian social formation. However, when such cultural forms arise at the level of the counterculture only, "their maturing within the womb of society is, as yet, incomplete." (Clarke, Hall, Jefferson, and Roberts, 1976:69–70).

These arguments are echoed by Brake (1980), who suggests that the countercultures are founded upon a fundamental rejection of the dominant social values of materialism and competitiveness. By dropping out from a society that alienates individuals, both from nature and from their true selves, the countercultural members are provided with an alternative set of social and productive relations—relations that at least contain the possibility of resolution and spiritual fulfilment. Muncie, too, contends that the countercultures anticipate utopian social formations.

> [Hippies]...advocated a revolution that would humanise society by reintroducing notions of romanticism, and would be based upon creativity and self-expression. The rational and scientific ideology of technocracy was to be replaced by a "new consciousness" centred on visionary experience, self-discovery and mysticism. It would be a "political end sought by no political means." (Muncie, 1984:113–114)

Similarly, Hebdige's work on subcultural style, in depicting the resolution of imaginary contradictions (thereby premised upon anticipatory forms of wholeness), can also be reinterpreted simply as a modern version of the romantic fashioning of personality. This will be discussed in greater depth in chapter 4.

In summary, it seems possible to suggest, from the ground covered thus far, that the explanation proffered by the CCCS is no longer as convincing as it once appeared. This case has been argued as follows: First, the traditional Marxist model of power provides an inadequate foundation for analyzing contemporary forms of social organization. The customary binary oppositions of powerful/powerless and domination/subordination lack the precision of an approach to power that focuses instead upon the distribution of certain practices, techniques, and routines to particular populations. Second, the pivotal Marxist theories of ideology and hegemony are inherently flawed. The concept of ideology is problematic as it is necessarily premised upon notions of falsity and the existence of a unitary subject, while the concept of hegemony is problematic since, like the juridico-discursive theory of power that supports it, it relies heavily upon the simplistic binaries of dominant class/subordinate class and coercion/consent. Finally, there are difficulties with the manner in which the notions of consciousness and culture are employed by the CCCS. In both cases, they are presented as totalized entities. Again, it is argued that this approach lacks the specificity of more recent theoretical accounts, accounts that have stressed the importance of a piecemeal understanding of human capacities and institutions. In general, then, as a result of these three criticisms, it is,

Adjusting the Focus on Subcultures

therefore, problematic to employ a model built upon these theoretical foundations.

As has been previously stated, the writers of the CCCS place youth subcultures within a logic of counterhegemonic struggle. They demarcate these groups as participants in a ritualized fight against the dominant social order—a part of the wider, ongoing conflict between classes. As has also been mentioned, this analysis assumes a coercive and centrally located understanding of power. Working-class subcultures are, therefore, the manifestation of the struggle of working-class youth with ruling ideology. However, on replacing the juridico-discursive characterization of power with that of government, this paradigm loses its supporting framework. As such, youth begins to look very different.

It can be argued, instead, that the category of youth has been formulated as an object of knowledge within a series of diverse disciplines that have posited youth as problem. For example, youth has been constructed and operationalized as a category through the different mechanisms and knowledges associated with law enforcement. The policing of youth has drawn upon rationales of behavior and discourses circulating within a variety of other terrains. Youth is defined as the object of expertise in areas ranging from psychology to orthopedics, social work to sociology. Youth is the center of a multitude of regulatory practices and techniques associated with pedagogy, and it is situated and interpreted in relation to the labor market by economists. Each of these knowledges plays a part in youth being positioned as the object of government.

By understanding the manner in which the category of youth is produced, in part, as an artifact of government, this allows for similar conclusions to be drawn about youth subcultures. Subcultures do not arise out of a well-spring of class consciousness and counterhegemonic struggle. They are not constructed as forms of resistance external to the exercise of power. Instead, to a certain extent, they can be best understood as the by-product of particular forms of government. Along with those already mentioned, these might include rationales and knowledges behind inner-city planning; various demographics of immigration; the rise of particular types of reporting and styles of media coverage; and specific technologies of marketing. Having moved away from his earlier CCCS-influenced framework, Hebdige (1988) addresses some of these issues in the essay, *Hiding in the Light: youth surveillance and display*:

> The category "youth" gets mobilised in official documentary discourse, in concerned or outraged editorials and features, or in the supposedly disinterested tracts emanating from the social sciences at those times when young people make their presence felt by going "out of control," by resisting through rituals...When young people do these things...they get talked about, taken seriously, their grievances are acted upon. They get arrested, harassed, admonished, disciplined, incarcerated, applauded, vilified, emulated, listened to. They get defended by social workers and other concerned philanthropists. They get explained by sociologists...(Hebdige, 1988:17–18)

Hebdige makes two important points here. First, and in keeping with the overall tenor of his postmodern analysis, he is contending that the category of youth is fashioned by, and emerges from, a multiplicity of diverse knowledges and contexts. Second, Hebdige is making the epistemological point that the CCCS cannot be regarded as adopting a position of analysis external to the categories it is attempting to describe. It is, in part, those who conduct research into youth, such as sociologist and social workers, who give the category its shape. As will be discussed shortly, the CCCS subculture research is itself implicated as one of the mechanisms by which the category of youth is formed and reformed.

Subcultures, too, can be partially located within the logic of a differentiating form of government. As Foucault (1977) notes in *Discipline and Punish: The Birth of the Prison*, by distributing and classifying individuals as classes of persons along an increasing number of axes, it becomes all the more possible to create a domain of government. This forms a crucial mechanism enabling power to be exercised in a far more comprehensive manner than was previously possible. He argues that in modern society, where power is generally anonymous and functional, there tends to be a strong process of individualization of those upon whom it is exercised. That is, those who do not conform to the norms (norms made available through technologies such as statistics and that locate individuals within a field of distribution), are the subject of the greatest attention. He states that "in a system of discipline, the child is more individuated than the adult, the patient more than the healthy man, the madman and the delinquent more than normal and non-delinquent" (Foucault, 1977:193). It is through the construction and demarcation of pathologies (such as the *juvenile delinquent*) that social, legal, psychological, and medical norms can be reinforced. According to Rose, this process is especially evident when addressing the young:

> It is around pathological children—the troublesome, the recalcitrant, the delinquent—that conceptions of normality have taken shape...expert notions of normality are extrapolated from our attention to those children who worry the courts, teachers, doctors and parents. Normality is not an observation but a valuation. (Rose, 1990:131)

As such, the focus on delinquent youth, and the categorization of some of them into subcultures, is part of the broader processes of measurement and judgment against a set of social norms. The delineation of characters such as *Bogans* and *Skeggs* (Denholm, Horniblow, and Smalley, 1992) creates yet one more scale, against which normal youth can be counterpoised, measured, and assessed. Indeed, Denholm, Horniblow, and Smalley actually go so far as to delineate a subcultural group called *Normals*. It even gives a description of just what it takes to be a member—to be considered normal. Curiously, it also describes this category as composed of "people who do not feel the need to do the same as everyone else" (Denholm, Horniblow, and Smalley, 1992:23). Employing the same logic while writing about the 1981 riots in the United Kingdom, Hebdige observes that:

> The *Sunday Times* ran an article providing a kind of consumer guide to the various rioting contingents. The categorisation was elaborate: rastas, punks, 2-Tone youths, mohawks. Each description was illustrated by an artists impression of the relevant type—an identikit for the breakfast voyeur. (Hebdige, 1988:34)

However, the construction of characters such as these is not a new phenomenon, even if it is more brazenly normative than usual. These subcultural ethnographies can be placed alongside much older forms of observation and policing. For example, between 1850 and 1880, the masturbating child was constructed as an archetypal object of knowledge within the sexual domain. This object not only acted as the benchmark against which the normal child could be measured, it also legitimated the intervention of a growing network of specialist knowledges. Similarly, the *adolescent* took shape in 1904 with the publication of G. Stanley Hall's massive text on the subject. This concept quickly became axiomatic to the way young people were understood and governed.

Essentially then, having stripped away the romance of subculture theory (and except for its liberatory aspirations), the CCCS approach is fundamentally no different in outcome to those knowledges which produced the *masturbating child* or the *juvenile delinquent* of the nineteenth century. This is not to suggest that youth subcultures are fashioned as objects of governmental knowledge directly, as was the juvenile delinquent. As previously mentioned, youth subcultures are *by-products* of particular forms of government. However, once formed, characters such as the *skinhead*, like the *juvenile delinquent*, act as pathologies against which conceptions of normality can be shaped.

A final tendency of subculture research into youth—as with a great deal of contemporary social theory—is that it has repeatedly supported its position by the use of global oppositions. In this particular field of research, the oppositions frequently include such familiar dichotomies as domination versus subordination, resistance versus conformity, and young versus old. As has been argued previously, the principal explanation for subcultures is based upon a relationship hitherto deemed to exist between dominant and subordinate social classes, between generations, and between those who conform and those who do not. Subculture members are consistently portrayed resisting their ideological and generational oppression, and this form of resistance (primarily through various forms of personal expression) is generally contrasted against the conformity of the *Normals*. Again, the Denholm, Horniblow, and Smalley (1992) article exemplifies this dichotomizing tendency. Not only are young people counterposed against adults, but the relationships that those young people have with adults are roughly polarized between characters such as *Gothics* and *Skeggs*, who avoid and hate adults, and oppose them bitterly as they represent authority respectively, and *Normals* who have a good to excellent relationship with adults and even consult adults with problems. This again also illustrates the recurrent polarization in youth research between those who are deemed to resist and those who are deemed to conform, to the extent that youth as a category has almost become synonymous with resistance.

The important criticism here is that this form of dichotomizing predetermines the conclusions of much of youth research; moreover it also often masks the complexity of any given field of debate. That is, if the central explanatory parameters of youth research are resistance/conformity, domination/subordination, and expression/regulation, then these are precisely the terms in which the results of that research will always appear. Furthermore, by painting the salient features of the debates over youth with such broad and primary brush strokes, this glosses over the piecemeal way in which youth has been differentially constructed as an object of knowledge.

To summarize this section—it is argued that characters such as *Bogans* and *Skeggs* are not engaged in a struggle against the power of the State. Rather, as will be demonstrated later in this book, they are constructed as artifacts at the intersection of a wide range of governmental strategies and as mechanisms of self-fashioning. As Foucault points out, power does not repress, it produces domains of objects and rituals of truth. Hopefully, attending to these rituals of truth will provide a more fertile ground for understanding the contemporary policing of youth than the repeated recourse to the romantic rituals of resistance described by the CCCS.

At this point in the argument, an objection could be raised. Even if subculture theory has some flaws, it is generally only applied to the study of social groups. A great deal of research into youth does not fit this model because it is issues based, instead. Surely this research is exempt from the problems discussed so far? And if this is so, what broader relevance do the criticisms of subculture theory have now? Both these questions can be answered by examining briefly some of the research conducted into the issue of youth homelessness.

From "Youth Homelessness" to "Streetkids"

During the 1980s, throughout almost all western countries, youth homelessness has been positioned as an important and pressing social problem. Within Australia alone, there have been numerous Federal Reports, for example, *Report on Youth Homelessness* (1982), *Homelessness—A Capital Problem* (1984), *Our Homeless Children* (1989); State Reports, for example, *Youth Homelessness and Responses* (WA—1982), *New Directions for Housing Young People* (SA—1986), *Girls at Risk* (NSW—1986); journal articles, for example, Rodney Fopp's (1983) "Youth Homelessness", Peter Van Reyk's (1985) "Shelter or the Streets", Peter Turley's (1988) "Homeless Young People"; and books, for example, Paul Wilson and Josie Arnold's (1986) *Streetkids*, John Embling's (1986) *Fragmented Lives*, Frank Donnelly's (1987) *The Youth Link Story*)—to name but a few. The question remains—how do the aforementioned criticisms of subculture theory relate to this body of ostensibly issue-based work?

First, some research into youth homelessness does employ subculture theory fairly directly. Wilson and Arnold's (1986) *Streetkids* is one example. In this text, streetkids are located firmly within the familiar subcultural realms of alienation and resistance: "Their silent scream and inner rage surface as they cut loose and take to the streets" (Wilson and Arnold, 1986:6–7). Furthermore, in the same way that the groups studied by the CCCS were seen to have possessed a common consciousness of their material circumstances, so streetkids are also deemed to have a unified outlook, a collective way of relating to their social environment:

> [streetkids] survive on their wits. Demoralised and debased, they feel under threat from the police and misunderstood by child care institutions because both are seen as punitive rather than supportive. Street kids feel exploited by almost everyone: the media, the pushers. the sex purchasers, the sociologists. (Wilson and Arnold, 1986:7–8).

The subcultural persona is further defined by research that notes that the typical streetkid also "has a history of drug problems or minor criminal offences" (Kissane, 1985:8). However, it should be noted that if, as has been discussed, subculture analysis presupposes class struggle and a shared consciousness (not to mention a certain stylistic cogency), then these elements problematize the use of a subculture framework for understanding youth homelessness. After all, young people end up on the streets for various reasons, and they experience street life in different ways. A limited number of shared interests (such as being young and without a place to sleep) is a meager ground to delineate a discrete, counterhegemonic subculture, or to validate the existence of a specific consciousness. Similarly, there are no grounds for a common decoding of their styles of dress. To date, there is no evidence to suggest that the young and homeless make a coherent fashion statement about their homelessness.

Irrespective of its seeming unsuitability for explaining youth homelessness, subculture theory retains a pervasive influence over the field. In "Homeless Youth and Streetkids," Sharad Gokhale (1987) actually attempts a subcultural delineation between these two groups. It is argued that although homeless youths and streetkids do have some similarities, group members also possess a variety of different characteristics. These differences, in turn, necessitate different social responses. Whereas both are socially and economically deprived, have low self-esteem and are affected by similar causative factors such as a broken home, poverty, and so forth, there are also important differences, which include considerations such as their likely age, problems, and requirements (Gokhale, 1987:16). Consequently, the issue here is not whether or not homeless youth can be understood in subcultural terms, rather, it is that on closer inspection, there are actually two subcultures present.

Setting aside the research that employs subculture theory directly, there also appears to be an alternative body of literature on youth homelessness which does not appear to employ any of the rationales associated with subculture theory at all. Although it may operate within contexts informed by the likes of *Streetkids* (and may have been driven by the moral panics associated with them), on the surface, this research adopts a different approach. Staying within the Australian context, the most visible example of this non-subcultural research into youth homelessness is the Burdekin Report (1989) *Our Homeless Youth*.

The Burdekin Report was the end product of a research project that incorporated twenty-one hearings conducted in 1987 and 1988, involving 330 witnesses, 160 written submissions, and visits to more than twenty refuges. The report is divided into six main parts: Background, The Dimensions of Youth Homelessness, Factors Contributing to Youth Homelessness, Income and Shelter, Other Services, and The Role of Government and Non-Government Sector. In general, the primary intention of the report was to uncover the causes and the extent of the phenomenon of youth homelessness. Significantly, it did so largely without overtly employing the conventional underpinning youth logic of resistance and shared consciousness.

Upon reading the Burdekin Report, however, it becomes obvious that several of the domain assumptions that support subculture theory are present. Although the nexus between youth and counterhegemonic struggle is no longer foregrounded, the Burdekin Report still exhibits characteristics already problematized in the subculture research dealt with earlier. First, youth is granted the status of an objectively valid category. That is, despite some awareness that the category of youth is a historical contingency, this seems to have few implications for the degree to which it is still used (both within general youth research, and within documents such as the Burdekin Report) as a stable, descriptive classification. This fact is evident not only from the title of the Burdekin Report itself, *Our Homeless Youth*, but also from the way the term acts as the focal point for each of the different sections, and from the unproblematic manner in which the term is used as a flexible catchall classification for anyone between the ages of twelve and twenty-four. Rather than being a fact-in-itself, the Burdekin youth is an artifact produced by an array of different mechanisms of information gathering. The substance of the Burdekin youth is actually an amalgam of data from numerous sites and problematizations including the health and welfare agencies, the schools, the criminal justice system, the Bureau of Statistics, voluntary organizations, family services, and so on. It is this youth which, in turn, acts as a target for policy and concern. So in reality, rather than simply describing what is happening to youth, research such as the Burdekin Report is instrumental in giving the category its shape and texture.

Second, the Burdekin Report makes several references to the importance of children being allowed to realize their total potential. Indeed, it quotes from the United Nations' (1959) *Declaration of the Rights of the Child*, which argues that children have the right to full and harmonious development (National Clearinghouse for Youth Studies, 1989:33). Again, this is a familiar line within youth research. In subculture theory, working-class youth is unable to find its ideal and complete form owing to the coercive effects of social inequality that force it into ritualized and spectacular configurations. That is, the capacities that working-class youth actually possess, are regarded as being either a distortion of, or a fraction of, the capacities that it might possess under ideal circumstances—capacities that are deemed to have their origins within youth itself. As previously mentioned, there are severe problems with this teleological and essentialist understanding of culture and cultural attributes. It can now be more convincingly argued that youth is constructed as an object of knowledge through the application of administrative and statistical calculation. That is, the attributes ascribed to youth are currently the contingent outcome of these techniques of government. They are thus not usefully assessed in terms of being a more or less limited part of some future whole.

Finally, the Burdekin approach to youth has normalizing implications, in that it gives a recognizable and, hence, governable shape to the homeless youth. This is not a criticism in itself. It is simply that, as with the CCCS research, such a consequence contrasts sharply with the report's emancipatory intentions. Just as Wilson and Arnold succeed in sketching out precisely what constitutes a streetkid, so the Burdekin Report describes some of the definitive attributes possessed by this social category. This category "survive(s) on the margins of society, begging, prostituting themselves, stealing, dealing in drugs and so on" (The Burdekin Report, 1989:49):

> The picture that emerges is a disturbing one. Amid family stress and economic hardship, a 12 to 14-year-old faces irreconcilable differences with her parents, and discouragement at school. A decision to leave home is made and then follows a process of sleeping out or drifting from one refuge to another, recourse to desperate sources of income, increasing alienation from society and eventual decline in health and self-esteem. (National Clearinghouse for Youth Studies, 1989:7)

Furthermore, the Burdekin Report even sets out in detail the characteristics that make a child at-risk of becoming such a streetkid. (The notion of the governmental construction of the at-risk youth is the subject of chapter 3 in this book.) These factors include family conflict, social rejection, physical, sexual or emotional abuse, poverty, unemployment, and so forth. Consequently, likely children can be measured against these indicators, assessed, counseled, and ultimately saved—with the characterization of the streetkid clearly visible as the price of failure.

Conclusion

The purpose of this first chapter has been to argue the following three points. First, recent research into youth has been dominated by the subculture theory associated with the Center for Contemporary Cultural Studies (CCCS). This paradigm characterizes youth in very specific ways, primarily by employing the concepts of counterhegemonic struggle, generational consciousness, and style as discourse.

Second, this theory has several problems. For instance, there are numerous difficulties associated with what Foucault characterizes as the *juridico-discursive* understanding of power, an understanding that underpins subculture theory. There are also problems identified with subculture theory's reliance upon the notions of hegemony, consciousness, and culture. In addition, there are difficulties with subculture theory's totalizing use of the notion of youth, the normalizing nature of the subcultural categories it produces, and the reliance upon conventional dichotomies, such as domination/subordination and expression/regulation. It was argued that, ultimately, youth subcultures are contingent social categories which, combined with various other governmental methodologies, chart the space between the normal and the delinquent.

Finally, it was argued that other youth research—while perhaps not adopting subculture theory directly—shares many of its methodological and theoretical presuppositions and, hence, its shortcomings. In the Burdekin Report into youth homelessness, youth was still granted objective validity as a category, the depiction of the homeless youth was still essentially normalizing (not a criticism in itself, but at odds with the intentions of the research), and the report still employed a teleology regarding the eventually complete development of the child.

In contrast to the above forms of youth research, this chapter has made a preliminary sketch of a model based not upon an *a priori* acceptance of the objective validity of youth as a stage of life, but rather upon a governmental interest in managing a constructed population. As will become more evident, this new approach not only seeks to avoid many of the problems described thus far, but it also permits a greater degree of historical specificity in the analysis of formations of youth. In attempting not to totalize (and thereby exhibit one of the central problems of the previous work), the focus will only fall upon some particular aspects of youth and the management of sex.

CHAPTER 2

Youth, Sex, and Government

This chapter outlines the first half of an alternative approach to youth research. This half of the approach presents the historical specificity of formations of youth. In particular, this chapter employs the concept of governmentality to examine the relationship between the category of youth and the management of its sex. First, governmentality as a form of rule is explained—how it evolved out of previous forms of rule based upon sovereignty, how particular effects of governmental programs largely dissolve the state/civil society dichotomy, and how specific analyses of the local effects of governmentality can be conducted utilizing the relationship between governmental programs, political rationalities, and governmental technologies. Second, this chapter addresses the notion of sexuality. Rather than regarding it as an inherent part of human nature, this chapter traces the way in which sexuality developed out of certain elements of Christian asceticism, and then was distributed through the machinery of government. This was possible primarily because of the dual governmental role that sexuality was able to play at the juncture between the important elements of the body and the population. Third, this chapter examines the emergence of youth as a category. It is argued that youth evolved out of previous concerns and debates over characters such as the child, the juvenile delinquent, and the adolescent, and that it has been produced as a governmental object at the intersection of certain legal, educational, medical, and psychological problematizations, especially ones concerning sex. Finally, this chapter addresses the questions concerning the limits of government. In what ways, and to what extent, can government be expected to modify the sexual conduct of youth, particularly in light of recent imperatives concerning HIV/AIDS?

Thus far, it has been argued that most youth research involves numerous recognizable characteristics. First, there is an essentialist and totalizing understanding of youth as a category. A general awareness that the current understanding of youth is historically contingent seems to have few implications for the degree to which it has been utilized in previous research as a stable descriptive classification. This issue will be dealt with later in this chapter. The second characteristic is that much of previous research into youth is underpinned by a foundational understanding of power as a global, coercive generality used in the process of subordinating young people. While the amount of scholarly work that positions power as lying in the hands of the ruling classes has decreased markedly, most youth research now appears to assign power to the state instead, using this assumption to support analyses that generally go on to chart the multiplicity of ways in which youth either falls victim to, or resists, that power.

Although the writers of the CCCS focus predominantly on coded cultural responses to the ruling class, they also have a fairly fixed and monolithic idea about the power inherent in the state. For example, with respect to securing effective hegemonic domination, Clarke, Hall, Jefferson, and Roberts (1976:38–39) argue that "the state is a major educative force in this process. It educates through its regulation of the life of the subordinate classes." This depiction of power relations is common within youth research. In *Making the Difference*, Bob Connell, Dean Ashenden, Sandra Kessler and Gary Dowsett make precisely this point when addressing power relations in the school:

> The teachers too are functionaries of the state, not just its employees; they bear certain powers over the kids which are not delegated to them by the parents...The teacher-pupil relation here is the carrier of a relation between state and subject, a coercive relation of a kind which always produces resistance, however muted. (Connell, Ashenden, Kessler, and Dowsett, 1982:138)

While not all analyses of the relationship between youth and state power are so reductionist, they are generally making the same point. In both Nicholas Dorn's (1983) *Alcohol, Youth and the State*, and in John Solomos's (1988) *Black Youth, Racism and the State*, the power invested in the monolithic state is still manifestly central to the analysis. Likewise, in his book on the history of Australian youth, Bob Bessant (1988) depicts the state as a single entity that organizes the lives of young people. Although this process is not necessarily portrayed as coercive, it is still seen as "mother state...extending her control over her little ones" (Bessant, 1988:28). Within this model, it is the state's desire to protect those at-risk that provides the rationale for intervention. (The theme of risk will be addressed at length in the next chapter.)

In "Youth and the State," David Kamens (1985:4) argues that the boundaries of the category of youth itself are a function of "the exercise of authority over society by modern nation states." Indeed, the changing status of youth in contemporary society is directly associated with "the rise of the omnivorous, universal state." John Muncie's (1984:184) *The Trouble with Kids Today*, concludes by arguing that recent social problems involving youth are, in part, the result of a growing state authoritarianism. That is, the state only seems able to respond to the young by markedly increasing its level of control over them. These conclusions are supported by two ethnographies of British youth, *Lads, Citizens and Ordinary Kids* (Jenkins, 1983), and *Growing Up at the Margins* (Coffield, Borrill, and Marshall, 1986). Both of these texts discern a greater mobilization of power from within the state, and this augmented state power is directed at controlling the social problems associated particularly with the category of youth.

In the light of these texts, it is obvious that a significant percentage of existing youth research employs the familiar doctrine that locates power within the state. Not only is that power itself totalized (that is, it is essentially unified and global in its effects), but the state is also largely presented in reified, unitary terms. As was argued in chapter 1, the belief that power emanates from a single source is one of the central characteristics of the *juridico-discursive* doctrine of power. This source can be a monarch, the ruling class, or the state. Although the age of the sovereign ruler is long past, Foucault (1976:88–89) suggests that the extensive and continuing utilization of this understanding of power merely goes to show that, metaphorically speaking, "in political thought and analysis, we have still to cut off the head of the king."

Within the *juridico-discursive* model, the binary opposition that characterized the exercise of sovereign power still operates, but now power has simply been allocated a new point of origin—the state. The state's power is still understood to be exercised upon a separate domain—civil society.

Foucault characterizes the dominant understanding of the state in terms of Friedrich Nietzsche's *monstre froid*, wherein the state is "the coldest of all cold monsters...(it) lies in all languages of good and evil; and whatever it says, it lies—and whatever it has, it has stolen...only there, where the state ceases, does the man who is not superfluous begin" (Nietzsche, in Rose and Miller, 1992:173). According to Nietzsche's logic, the search for true freedom can only commence in that realm beyond the direct and immediate reach of the state, in the domain of civil society. In direct contrast to the sphere of anonymous and coercive state power, civil society (where the state ceases...) promises a counterposed region of autonomy and liberty.

This, Foucault argues, is a misconception. First, power does not have its genesis in any specific location—be that location a person (the monarch) or a group (ruling class/state)—and, as such, it is not mandatorily utilized in their interests. There is no "binary...opposition between rulers and ruled" (Foucault, 1976:88). Instead, power is exercised from innumerable points and should be analyzed as something that circulates throughout a complex of social techniques, practices, and routines. Second, with regard to the notion of the *monstre froid*, he declares that the state "does not have this unity, this individuality, this rigorous functionality, nor, to speak frankly, this importance" (Foucault, 1991:103). He argues that rather than the state's having come to dominate society during the last two hundred years, the state has become governmentalized. In reality, the state is merely one modality with a much broader vocabulary of governmental alternatives—and one whose importance has been repeatedly overestimated. Finally, he argues that the dichotomy between state and civil society is illusory. This illusion obscures the way in which modern society is actually governed. That is, to retain theories based upon the state/civil, public/private split, is to be blind to more productive ways of approaching contemporary social analysis:

> The language of political philosophy: state and civil society, freedom and constraint, sovereignty and democracy, public and private plays a key role in the organisation of modern political power. However, it cannot provide the intellectual tools for analyzing the problematics of government at present. Unless we adopt different ways about thinking about the exercise of political power, we will find contemporary forms of rule hard to understand. (Rose and Miller, 1992:201)

As a consequence of these observations, it is the contention of this chapter that employing the Foucaultian notion of governmentality not only avoids the problems associated with employing a coercive model of power tied to the state/civil society split, it also ultimately permits an analysis of youth that accounts for its historical specificity.

Governmentality

The question now is: what precisely is meant by governmentality? This question is answered most coherently in Foucault's (1991) article of the same name. In this piece, he sets about outlining his ideas on the modern exercise of power. He begins this task by first examining some of the forms of rule that preceded it—starting with the principles of government described in Niccolo Machiavelli's *The Prince*. In this sixteenth-century text, Machiavelli sought to give advice to the sovereign as to how to retain his principality in the face of threats to his rule, both from inside and outside his territory. Foucault (1991:87) argues that the book's most telling characteristic was not the specific nature of that advice, but rather an exposition of the relationship between the state and the prince himself. Because the prince normally acquired his land through inheritance or conquest, his relationship to that land is always one of externality. There was no "fundamental, essential, natural and juridical" connection between ruler and realm (Foucault, 1991:90). That is, the rule of the prince was not an internal part of the principality. Ruling successfully simply meant successfully protecting his link to his territory, not improving the conditions of life of his subjects.

This doctrine provoked a number of criticisms. Foucault (1991:90) reviews some of the appraisals and looks in particular at those writers who were suggesting a new approach to rule, one not based upon a necessary relationship of externality. He refers to this new approach as the art of government. He cites La Perriere's (1576) *Miroir Politique*, whose vocabulary of government repeatedly draws analogies to governing domains such as households, convents, families, and children. As Foucault points out, these are telling examples, after all:

> All these other kinds of government are internal to the state or society. It is within the state that the father will rule the family, the superior the convent, etc. Thus we find at once a plurality of forms of government and their immanence to the state: the multiplicity and immanence of these activities distinguishes them radically from the transcendent singularity of Machiavelli's prince. (Foucault, 1991:91)

Consequently, there is a conceptual break between the form of rule advocated by Machiavelli and that associated with the art of government. Within this new logic, then, successful rule is not accomplished merely by managing to remain in control, but, rather, is accomplished by ensuring that the family itself prospers, as the head of the family is responsible for all aspects of that family's life. The art of government primarily involves meticulously, correctly, and wisely looking after the economy of the household—the members, goods, and wealth of the entire family. As Foucault (1991:92) states: "this, I believe, is the essential issue in the establishment of the art of government: introduction of economy into political practice." To govern effectively now meant to expand the limited model of managing the family to the entire state.

Initially, the art of government was, at best, quite undeveloped. Foucault (1991:96) suggests that it proliferated principally owing to contingencies such as the emergence of governmental apparatuses, the development of new techniques for amassing knowledge about the state, and the advent of mercantilism and the Cameralists' science of police. It was, in part, these additional factors that accelerated the shift from the limited Machiavellian approach to rule, to the art of government. As Colin Gordon (1991:11) observes, "police science, or 'Cameralism' is also, in conjunction with the allied knowledge of mercantilism and political arithmetic, the first modern system of *economic sovereignty*, of government understood as an economy."

This new form of power/rule, however, was not able to develop unimpeded. Until the early eighteenth century, the art of government remained yoked to imperatives of sovereignty. To exemplify this claim, Foucault (1991:97) uses the example of mercantilism—"running the state like a set of enterprises" (Weber, cited in Gordon, 1991:12)—arguing that its success was unavoidably hindered as it still considered its fundamental goal the wealth of the sovereign. Furthermore, it also still utilized the blunt instruments of sovereign rule—laws, decrees, and regulations. So even though mercantilism, like police theory, sought to operate within the new logics associated with the art of government (in that it "strives towards the prudential by cultivating the pastoral" (Gordon, 1991:10), it remained tethered to both the structure and the objectives of sovereignty:

> On the one hand, there was this framework of sovereignty which was too large, too abstract and too rigid; and on the other, the theory of government suffered from its reliance on a model which was too thin, too weak and too insubstantial, that of the family: an economy of enrichment still based on a model of the family was unlikely to be able to respond adequately to the importance of territorial possession and royal finance. How then was the art of government able to outflank these obstacles? (Foucault, 1991:98).

To answer his own question, Foucault (1991:100) suggests that "derestriction of the art of government" evolved in a several ways, all involving the pivotal notion of the population. First, the family was abandoned as the central model of government. The increasing deployment of statistics had shown the population to have its internal configurations and regularities. These were irreducible to a simple template of the family. Indeed, the family was now to be relocated inside the wider umbrella of the population, where it was to become an instrument of, rather than a model for, government. Second, the population became the new raison d'etre of government. Before this time, government had, in a sense, been its own purpose, operating almost exclusively in the interests of the sovereign. It was now to be focused upon the population, both directly and indirectly, not only in improving its conditions, but also in managing its habits, aspirations, and interests. Government would, therefore, become the conduct of conduct (Gordon, 1991:2). Finally, the population becomes the pivotal point of intervention into the new field of political economy. It marks the transition in the eighteenth century from a "regime dominated by the structures of sovereignty to one ruled by the techniques of government" (Foucault, 1991:101). The new science of government, employing the problem of the population, shifted the old notion of economy (within the metaphor of the family) to the domain of what is now referred to as the economic.

This is not to suggest that sovereignty now became a non-issue—far from it. Foucault (1991:101–102) suggests that the rise of governmentality meant that questions concerning sovereignty were raised with renewed vigor. Likewise, the emphasis on discipline, which had its genesis in the seventeenth and eighteenth centuries, was augmented rather than diminished when employed in the management of populations. Thus, the important point is made that discipline did not replace sovereignty, only to be replaced itself by government. Rather, "one has a triangle, sovereignty-discipline-government, which has as its primary target the population..." (Foucault, 1991:102). Foucault abridges his account of governmentality in the following manner:

> By this word I mean three things:
> 1. The ensemble formed by the institutions, procedures, analyses and reflections, the calculations and tactics that allow the exercise of this very specific albeit complex form of power, which has as its target population, as its principal form of knowledge political economy...
> 2. The tendency which, over a long period and throughout the West, has steadily led towards the pre-eminence over all other forms (sovereignty, discipline) of this type of power which may be termed government, resulting...in the formation of a whole series of specific governmental apparatuses...
> 3. The process, or rather the result of the process, through which the state of justice of the middle ages, transformed into the administrative state during the fifteenth and sixteenth centuries, gradually became "governmentalised."
> (Foucault, 1991:102–103)

Through the above reasoning Foucault is able to downplay the importance of the state. First, he argues that a continual analytic reliance upon the state brings with it a unitary (and hence reductionist) understanding of the functioning of power. In contrast to this, the notion of governmentality is constructed around a conceptual framework wherein power is exercised toward a multiplicity of ends not anchored in the unity of the state. Second, he argues that it is only because the state became governmentalized that it has survived at all. Therefore, to place it at the center of the analysis, as many theorists have, and to assign to it the power befitting a *monstre froid*, is to position government as a function of the state, rather than the other way around.

Having introduced the notion of governmentality and having discussed some of the historical circumstances of its emergence, in order to address effectively the relationship between governmentality and youth, it is now necessary to examine some of governmentality's workings in more detail. This involves examining the relationship between specific governmental programs, the political rationalities that these programs articulate, and the technologies of government that enable them to be put into practice.

Nikolas Rose and Peter Miller (1992:181) argue that, first and foremost, government is a problematizing activity. They suggest that the history of government could be written solely in terms of a history of the problematizations that it seeks to address. Thus, it is primarily the identification of various sites of failure that provide the raison d'etre for the countless programs of intervention characteristic of contemporary government. Governmentality is programmatic for two further reasons.

First, it is programmatic in that there has been rapid and ongoing expansion in the number of existing programs that seek to reform reality: "government reports, white papers, green papers, papers from business, trade unions, financiers, political parties, charities, academics proposing this or that scheme for dealing with this or that problem" (Miller and Rose, 1990:4). Second, governmentality is programmatic in that it is premised upon the fundamental assumption that reality is actually programmable, and that it is a "a domain subject to certain determinants, rules, norms and processes that can be acted upon and improved by authorities" (Rose and Miller, 1992:183).

However, there is nothing self-evident about the problems upon which governmental programs are focused. Because power is no longer seen as emanating from a single source (such as the state), possessed of a single underpinning purpose, questions now have to be asked concerning how, why, and when government should operate. That is, governmental programs must be positioned within a broader field—a field that articulates various ideas concerning the appropriate ends and means of government in general. These ideas—*political rationalities*—give shape to social reality and determine the way in which problems are generated, defined, and ranked, and how they might be responded to, and by whom. Rose and Miller (1992:178–179) suggest that differing political rationalities determine issues such as how tasks are distributed and which principles should direct which aspects of government; they express a knowledge of the objects to be governed; and they provide the framework for "rendering reality thinkable in such a way that it is amenable to political deliberations." While governmental programs are not directly derived from political rationalities, there is a relationship of translation between the two—the latter providing the language within which the former can be addressed.

However, as Miller and Rose (1990:8) note, government is not only a matter of representation, it is also a matter of intervention. Furthermore, the analysis of this intervention should commence, not with the most grandiose forms of legislation or visible examples of state jurisdiction and control, but, rather, with the mundane and routine administrative mechanisms through which government becomes possible. This includes such seemingly trivial technologies as techniques of notation, computation, and calculation, the invention of surveys and presentational forms such as tables, the standardization of training systems, and so on. It is these technologies that permit the "inscription of reality in a form where it can be debated and diagnosed" (Miller and Rose, 1990:7):

> If political rationalities render reality into the domain of thought, these *"technologies of government"* seek to translate thought into the domain of reality, and to establish 'in the world of persons and things' spaces and devices for acting upon those entities of which they dream and scheme...It is through technologies that political rationalities and the programs of government they articulate become capable of deployment. (Miller and Rose, 1990:8)

This relationship between governmental programs, political rationalities, and governmental technologies forms the core of Foucault's notion of governmentality. These elements permit an analysis of the exercise of power in advanced liberal democratic societies that is not tied to the pre-existing dichotomies of state/civil, sovereignty/autonomy, and coercion/consent.

It is arguments specifically concerning the opposition between state and civil society in particular that provide a point of entry for a number of recent writers on governmentality, such as Graham Burchell, Colin Gordon, and Nikolas Rose. This work is important as it will later provide two useful conceptual instruments for addressing the government of youth. The first of these conceptual devices is the notion of government at a distance, and the second is an emphasis upon the role of expertise within contemporary government. Both these features will be discussed at some length after a more general analysis of this work on governmentality.

Primarily, Burchell, Gordon, and Rose argue that any understanding of governmentality must also include the effects of what they see as a significant change in eighteenth- and nineteenth-century society, a change that came about, in part, as a challenge to *raison d'état*: the advent of liberalism. It is argued by these writers that the philosophical ideas of John Locke and David Hume, as well as the economic theories of Adam Smith, were instrumental in formulating a series of concerns about the limits of government. It is also suggested that the publication of Smith's *The Wealth of Nations* resulted in both a change in political and economic thinking, and more importantly, a shift in the relationship between knowledge and government (Gordon, 1991:14). Although this shift originated in European states (Polanyi, 1944; Foucault, 1989), similar changes soon occurred in North America (Orren, 1991; Appleby, 1992*)* and in Australia (McIntyre, 1991).

In contrast to the logic of Cameralism (wherein the science of government is homologous to the activities of the state), liberal political economy depends upon a certain distance from matters of state—a state with inherent limitations in its ability to know. That is, according to Burchell (1993:269), liberalism was skeptical both about the state and state reason, and also about the ability of the state "to know perfectly and in all details the reality to be governed." As Rose (1993:289) observes, the advent of liberalism marks the abandonment of the belief in the possibility of a totally administered society. After all, not only was the population now understood to have its own natural and inherent characteristics (beyond the reach of sovereign will), but also that the *a priori* opacity of the field of economic exchange disqualified it from sovereign knowledge or intervention (Burchell, 1991:134):

> Liberalism can thus be accurately characterized in Kantian terms as a *critique of state reason*, a doctrine of limitation and wise restraint, designed to mature and educate state reason by displaying to it the intrinsic bounds of its power to know. Liberalism undertakes to determine how government is possible, what it can do, and what ambitions it must needs renounce to be able to accomplish what lies within its powers. (Gordon, 1991:15)

Thus, what is important about liberalism for the issue of governmentality is not its role as a political philosophy nor its adoption as a generalized template for living, but rather its place as a formula of rule (Rose, 1993:283), or as a style of thinking quintessentially concerned with the art of governing

(Gordon, 1991:14). Furthermore, liberalism took as its central problem the demarcation of the governable from the ungovernable, of those areas of necessary state intervention from those of autonomy. However, it is argued that those domains where governmental intervention is deemed inappropriate only exist as a result of more subtle forms of governmental management, such as those operating within the family. In order to construct the family in this manner it has been necessary to develop mechanisms of government that operate at a distance. It is through expertise associated with disciplines such as family guidance, welfare, psychology, community medicine, counseling and pedagogy, that the family can at once be private and autonomous, while simultaneously being one of the most important sites for instilling the capacities, aspirations, and habits required of the population.

At this point, it should be noted that, although the central principle of liberalism has remained constant (that is, setting limits to government), government itself has experienced numerous important modifications. Rose and Miller (1992) outline two of the most important of these modifications to classic liberalism. First, they argue that the late nineteenth and early twentieth centuries witnessed an increasing conviction that classic liberalism was failing to produce the kind of society that many desired. In response to this dissatisfaction, many western societies became welfare states. This did not signal the founding of a new form of state; rather, it initiated a new mode of rule. Again, the welfare state cannot accurately be depicted as a central entity that extended its tentacles throughout society (Rose, 1993:295). Instead, it is best characterized by the deployment of new ideas about how best to govern. In general, these ideas attempted to transform the state into a center which, while retaining a distance from those domains in need of intervention (in classic liberal tradition), still succeeded in their effective management:

> Welfarism is not so much a matter of the rise of an interventionist state as the assembling of diverse mechanisms and arguments through which political forces seek to secure social and economic objectives by linking up a plethora of networks and aspirations to know, program and transform the social field. (Rose and Miller, 1992:192)

The aforementioned securing of social and economic objectives was primarily to be accomplished through the medium of expertise. In this instance, welfarism uses expertise as the link between a centrally controlled network and a series of domains in which political decisions are dominated by technical calculations (Rose and Miller, 1992:196). As previously mentioned, these new techniques of government would still succeed in retaining the public/private split characteristic of liberalism. Within the political rationality of welfarism, the notion of social responsibility played a pivotal role. As Rose (1993:285) notes, persons and activities were to be governed through society, not only in that social norms formed one of the crucial instruments of government, but also that experiences were to be constituted in a social form.

In part, it was this very emphasis on the social that provided the counterpoint for the second important mutation in classic liberalism—the rise of neo-liberalism from the mid-1970s onward. As with classic liberalism, neo-liberalism concerns itself primarily with setting limits to governmental intervention. It characterizes welfarism in terms of an excessive and counterproductive expansion of the state. Because the state is inherently unable to deal with the marketplace, it should all but leave it alone. Furthermore, the principles of the market should be applied more widely within society, even to the level of the construction of a particular type of subjectivity. As will be discussed in chapter 4, the new notion of the entrepreneur of the self successfully aligns the self-regulating capacities of individuals with broader governmental objectives. Burchell (1993:271) concludes that, within the logic of neo-liberalism, "the rational principle for regulating and limiting governmental activity must be determined by reference to...the free, *entrepreneurial* and *competitive* conduct of economic-rational individuals." This understanding of the relationship between neo-liberalism and the formation of certain types of person is also held by Rose and Miller, who state that within neo-liberalism:

> Economic entrepreneurship is to replace regulation, as active agents seeking to maximise their own advantage are both the legitimate locus of decisions about their own affairs and the most effective in calculating actions and outcomes. And more generally, active entrepreneurship is to replace passivity and dependency of responsible solidarity as individuals are encouraged to strive to optimise their own quality of life and that of their families. (Rose and Miller, 1992:198)

This is not to suggest that expertise plays no part within neo-liberalism. Independent entrepreneurial individuals do not now simply choose their own social trajectories from the range of social alternatives made available to them. On the contrary, expertise is still central to the machinery of neo-liberal government; however, it now operates in a different manner. Whereas welfarism employed expertise in its attempts to govern through the foundational concept of society, neo-liberalism utilizes expertise to manage the choices of individual citizens. Furthermore, expertise was no longer to be directly and obviously coupled with the political apparatus of rule; rather, experts were to be relocated "within a market governed by the rationalities of competition, accountability and consumer demand" (Rose, 1993:285). And far from reducing the governmental potentiality of expertise, this new distance from formal government has resulted in the establishment of new mechanisms of accountability, such as audits, budget disciplines, and accountancy. The deployment of these technologies effectively breached many of the enclosures of expertise that had thrived under welfarism—Rose and Miller (1992:200) cite the example of market encroachment into areas such as operating theatre administration, where managers rather than medical consultants now become the most powerful actors.

Rose (1993:285) is quick to point out that the liberalism/welfarism/neo-liberalism shifts should not be understood in terms of periodization. Instead, they are simply effective ways of examining loosely demarcatable problematizations of rule. That is, if it is accepted that liberalism played as important a role in the shaping of contemporary government as did, for example, Cameralism, then these mutations are worthy of investigation. However, this assertion itself is not without its critics. In his paper, "In What Sense is Liberal Government 'Liberal'?" Hunter (1993c) articulates numerous misgivings over the central role allocated to liberalism. He argues that the prominent influence of specific liberal philosophers indicates a history of ideas approach. He also maintains that many of the mechanisms constituting government at a distance, which have been attributed to liberalism, may actually have originated elsewhere. Irrespective of this debate, Hunter (1993c:1) states that he is not challenging the importance of the notion of government at a distance. He agrees that, in contemporary western societies, government exists principally through the expert management of numerous relatively autonomous domains, which, in turn, shape the conduct of self-disciplining and self-acting individuals.

It is now more evident that the notion of "government at a distance" and a concomitant focus upon expertise provide important conceptual tools for understanding the government of categories such as childhood and youth. After all, having made a case against a dichotomous social model that features the state exercising power over civil society, the question remains—how then is the category of youth organized and administered? It will be argued here that an investigation of quasi-autonomous governmental domains, such as the family, the school, and the workplace, will provide some answers.

Addressing government at a distance first—in *The Policing of Families*, Jacques Donzelot (1979) points out the central role of the family in the government of children. As previously mentioned, the means of sovereign rule—laws, decrees, and regulations—are blunt instruments, indeed. Donzelot argues that a far more effective way of governing childhood involved the enlistment of the family in the production of good children. This production was overseen by medical, educational, and psychological experts who successfully bridged the gap between the inner workings of the family unit and the broadest objectives of government. By what Donzelot (1979:169) refers to as the subtle regulation of images, it became possible to construct desirable and effective norms of family life, motherhood, and childhood, without resorting to the legal system at all. Thus, sites such as the family became crucial in establishing a useful grid of norms—norms that were instrumental in constructing the capacities and aptitudes expected of normal, healthy children.

Although Donzelot's analysis is solely concerned with French history, in "Minding the Family: Donzelot and His Critics," Terry Counihan (1982) correctly indicates that these same arguments have wider application. In other contemporary Western societies, including Australia, the family is similarly enlisted as an effective mechanism through which to govern at a distance. In *The Disenchantment of the Home*, Kerreen Reiger (1985) examines some of the changes that occurred in the structure of the Australian family between the 1880s and the 1930s. Although she employs a Marxist explanatory framework, which Donzelot does not, she also argues that the family was enlisted in the production of good children. In a chapter entitled

"Producing the Model Modern baby," she notes that motherhood became a skill which required learning. No longer were women deemed to be innately possessed of the ability to raise children, rather maternal common sense became something that had to be taught (Reiger, 1985:132).

> With the institutionalisation of the infant welfare movement, "mothercraft" had emerged as a new domain of knowledge, now under professional control and ready for popular dissemination through the women's magazines and feature pages of the newspapers. The major theme was that of maternal ignorance and the need to educate parents and mothers in particular, because...they're "on duty unremittingly night and day." (Reiger, 1985:128–129)

Women were deemed to need expert guidance in order to fulfill their maternal responsibilities, with the notion of infant welfare providing one of the rationales for the construction of the good mother—the character that formed the central foundation for effective government at a distance within the family.

The importance of government at a distance is also examined in Vikki Bell's (1993) "Governing Childhood," an analysis of the relationship between government and the family in contemporary Great Britain. Bell (1993:394) contextualizes her argument by contending that the classical liberal approach of *laissez-faire* had been applied directly to the family. Although simultaneously articulating the privacy of the domestic domain, various governmental programs also gave parents (ostensibly voluntary) tasks concerning the rearing of their children. Thus, she argues, *laissez-faire* was a theory held but not practiced. Although the cooperation of the family was ostensibly voluntary, this very cooperation was actually vital to the processes of normalization within liberal societies. Consequently, "the maintenance of a discourse of public/private was part and parcel of the way in which power worked" (Bell, 1993:394).

Bell goes on to discuss the relationship between government and the family within neo-liberalism. She argues that this contemporary form of rule also stresses the importance of domestic autonomy, while simultaneously employing the family as a governmental site. The heavy emphasis upon individualism and personal responsibility, however, characteristic of neo-liberalism, has brought with it a different set of problematizations regarding the government of the family. Unlike its forebear, neo-liberalism no longer subordinates the rights of the child to that of the family.

> Neo-liberalism is in a sense the governmental outcome of the tension which welfarism generated, posing as it does the primacy of both the family and its individual members. That is, it seeks to rejuvenate a sense of autonomy for the family as an autonomous and central social unit at the same time as it treats the family as a dangerous space where all members (but particularly children and women) are potentially in need of support against that unit. (Bell, 1993:395)

Bell (1993:397) discusses this tension in the light of the Children Act of 1989, which legislates aspects of the relationship between children's rights and parental authority. She argues that the main practical outcome of this legislation is the implied message that responsible parents do not use the courts in the process of bringing up their children. It follows on from this legal judgment that, by reinforcing the merely supportive role that the state ought to play in child-rearing (while simultaneously stressing the vital importance of proper child care and supervision) and by formalizing the concept of parental responsibility, this necessarily augments the significance of the mechanisms by which the child is "governed at a distance" through the family.

In combination with the notion of government at a distance, the emphasis on expertise provides the second important conceptual tool for addressing the contemporary government of youth. Indeed, it is this expertise that permits government at a distance to operate effectively. Within locations such as the family and the school, parents and teachers are themselves recruited as relays between this external expertise and the child itself. In cases where the parent and the teacher are inadequate to deal with the complexity and delicacy of ensuring proper social adjustment, external expert guidance is then employed. Increasingly, it is the role of a network of experts in subjectivity (not just psychoanalysts, but educational and clinical psychologists, psychiatrists, guidance counselors, social workers, and Human Relation Education teachers) to ensure the normal mental and moral development of youth. Psychological expertise has been especially significant in the government of the young:

> Psychology has played a key role in establishing the norms of childhood, in providing means for visualising childhood pathology and normality, in providing

> vocabularies for speaking about childhood subjectivity and its problems, in inventing technologies for cure and normalisation...The soul of the young citizen has become the object of government through expertise. (Rose, 1990:131)

In the specific case of sex, the successful creation of the well-balanced adult is often deemed to rely upon appropriate expert management of the adolescent's sex. Irrespective of the psy-disciplines' current self-depiction as leading the struggle against the structures of social, psychical, and sexual repression, the knowledges of the psy-disciplines are still largely governmental in function. Indeed, the deployment of child psychology within the classroom originated as part of a wider concern over distinguishing between normal and abnormal children. Furthermore, it has primarily been through psychological expertise that the criteria for the normal healthy child have been refined, as well as the mechanisms for assessing that normality. The contemporary classroom played an important role in this process, as it contained large numbers of children of the same age, which enabled a broad range of rigorous comparisons, through which a grid of norms could eventually emerge. Arguably then, the success and expansion of the psy-disciplines owe little to their epistemological claims, as these claims bear limited direct relation to the practical and tactical deployment of psychological expertise within particular governmental strategies played out in the homes, the classroom, the clinic, and the courts.

As will be demonstrated, the importance of expertise, in tandem with domains such as the family and the school, is particularly evident when addressing the issue of youth and the management of its sex. However, this book will not take the approach that expertise plays a part in channeling the sexual energies of youth in appropriate directions, a self-characterization common to the sex education literature. For example, in *Sex Education in the Eighties*, Mary Calderstone states:

> Our children are sexual; they are born that way and it would not be considered normal if this were not so. It is our responsibility to help parents not to fear or repress their children's sexuality, but to help it mature safely along with all the other wondrous endowments that are part of being a human child. (Calderstone, 1981:251)

Calderstone unknowingly demonstrates the characteristic governmental links between expertise and autonomous domains such as the family. She also outlines most of the central tenets of an essentialist model of sexuality—a model rejected by this book. That is, rather than adopting the familiar position that sexuality is an inherent drive that society then either represses or channels, it will be argued here that sexuality has its origins in Christian asceticism, which the machinery of government then relayed to a wider population. However, before addressing the central focus of chapter 2—the relationship between youth, sex, and governmentality—Foucault's arguments concerning the governmental nature of sexuality need a little development.

Sexuality and the Emergence of Childhood

Within most of the literature, the concept of sexuality has consistently been represented as the most fundamental axis of life. It appears to furnish a bedrock for the process of self-definition and is the most obvious conduit between humankind and nature. This essentialist characterization of sexuality provides the central theoretical orthodoxy for all but a few texts on the subject, such that within these texts, sexuality:

> is conceptualised as an overpowering force in the individual that shapes not only the personal but the social life as well. It is seen as a driving, instinctual force, whose characteristics are built into the biology of the human animal, which shapes human institutions and whose will must force its way out, either in the form of direct sexual expression or, if blocked, in the form of perversion or neuroses. (Weeks, 1981:2)

This approach is typified by the works of the influential sexologist Henry Havelock Ellis, his *Studies in the Psychology of Sex* (seven volumes, published between 1897–1928). He located the two great, fundamental human drives as being for food and sex, and from these drives come the energy to construct culture. After all, a man is what his sex is (Ellis, 1946:3). Consequently, Ellis attempted to construct an encyclopedia of the various forms in which the sex drive manifested itself, arguing that the sex drive becomes refracted through various diverse cultural filters. Although these filters produce diverse forms of sexual conduct, all are still tied to an original motivating essence. This approach to sex presupposes more than just the existence of a fundamental human sex drive, it also assumes that this impulse manifests itself in terms of a unified sexuality. Humans are deemed to have a sexuality in the same way that they have a personality. It is depicted as a singular, bounded sphere, a demarcated capacity. Just as youth is understood and utilized as a coherent category, so sexuality seems to describe an unproblematic thing-in-itself, a fact of nature—everyone has a sexuality.

However, the view that humans are endowed with a singular sexuality which, although expressed in diverse forms, is still grounded in nature, is not without its critics. Jeffrey Weeks (1981:3) suggests that despite the divisions that exist between counterposing theories of sexuality, they have sufficient ground in common to permit the construction of a collective criticism of the established model. Generally, this collective criticism rejects the most crucial foundation of the essentialist paradigm: that there exists a fundamental sexual drive responsible for the establishment of a sexuality. Feminist writers have long regarded the work of sexologists such as Ellis with suspicion, understanding that by constructing sexuality within an essentialist framework this necessarily inscribes a biological authorization upon existing gender inequalities. Because this essence of sexuality naturally differed between the sexes, men have accordingly been inexorably driven by a predatory sexual impulse. Margaret Jackson (1984:53) sums up a popular feminist position on Ellis, by stating that his "'science' of sex constitutes above all an apology for and a justification of precisely that form of male sexuality which contemporary feminists were challenging: a sexuality based on 'uncontrollable urges,' power and violence." Likewise, social interactionists also reject this deterministic model of sexuality. They argue that there is nothing intrinsic to any behavior that makes it inherently sexual. Sexual conduct is neither fixed in nature nor by the organs themselves (Gagnon and Simon, 1973:9). Rather, it is the meaning assigned to that behavior by the actors concerned that determines whether a situation or activity is sexual or not (Miller and Fowlkes, 1987:153).

In *The History of Sexuality*, Foucault (1976) also rejects the essentialist notion of sexuality as a self-governing domain. Rather, he contends that Western societies created and deployed a new apparatus for ordering sexual relations—sexuality. According to this argument, sexuality is simply a historical construct, in part a complex mechanism for the policing of populations, and in part a legacy of Christian confessional practices. To support this latter claim, Foucault (1976:63) argues that the practice of confession, once restricted to penance, spread to a broad range of new contexts. The central intention remained the same—the production of truth—but the governmental possibilities multiplied. Confessions regarding sex, originally heard once by the priest and then lost, were now recorded, assembled, and classified by experts of all kinds (doctors, teachers, psychologists, welfare workers, sexologists). An entire confessional technology evolved:

> Nearly one hundred and fifty years have gone into the making of a complex machinery for producing true discourses on sex: a deployment that spans a wide segment of history in that it connects the ancient injunction to confession to clinical listening methods. It is this deployment that enables something called 'sexuality' to embody the truth of sex and its pleasures. (Foucault, 1976:68)

Thus, an existing means of organizing conduct—the confession—was taken up within a series of sites inquiring into the truth of sex. *Sexuality* evolved as a product of these inquiries, with the process of embedding sexuality eventually being so successful and pervasive that it has now come to be posited as the truth of our being. It is by this reasoning that Foucault contends, rather than constituting a relatively autonomous part of human nature outside discourse and to which discourse merely refers, sexuality is actually created within discourse itself as a form of power-knowledge:

> It is the name that can be given to a historical construct: not a furtive reality that is difficult to grasp, but a great surface network in which the stimulation of bodies, the intensification of pleasures, the incitement to discourse, the formation of knowledges, the strengthening of controls and resistances, are linked to one another, in accordance with a few major strategies of knowledge and power. (Foucault, 1976:105–106)

Foucault argues that before the development of sexuality, sexual relations had given rise to a deployment of alliance. This system of governing marriage, kinship ties, and the inheritance of names and possessions declined in importance as economic processes and political structures required more flexible instruments and supports. That is, the machinery of alliance is firmly tied to the economic, primarily through imperatives concerning the transmission of wealth; it operates through the rules demarcating the permitted from the forbidden; also, it is centered around the relationship between partners and fixed laws. However, this apparatus was eventually augmented/superseded by the deployment of sexuality. The machinery of sexuality is more subtly linked to the economic through a number of relays—such as via the body that produces and consumes; it operates through more numerous, flexible, and contingent modalities of power; also, it centered around the sensations and pleasures of the body. This is not to suggest, however, that the deployment of sexuality ended, or ever acted against, the deployment of alliance:

> The machinery of sexuality arose out of the machinery of alliance. Indeed, it is in the family, at the heart of the alliance machinery that the principal elements of the sexuality machinery have been developed...The modern family must not be seen as a social, economic and political structure of alliance that excludes or limits sexuality. On the contrary, it has provided sexuality with a permanent support. It has made possible the production of a sexuality quite different in nature from alliance, while allowing the systems of alliance to be permeated with a whole new tactics of power. (Sheridan, 1980:188)

Significantly, Foucault's notion of bio-power—a contemporary form of power directed at administering the conditions of life—found its greatest and most useful instrument in sexuality. Sexuality effectively straddled bio-power's two most important forms—the "anatomo-politics of the human body" and the "biopolitics of the population." The first of these forms centered on the body as a machine, wherein its capacities were to be maximized, its usefulness augmented, and its docility ensured. This process occurred primarily through the use of the disciplines. The second form addressed itself to the new *raison-d'etre* of government—the population. Government sought to regulate factors such as its health, life expectancy, and birth rate, not merely through the legal system, but through the establishment of an effective grid of governmental norms. Therefore, as the machinery of sexuality is pertinent to both these domains, at the juncture of the body and the population, it became a crucial target of a power organized around the management of life rather than the menace of death, as had been the case in Foucault's characterization of the *juridico-discursive* (Foucault, 1976:147).

Foucault maintains that the past three hundred years witnessed an increasing pre-occupation with sexual matters, such that they now occupy a unique position in our society. Foucault argues that the contemporary understanding of sexuality is dependent upon a wide historical legacy of interrelated knowledges and practices. Although he limits his analysis to specific eras, he has been instrumental in opening up the field for a number of similar studies, which have now staked out the main contours of the sexual terrain (Weeks, 1981, 1986; Mort, 1987). These studies suggest that to understand the mechanisms by which sexuality occupies its current form, it is necessary to trace the diverse trajectories of an assortment of knowledges, disciplines, and practices. These would include influences such as the moral regulation of the Church; the rise of libertarianism and the freedom of sexual expression; the biological determinism of Darwin (which lay the foundation for all ensuing essentialist theories of sexuality); the Eugenicist/Social Darwinist movements (locating sexuality within the realm of racial survival, birth control, and the management of the population); Feminism and the Moral Purity movements, (which sought to police the sexual activities of men); and the medicalization of sexuality (which cordons off sexuality as, first and foremost, an object of scientific knowledges, and which includes medicine, psychology, psychoanalysis, and sexology). By refusing to assign a priority to any of these specific truth claims, Foucault concludes that there are no grounds for believing that sexuality exists independent of discourse, but, instead, that it is an aggregation of discourses concerned with sex.

It is, in part, Foucault's discursive conception of sexuality that leads to his rejection of the repressive hypothesis concerning Victorian sexuality. This hypothesis, taken as an *a-priori* truth in most literature, argues that the high level of sexual freedom taken for granted by the inhabitants of Europe until the end of the sixteenth century was increasingly repressed—concomitant with the rise of capitalism and the Victorian bourgeoisie. Furthermore, the all-pervasive nature of this repression has meant that the twentieth century is yet to rid itself completely of its unwanted effects. Foucault points out that subscribing to the repressive hypothesis concerning Victorian sexuality is to ignore that fact that there was a hyperbolic increase in the number of discourses on sexuality from the eighteenth century onward. As he observes: "Surely no other type of society has ever accumulated—and in such a relatively short space of time—a similar quantity of discourses concerned with sex. It may well be that we talk about sex more than anything else..." (Foucault, 1976:33).

Foucault stresses that there was no overall logic or design behind the various discourses clustered around sex at this time. However, as the amount of sexual knowledge increased, there gradually emerged four strategic unities that formed specific mechanisms of power and knowledge centered on sex. These include: a hysterization of women's bodies, a socialization of procreative behavior, a psychiatrization of perverse pleasures and, of relevance to this chapter, a pedagogization of children's sex:

> A pedagogisation of children's sex: a double assertion that practically all children indulge or are prone to indulge in sexual activity; and that, being unwarranted, at the same time "natural" and "contrary to nature," this sexual activity posed physical and moral, individual and collective dangers; children were defined as preliminary sexual beings, on this side of sex, yet within it, astride a dangerous dividing line. Parents, families, educators, doctors, and eventually psychologists would have to take charge, in a continuous way, of this precious and perilous, dangerous and endangered sexual potential: this pedagogization was especially evident in the war against onanism, which in the West lasted nearly two centuries. (Foucault, 1976:104)

The concern over masturbation was at its zenith in Britain and America between 1850 and 1880, although in Germany and France it continued as a familiar representation of childhood until the 1920s (Sommerville, 1982:205). As such, the masturbating child became constructed as an archetypal object of knowledge within the sexual domain. Experts within the fields of medicine, psychology, and pedagogy all deemed onanism to be responsible for a myriad of childhood disorders, both moral and physical. However, this is not to suggest that masturbation provided the only axis along which the relationship between sex and young people was policed— far from it. As Foucault (1976:98) points out, the body of the child provides an important focus for power-knowledge, since the child is "under surveillance, surrounded in his cradle, his bed, or his room by an entire watch-crew of parents, nurses, servants, educators, and doctors, [who are] all attentive to the least manifestation of his sex..." Again, the presence of these forms of expertise permitted the realization of a broad range of governmental aspirations concerning the child, while not directly compromising the autonomy of the family. After all:

> Childhood is the most intensely governed sector of personal existence. In different ways, at different times, and by many different routes varying from one sector of society to another, the health, welfare, and destiny of children has been linked in thought and practice to the destiny of the nation and the responsibilities of the state. (Rose and Miller, 1990:121)

Before examining in greater detail the relationship between the child and its sexuality, it is first necessary to emphasize the contingent nature of childhood. Like youth, childhood is not a fact in itself. Both emerged from within a number of historically specific sites (indeed, it will be argued later that, in part, youth emerged from previous objects like the child, the adolescent, and the juvenile delinquent). Regarding the historical contingency of childhood, in *Centuries of Childhood*, Philippe Aries (1960) advances the proposition that before the sixteenth century, the category of the child did not exist. Pre-adulthood consisted solely of being an infant, a category that lacked any real importance. Upon reaching the age of six or seven, they were immediately accorded the full status, rights, and obligations of adults. That is, those too fragile to be considered adult simply did not count.

From the sixteenth century onward, Aries (1960:125–126) argues, the single status of adult started to fragment. Young people from the upper classes began to be represented distinctively in art, not just in the structure of their faces, but also in that they were clothed in a different manner from adults. Eventually, Aries claims, a separate status of child was demarcated from the broader status of adult. He argues that the idea of coddling provided the focal point around which childhood was eventually to crystallize, in that children became a source of amusement and relaxation for the women who looked after them. While this occurred within the family circle, however, a parallel set of imperatives began to impinge upon the new space of childhood from outside the family. An assortment of churchmen and social moralists also began to take interest in childhood, but rather than lauding it for its simplicity and sweetness, they regarded the child to be in need of safeguarding and reformation. The family should provide protection and instruction for what were, indeed, future adults. Consequently, children were no longer to be dressed and treated as miniature adults; instead they were conceived of as a form of property to be admired, cared for, disciplined, and especially, protected.

That children needed to be protected forms an integral part of defining and articulating the aspects of the relationship that existed between childhood and sexuality at that time—a relationship primarily based upon the notion of childhood as innocence (Finch, 1993:70). This characterization of the child had its inception firmly within the rationalities associated with the bourgeois family. Axiomatic to this understanding of childhood was the pre-requisite belief that children were intrinsically pure and innocent (Weeks, 1981:49). By shielding them from the corruption of society (a corruption most normally characterized by the lifestyles of the working classes) for as long as possible, they could be equipped with the necessary moral faculties to cope by themselves. Aries (1960:116) states that: "the ideas of childish innocence resulted in two kinds of attitude and behaviour towards childhood. First, safeguarding it against pollution by life, and particularly by the "sexuality" tolerated if not approved of among adults; and second, strengthening it by developing character and reason." This argument is supported by Donzelot (1979:78), in *The Policing of Families*, who argues that many of the philanthropic crusades on behalf of children (such as the age of consent campaign) were focused around the themes of the corruption of innocence—sexual corruption in particular.

These, however, were still essentially bourgeois concerns. Sexuality was not immediately and evenly deployed across the entire social body. Rather, it was initially addressed within quite restricted circles. Contrary to arguments that follow from the repressive hypothesis, these circles were not the working classes—powerless groups, dominated through a new and pervasive form of social control. Instead, it was among the most privileged in society that the various techniques and practices that constitute the governmental machinery of sexuality first began to be applied. It was within the bourgeois family that the sexuality of children first became an important issue. Foucault (1976:121) rightly observes that the great anti-masturbation campaigns of the nineteenth century were not waged against the children of the lower classes, instituted by concerned factory owners. They were directed at the secret habits of the nation's future leaders, whose onanism threatened not only their intellect and moral fiber, but also their ability to guarantee a healthy line of descent for their family. This was no fleeting concern. The machinery of sexuality began to play a strategic role in the marking out of caste boundaries. Claims to difference/superiority from subordinate classes would now be supported through the knowledges associated with disciplines such as biology and eugenics. Aristocratic "blood" was now converted into "a sound organism and a healthy sexuality" (Foucault, 1976:126). After all, certain sexual practices were associated with degeneracy in offspring, which, in turn, threatened the line of descent and the reproduction of privilege. Thus, it is argued, sex became central to bourgeois self-definition.

It took some considerable time for the deployment of sexuality to extend to the working classes. Initially, there was neither interest nor concern over their sexual practices. However, congruent with the increasing governmental centrality of the notion of the population, there developed numerous anxieties over the levels of crime, disease, and immorality within the dark, forbidding and largely unexplored regions of the urban rookeries. These problems, driven by political rationalities pertaining to the health of the nation, were instrumental in the deployment of diverse techniques and practices that constitute the machinery of sexuality. The numerous programs associated with this deployment were not all set in motion simultaneously, however. Foucault (1976:122) suggests that this process actually occurred in three phases from the end of the eighteenth century through to the end of the nineteenth century. The first involved concerns around birth control and the administration of reproduction. The second involved the earliest attempts to position the family as one of the main instruments of government. The final phase involved the aspiration of government for the moral reformation of the poor, concentrating on the juridical and medical control of perversions. Although the manner of its deployment was not identical in all locations, "this was the moment when the deployment of 'sexuality,' elaborated in its more complex and intense forms, by and for the privileged classes, spread through the entire social body" (Foucault, 1976:122).

As Finch (1993:78) points out, however, even within the safe bounds of the bourgeois family, the young child occupied an increasingly tenuous sexual position. Although the child was deemed to be naturally without a sexuality, the belief existed that they could potentially be sexualized. Such ambiguity became the subject of open debate from the late 1860s onward. Some, such as Henry Maudsley, regarded childhood sexuality as an entirely natural and essential part of being human, in much the same way as it is most widely characterized now. Finch argues, however, that most theoretical work of the period located childhood sexuality in terms of pathology, with any visible sexual behavior generally explained away using environmentalist logic. For example, such logic often characterized the innocent sons of the bourgeoisie being despoiled by working-class servant girls, in whom sexual lasciviousness was expected. In support of this position, Finch (1993:79) cites Krafft-Ebing's (1886) seminal *Psychopathia Sexualis* that positioned childhood sexuality as an analog of masturbation, arguing the practice demonstrated a neuropathic constitution condition. It was not until the publication of Sigmund Freud's *Three Essays* in 1905 that the notion of the sexual child slowly began to become the orthodoxy.

Finch (1993:85) argues that the sexualizing of childhood brought with it its own problems. The initial separation of the personage of the child from that of the adult, and the allocation of a special place for that personage within the bourgeois family unit, was largely based upon a presupposition of sexual innocence. With this underpinning assumption removed, it is not surprising that sexuality became a constant preoccupation and, thus, an obvious target of government. As seems to be consistently true of governmental programs, the history of the various attempts to regulate the sexuality of the young could generally be written in terms of their limited success:

> The mother of the middle class family had a special role, guarding her children's sexuality, but throughout the twentieth century working class families were seen to be deficient in this role. The non-respectable who left their children to raise themselves in the streets had provided the depraved with a supply of precociously sexual children, and had left middle class society, primarily through medical science, with the problem of policing the behaviour of these sexual children. (Finch, 1993:85)

Despite the focus thus far falling upon the sexual management of children within the family, however, governmental aspirations were also being realized at a distance within the confines of the school. Foucault reinforces this contention by illustrating how, for example, the issue of sex was central to the construction and functioning of the secondary school. The sexual preoccupation can be seen in the overall architecture of the school to the internal layout of classrooms and dormitories, in the rigorous standards of behavior expected of students to the correlative mechanisms of punishment for transgressors, in the hierarchies of authority that policed the school itself, and in the technologies that were instrumental in positing childhood sexuality as a crucial domain of governmental intelligibility (Foucault, 1976:27–28). Although sex education itself may not have been on the curriculum, domains such as the school still provided a site wherein a broad range of governmental imperatives pertaining to sexual self-management could be realized.

Thus, along with the pedagogic family, mass schooling became one of the most important and convenient mechanisms for implementing specific forms of self-cultivation and distributing them to a mass population. These ends, however, could not be realized satisfactorily solely through the mechanisms available at the beginning of the nineteenth century—that is, either the strict regimen of monitorialism or the pastoral care of the Sunday school. David Stow (1850), a nineteenth-century educational reformer, argued for a form of schooling that allowed a greater level of freedom than previously possible within the monitorial school, and yet which still permitted the subtle imposition of required social norms. This child-centered pedagogy successfully combined the strategies of pastoral care with those of social investigation and administration. It also promoted a sympathetic relationship between teacher and pupil, in the form of the concerned teacher who observes and directs the moral development of children. However:

> The move to overcome "mechanical" teaching and the remoteness of the classroom from "life" through a new "child-centred" pedagogy was, therefore, no fundamental opposition to the disciplinary normalisation of whole populations. Quite the reverse: it was the means by which the latter could be most successfully achieved. (Hunter, 1993b:25)

As Hunter (1984:69) indicates, the appearance of the modern classroom had the dual effect of regulating the behavior and bodily demeanor of large numbers of children while simultaneously supplying them with various skills and capacities related to appropriate self-regulation. Even in those educational sites generally characterized by their child-centeredness, such as the kindergarten, pastoral care is combined with social investigation and management. These do not represent a fundamental opposition; rather they are two tactics that form part of a wider strategy aimed at the correct training of young people.

In support of this contention: the correct training of young people provides the focus for much of Debbie Tyler's (1992) work on the 1930s kindergarten. Specifically, she discusses the implications of the categorizing of a five year old girl as a problem child, owing largely to her occasionally "going like a boy"—urinating standing up. Her status as a problem hinged upon the unsuccessful attempts of the school to enlist the girl in the process of becoming a better child—that is, one who urinated appropriately. It is important here that the quirk of "going like a boy" was only made visible due to the surveillance techniques of the kindergarten. Within this specialized context, the most private of practices are made visible and recorded, cases are compared, norms constructed. Tyler (1992:1) realizes the significance of the ability to mark out this behavior as a specific type of problem, noting that "while the kindergarten spoke of 'the child' as a type of person undifferentiated by sex, its techniques for inscribing individual differences also made visible sex differences in the capacity of children to learn its lessons." Eventually, the development and deployment of techniques like the chi-square (which tested the validity of differences) resulted in the emergence of sex as a statistically significant indicator. Differences materialized between male and female populations concerning factors such as speech development, aggression, and sleep patterns (Tyler, 1992:22–24). It would appear then, that the application of governmental technologies to the kindergarten population produced (in part) a new variable—sex—and, hence, a new target population—the schoolgirl. Although there are no longer governmental programs explicitly aimed at producing better children, Tyler (1992:25) notes that there exist strategies aimed at forming other types of children, such as "girls who will choose to take science subjects, or who will wish to enter 'non-traditional' careers." These strategies are dealt with in greater depth in chapter 3, where it is argued that risk is used within schools as a governmental rationale for managing the sex of young people. Within these concerns over the management of children's sex, there are traces of a broader theme common to depiction not only of childhood, but also of adolescence and youth—the romantic notion that there is a natural state which, given the opportunity, young people can manifest. This is, in part, a legacy of the belief that categories such as childhood and youth are somehow timeless and unchanging, and that society represses and distorts the real person inside. Indeed, the presumption of the existence of the natural child has formed the basis for a great deal of education research and so-called progressive practice. As A.S. Neill (1968:114), the best-known advocate of free-schooling, states in the influential *Summerhill*: "the whole idea of Summerhill is release: allowing the child to live out his natural interests." In a section of Tyler's (1993:44) "Making Better Children," entitled "Training to Be a Natural Child," she discerns within the 1930s child development literature an exhortation toward helping children achieve rationality, autonomy, and self-regulation. These aspirations are deemed to be desirable results, and yet simultaneously part of the child's nature. According to the advocates of kindergarten education:

> These "better children," children who were "better" at performing the tasks that child psychologists decreed indicated levels of development and foretold competence at the work of being an adult citizen, were produced by locating the child within the space of the kindergarten. (Tyler, 1993:44)

She notes the explicit belief that appropriate intervention within the school (utilizing available techniques of surveillance, normalization, and individuation, as well as additional expertise where necessary) will sort out most abnormalities, and permit optimum natural development. Tyler (1993:45) argues that the closely regulated space of the kindergarten produced the "kindergarten child"—a child that could be differentiated from other children owing in part to augmented capacities of self-regulation, inculcated via the techniques of normalization and surveillance operating there. Tyler uses the example of the Lady Gowrie Centers, built during World War II and still a popular form of kindergarten. Within these institutions, there operates a variety of subtle measurement and surveillance techniques. The measured organization of bodies in space permits the teacher to assess each child against graded developmental norms at a glance, while a number of unseen observation posts are incorporated into the standardized design of the buildings themselves. Furthermore, careful records are kept of each child, a crucial component in the dual strategies of normalization/differentiation.

These techniques, however, are not restricted to the kindergarten. It will be argued that youth itself is also generated within interrelated strategies that regulate the relations of time, bodies, and forces (Foucault, 1977:157), and also sort, classify, and differentiate individuals as members of classes of person. It will also be argued that the category of youth emerged from earlier personages and debates, such as those over the child, the adolescent, and the juvenile delinquent.

Youth, Sex, and Governmentality

Foucault (1977:157-158) contends that contemporary society is, in part, characterised by techniques for taking charge of the time of individual existences. This does not simply extend to the rigorous demarcation of the working day. Rather, it is composed of a minute positioning in relation to the pervasive division of time—the organization of time into successive or parallel segments; the arrangement of these segments into a graded, cumulative series of increasing complexity; and the connecting of these series into an overall, developmental plan. This is especially evident within contemporary schooling. As Foucault points out:

> disciplinary time...was gradually imposed upon pedagogic practice—specialising the time of training and detaching it from adult time, from the time of mastery, arranging different stages...drawing up programs...qualifying individuals according to the way they pass through these series. (Foucault, 1977:159)

This disciplinary logic is characteristic of the modern curriculum and is even evident within school-based attempts to manage the sexual conduct of pupils. In the recent guidelines for the implementation of Human Relations Education in Queensland schools, a ranked set of evolutionary categories has been developed, such that the general status of pupil is divided into four subcategories of chronological age—early childhood, middle childhood, adolescence, and young adulthood. Specific capacities are then allocated in relation to these categories, capacities against which knowledge about sex can be graded. Pupils in Early Childhood display "a natural curiosity about sex and development", whereas those in Middle Childhood are "more consciously aware of their own uniqueness in their relationships with others". The category undergoing Adolescence are "developmentally ready for a formal study of their physiological and emotional changes", and those demarcated within Young Adulthood "develop a personal responsibility for relationships" (Queensland Department of Education, 1988:3).

It follows from this logic that categories such as adolescence and youth actually spring from historically specific methods of classifying individuals as members of classes of person, and subdividing time. By placing individuals within the disciplinary space and time characteristic of mass schooling, observable differences could then appear. At the same time, these disciplinary arrangements permitted, for example, the production of norms of human sexual development and their application to the population. Thus, youth can be understood as part of the process of subdividing and ranking time within a segmented (but linear and teleological) model. Youth becomes an artifact of disciplinary methods that characterize and utilize categories of person according to the stage in the series they are encountering, in this instance, the intention is to produce adults who can manage their own sex.

In addition to the embedding of time within the body, the implementation of disciplinary technologies also involves sorting and classifying different categories of person. Primarily, this consists of the combined processes of normalization/differentiation. For example, in addition to its formation within the family, the child also came to be constructed as an object of knowledge within the institution of the school. Central to these mechanisms were the dual strategies of hierarchical observation and normalizing judgment—procedures still axiomatic within contemporary education. The architectural and spatial arrangement of the homogeneous-age classroom enable the ready compilation of academic, physical, social, psychological, and disciplinary norms. The augmentation of these norms then permits an ever more rigorous web of governmental intelligibility through which differentiation occurs. Consequently, with the category of youth, it is now possible (within a number of contexts, which do not necessarily specify the same object) to "measure gaps, to determine levels, to fix specialties, and to render the differences useful by fitting them to one another" (Foucault, 1977:158). Rose (1985) suggests that, by increasing the complexity of the grid of norms against which young people were measured, it became possible to construct a scientifically legitimated causal correlation between two increasingly recognizable personages—the maladjusted schoolchild and the juvenile delinquent. It was from various concerns over objects such as these (as well as the adolescent) that youth finally emerged in its own right. These concerns included:

> Abnormal behaviour, antisocial conduct, neuroses, eccentricities, making friendships too easily or not at all, quarrelling or being withdrawn, grieving or fearing too much or too little—all these departures from the norm could be linked together as maladjustments, and as predictors of troubles to come. (Rose, 1985:165)

Operating in conjunction with these two prominent characterizations was a newfound vocabulary of normative disturbances and disorders, a vocabulary which still underpins those aspects of contemporary psychology directed at youth. Such problems, left untreated or unrecognized, are still regarded as preliminary indicators of more serious future trouble. Implicit within the structures of the modern family and school, however, are the assumptions that most problems can almost always be avoided by acceding to governmental practices and interventions designed to promote the correct training of young people.

David McCallum (1993) also writes about problem children. He argues that, like the broader concept of the child itself, this figure does not have any essential, transhistoric validity as a category. Rather, the problem child is an artifact produced at the intersection of a number of governmental strategies, and is shaped by professional knowledges circulating within "the matrix of social workers, psychologists, psychiatrists, child guidance experts and family counsellors overseeing the child" (McCallum, 1993:138). He also concurs with the previous arguments that challenge the unitary and coercive role of the state, contending instead that the processes that fashion the problem child cannot be understood simply in terms of social control. Rather, these processes must be reinterpreted in terms of the formation of a new domain of power-knowledge. McCallum maintains that it is primarily through the burgeoning of various governmental techniques of information gathering and collating that new types of person—such as the problem child—first were identified and, subsequently, became the object of administration. This is not to suggest that certain legislative changes did not also have an effect upon existing understandings of preadulthood. McCallum (1993:132) maintains that legal changes delineating between different types of offender, also began to produce numerous new categories of person. Figures such as juvenile criminals, criminal children, and neglected children gained currency as characters requiring intervention and reformation. Significantly, these characters were not endowed with innate anti-social or criminal tendencies. Instead, they were now seen to be the product of their environments, and, more often than not, the product of a family that failed in its duty of care.

The problem child or juvenile delinquent is not, however, the most influential of the new categories of person that emerged from concerns over childhood. This distinction undoubtedly fell upon the adolescent. Although some concerns had been expressed over adolescence during the latter part of the nineteenth century, these did not assume any coherent shape until the publication of G. Stanley Hall's massive study in 1904. Hall's adolescent was firmly rooted within the realm of biology; the book contained numerous chapters on subjects such as physical growth, instincts, and (as a result of Hall's intellectual debt to Darwin) evolution. Furthermore, his emphasis on storm and stress came to form one of the central foundations of ensuing depictions of the adolescent persona.

> Dominant in all aspects of adolescence is the note of an equilibrium relatively less secure than what has preceded, of an old anchorage broken, of elements less harmonized, of coordinations yet incomplete, of adjustments to the environment less fine and less settled, of insecurity and ever-impending danger of mental or physical relapse, at the same time, of the promises and potencies of a slow but ever higher development. (Hall, 1914:49)

Unlike the notion of the child, the adolescent was also a personage to which the psy-knowledges attributed an active sexuality. Not surprisingly, Hall's adolescent reflected most of the dominant theoretical understandings of sexuality of the time. Male adolescents were seen to develop in terms of strength and aggression, while the development of female adolescents was interpreted predominantly in terms of preparation for maternity. Thus, not only was sex treated as a powerful drive that "asserts its mastery in field after field" (Hall, 1904:XlV), but this depiction also, within the scientific arena of the biology lesson, reinforced the naturalness of gender divisions for young people.

Despite the pervasiveness of the category adolescent, however, retrospect suggests that the adolescent was simply the product of the intellectual milieu of the time in the field of psychology, along with Hall's own eclectic background, rather than anything more concrete. Bruce Smith suggests that the adolescent was:

> an amalgam of neurological research, literary romanticism and nineteenth-century American child rearing advice—an amalgam which did not succeed in forming its constituent elements into a coherent object. With the somatic base of much of Hall's evidence discredited...the adolescent became abstracted as merely a figure of storm and stress, without any determinate content upon which educational policy or technique could be formulated. (Smith, 1989:8–9)

Two points are of note here. First, irrespective of its being undermined, residual elements of the storm and stress depiction of the adolescent still influence a significant amount of youth research. In the participants' manual for the 1990 "Youth Sector Training Program," issued to youth workers in Queensland, youth is described as a natural period of exploration, confusion, and guilt (particularly concerning sexuality); a time when their hormones are running wild and when they need to express their sexual feelings (Crane, Embelton, Harris, and Stokes, 1990:3.3). Such domain assumptions are particularly evident in the area of youth suicide research. Texts such as Peter Cimbolic and David Jobes (1990) *Youth Suicide*, Gail Mason's (1990) *Youth Suicide in Australia,* and John Davis and Johnathon Sandoval's (1991) *Suicidal Youth* all emphasize the vulnerability of youth to potentially dangerous levels of stress and turmoil. They also draw direct links between suicide and the stress induced by an emerging sexuality (Davis and Sandoval, 1991:194). Similarly, various problems over sexual identity, and an inability to deal with sexual disappointment, are both deemed to be crucial elements in explaining the high levels of youth suicide (Sugar, 1990; Bell, 1987). In all these cases, the legacy of G. Stanley Hall's storm and stress adolescent is still clearly visible.

Second, Smith's (1989) contention that the category of adolescent is largely a composite of various knowledges, is echoed in this book's approach to the category of youth. Youth does not constitute a unitary object.

Rather, this concept has been discontinuously constructed across a number of terrains and, as such, it has neither a linear history nor a clearly demarcated present. Youth has been produced as a governmental object at the intersection of certain legal, educational, medical, and psychological problematizations. These include debates over legal definitions of consent and criminal liability, changes in strategies regarding juvenile delinquency, and concerns over venereal disease and public morality. Despite this fragmented history, however, youth has repeatedly been regarded as one of the most important contemporary social problems:

> Young people have probably attracted more public criticism...since the Second World War than almost any other social group. Both academic and popular analysis of their behaviour, lifestyle and leisure pursuits have resulted in their definition as a major social problem. The very category of "youth" seems to attract adult censure and moral outrage. (Muncie, 1984:9)

Moreover, the problem of youth is itself taken as an accurate indicator of the wider health of the social body. Just as youth is familiarly characterized by the problems of violence, crime, drug abuse, delinquency, and unemployment, these problems are themselves taken as indicators of more fundamental social ills, such as family breakdown, educational, and economic failure (for example, "Apple Isle Follows its Youth Down the Drain"—headline in *The Australian*, April 8, 1989:1).

However, far from deserving its status as self-evident object and signifier, the construction of the problem youth is contingent upon a range of expertise and modes of information gathering. It is a collage of information assembled from diverse locations and sources, in that it is produced and defined through the expertise of statisticians, youth workers, aldermen, sociologists, doctors, and police. A more specific example involves the Burdekin Report's homeless youth, itself taken as a measure of the poor condition of Australian society. As discussed in chapter 1, this character is actually an amalgam of data from numerous sites and problematizations—health and welfare agencies, the schools, the criminal justice system, the Bureau of Statistics, voluntary organizations, family services, and so on.

Prostitution among the young is, in several ways, a similar issue to youth homelessness. First, the existence of the youth prostitute is also taken as an indicator of the nation's poor health. This is nothing new. In 1885, there was published in Great Britain an influential set of articles in the *Pall Mall Gazette* entitled "Maiden Tribute of Modern Babylon", articles credited with precipitating the passing of the "Age of Consent" legislation in both Britain and Australia (Finch, 1993:77). As a measure of the social failure of Victorian London, the articles detailed the circumstances of innocent young girls who were prostituted for the pleasure of depraved male clients. More recently, Ian O'Connor (1989:114), in *Our Homeless Youth: Their Experiences*, states that "it is an indictment of this society" that Australian youth is being forced into prostitution. Likewise, the Interim Report of the Select Committee on HIV, Illegal Drugs and Prostitution (1991:53), *Prostitution in the ACT*, draws almost identical conclusions as do the 1885 articles when it directly equates the existence of youth prostitution with social failure and states that "some of our disaffected, and predominantly homeless, young people are being sexually exploited and abused by...rapacious adults."

The second similarity between the homeless youth and the youth prostitute is also evident in the above quote from *Prostitution in the ACT*: the two categories overlap significantly. Indeed, the *Final Report* of the Victorian State Government's (1985:98) inquiry into prostitution contends that separating the streetkid from the young person engaging in prostitution (for the governmental purpose of calculating their respective numbers), is very difficult, owing to the lack of differentiation between the two. Again, in *Regulating Morality*, the Criminal Justice Commission's Inquiry into Prostitution in Queensland (1991:205), the correspondence is pointed out between the homeless youth and the youth prostitute. Likewise, this correlation is central to many other analyses of homeless youth—Myron Brenton's (1978) *The Runaways*, Paul Wilson's (1982) "Runaway Behaviour and Its Consequences," Wilson and Arnold's (1986) *Streetkids*, the Burdekin Report (1989), and so on.

The third similarity involves the manner in which the youth prostitute is constructed. Just as Burdekin's homeless youth is an amalgam of data, so the youth prostitute is assembled with information garnered from diverse locations and through different instruments of government. The various state reports into prostitution utilize information from police, court, and family services records; data are supplied by welfare agencies, voluntary and community organizations, religious pressure groups, newspapers, universities, and sex worker unions; and statistics are garnered from government departments, brothels, hospitals, private research firms, and other public inquiries. Thus, it can be argued that the youth prostitute, like youth itself, is an artifact produced through different mechanisms of information gathering. The piecemeal construction of various subcategories of youth has been particularly evident within numerous other studies. For example, William Connell et al.'s (1975) influential *12 to 20: Studies of City Youth* employs a range of mechanisms of information gathering to piece together a profile of the city youth. Not only is the city youth constituted through research instruments such as surveys, government statistics, physical measurements, psychological tests, ethnographic observation and anecdotal evidence, but also the city youth itself appears as an amalgam of specific attitudes, practices, capacities, and interests.

Finally, like the homeless youth, the youth prostitute is shaped and managed through expertise. Each of the above mechanisms of information gathering has associated forms of expertise, whether they be medical, legal, criminological, administrative, pedagogic, statistical, sexological, sociological, or psychological. Psychological expertise in particular has a large role to play in the construction of the youth prostitute. A sizable body of psy-based literature exists that examines the reasons young people (predominantly women) become prostitutes. It arrives at assorted contributory conclusions—bad relationships with their father (Chesser, 1971), guilt over incest fantasies (Winick and Kinsie, 1971), psychological susceptibility (Potterat, 1985), compulsive individuals, psychoneurotically driven to prostitution (Benjamin and Masters, 1964), and abusive families (James and Mayerding, 1977). This final reason, the abusive family, is the most frequently mentioned causal factor in the construction of the youth prostitute. In "Entrance into Prostitution," Mimi Silbert and Ayala Pines (1982:476) argue that an economically impoverished home background is not a significant contributory factor in becoming a prostitute. Instead, they point to other domestic influences:

> It is clear that the entrance [into prostitution] was motivated much more by an attempt to avoid or escape extremely negative conditions in the environment than by an attraction to the life of prostitution. In terms of pre-disposing factors, most subjects came from homes marked by crime, violence, and substance abuse, where

many were abused physically, emotionally, and sexually. (Silbert and Pines, 1982:489)

The link to the family is a familiar one. Not only is youth prostitution explained in terms of the failed family, but so, too, are most other problems associated with youth—delinquency, suicide, violence, drug abuse, stealing, and so on. Indeed, governmental programs aimed at these concerns have been directed both at the problem youth itself, and in equal measure, domains such as the family (and the school). Thus, as discussed earlier, youth can be effectively governed at a distance. This latter strategy indicates a significant change in emphasis from the punishment of offenses committed by young people to a concern with their rehabilitation. Currently, the segregation of young offenders remains secondary to the concerted attempts made to reform the potential problem youth while still within the bounds of the family. This focus on families has resulted in the formation of a new network of experts (welfare officers, guidance officers, teachers, health visitors)—a network that has attempted to align the practices and aspirations of the family to a broad range of wider governmental imperatives, while simultaneously observing the liberal dictum that demands a high level of family autonomy from state interference:

> The strategy of family privacy might appear to stand in opposition to all those attempts to police and regulate the family mechanism over the past 150 years. But the reverse is the case—it stands rather as a testament to the success of those attempts to construct a family that will take upon itself the responsibility for the duties of socialisation and will live with them as its own desires. (Rose, 1990:208)

Kerry Carrington (1993:89), in *Offending Girls*, makes some similar observations. For the vast majority of the population, parents become willing recruits in various governmental programs aimed at avoiding the production of problem youth. While families are at liberty to enjoy what Donzelot (1979:47) refers to as supervised freedom, this liberty is premised upon the assumption that parents will meet certain basic social expectations. When parents fail in the management of their children—that is, fail to provide a proper childhood, the family is then subject to a number of graded interventions—with the child eventually being taken into care.

Carrington (1993:90–91) argues that in her particular study of problem youth—largely dealing with aboriginal and working-class girls—the evidence suggests that the balance between successful government at a distance of the family, and direct intervention has been askew. According to writers such as Rose and Bell, however, this kind of disagreement over precisely how and where to set governmental limits has been a recurrent feature of neo-liberalism, particularly in relation to the family:

> The successful government of the parent/child relation is crucial to neo-liberalism, but a central dilemma opens up: how does neo-liberalism maintain the notion of a "contract" with the parents which gives them this sense of distance and of the possibility of autonomy whilst continuing to monitor their performance, especially around child-care? (Bell, 1993:395)

Certainly, Bell's observations concerning the government of the family illustrate liberalism's dilemmas: how to produce the desired regulatory ends, without compromising the independence of the various autonomous zones that liberalism itself helped establish. To put it another way, liberalism constantly has to balance the undesirability of governmental intervention against counterposed anxieties over the dangers of governmental inaction (Rose, 1993:292).

Youth, Sex, and the Limits of Government

Far from being a problem, Gary Wickham (1993:9) argues that a perpetual dissatisfaction with government is actually essential to its continued operation. While not decrying the many mundane achievements of contemporary government, he suggests that government is necessarily never complete, never totally successful. Indeed, if it did not continue to fail, there would be no government. It is through the continually disappointed reassessment of governmental outcomes that more effective programs are introduced, in time only to be replaced themselves by newer and even more effective programs. Wickham is not alone in his assessment. Rose and Miller (1992:190) also consider government to be a congenitally failing operation. They note that the very nature of governmental programs often make them ambiguous, contradictory, partial, and inexact. This heterogeneity ultimately results in the targets of government "refusing to respond according to the programmatic logic that seeks to govern them."

The need to manage the sexual conduct of youth exemplifies some of the problems of government. Although different knowledges and programs have targeted the sexual conduct of youth indirectly through the family (thereby preserving a sense of distance), it has been programs such as formal, school-based sex education that encroach upon family autonomy and deal with young people directly that engender debates over precisely where to set limits to government. In addition, not only have there been problems over deciding how best to manage the sexual conduct of youth (in relation to the public/private dilemma), but also the various programs directed at youth often lack success. Attempts to alter the sexual habits of youth (such as those involving the tactic of formal sex education) have generally only succeeded in demonstrating the limits of government in relation to self-formation. That is, they have limited success in reforming the conduct of the sexually irresponsible youth.

Much of the recent literature on HIV/AIDS education has questioned how much success governmental programs have actually had in modifying the sexual conduct of young people. Whereas the central mechanisms of HIV/AIDS transmission now appear to be common knowledge within this social category, Roger Ingham, Alison Woodcock, and Karen Stenner (1992:164) claim that this knowledge is not then transferred into the widespread adoption of safe sex practices. Tamsin Wilton and Peter Aggleton (1991), in an article on the limits of HIV/AIDS education, argue that it should not come as a surprise that the governmental programs aimed at the sexual practices of youth have not resulted in immediate and clear-cut changes in behavior. After all, they claim that governmental programs are never directly nor unproblematically translated by the target groups concerned into the desired forms of self-government. New programs, such as those dealing with HIV/AIDS, often clash with older programs, doctrines, forms of conduct, and subject positions:

> In the case of AIDS, the conceptual matrix into which safer sex information must be fitted also includes not only lay beliefs about the origins, aetiology and effects of the syndrome but also socially, culturally, ethnically, religiously and politically specific significations of sexual desire and practice. (Wilton and Aggleton, 1991:149–150).

As an example of the complexity of the field in which governmental programs operate, Janet Holland et al. (1991:1992) address the use of safe sex practices among female youth. Campaigns aimed at constructing a specific character—the modern yet sexually responsible young woman—impinge upon much older forms of conduct among young women—conduct shaped by the contradictions and tensions of heterosexual relationships. They argue that the practices associated with a traditionally feminine sexual habitus often restrict the likelihood of obtaining condoms, let alone an insistence upon their usage.

Another example of the contradictions associated with the implementation of HIV/AIDS prevention programs is to be found in Tim Rowse's (1992) work focusing on a remote aboriginal community. He argues that the western notion of sex education bears little resemblance to the existing kinship-based forms of sexual tutelage. Indeed, the western model of sexuality even appears inappropriate within a culture where different modes of personhood exist (as will be discussed in chapter 4), and where sexual conduct is organized by such factors as "skin law" taboos related to kinship. Therefore, strategies aimed at producing the sexually responsible youth within *Bushtown*, must necessarily cut across ancient and complex cultural practices. These preexisting features in turn modify, negate, or garble differing elements of the introduced programs. As a consequence, such programs have had limited success (or are quite slow) in producing the kinds of new subject-positions intended.

This is not to suggest that the HIV/AIDS campaigns have been a total failure. Far from it. Mitchell Cohen (1991:19) argues that the programs that targeted the conduct of gay men have succeeded in drastically altering their sexual practices. It can also be argued, however, that the very programs that delineated gays as high-risk appear not only to have failed to modify the conduct of those who considered themselves far removed from this community, but they also appear to have given them a sexual carte blanche. A wealth of literature exists that records the belief among youth that HIV/AIDS is a gay problem (intravenous drug use aside), and that you have to be gay, or very unlucky, to get it (Wellings, 1988; Pilkington and Sara, 1991). As Hilary Homans and Peter Aggleton (1988:160) note, in "Health Education, HIV Infection and AIDS," health programs aimed at reforming conduct, such as those implemented in the mass media, tend to produce a short-lived increase in knowledge and only slight changes in attitudes and conduct. Furthermore, they cite Gatherer et al. (1979) who have observed that sometimes there may even be shifts in attitude in the opposite direction to that desired.

While government has had some success in targeting the conduct of certain sections of society, such as the gay community, it has been less successful with other groups. In "Reaching the Hard to Reach," Tim Rhodes and Richard Hartnoll (1991) discuss the problem associated with the effective government of some of the more marginal social zones. They detail the difficulties associated with attempting to manage the sexual (and narcotic) conduct of homeless youth (as well as other categories such as prostitutes, IV drug users, and prisoners). In each case, numerous different programs have been initiated. With these particular governmental targets, however, management problems are compounded by recurrent difficulties in assessing their effects. That is, the marginal nature of these groupings damage the evaluative feedback loop—a loop that is so vital to the continuing processes of governmental self-assessment, analysis, and adjustment.

Finally, the evidence would suggest that the governmental tactic employing formal sex education in schools has also had limited success in restructuring the subject. Dilys Went (1985) cites a wide range of data supporting the contention that sex education has little effect on the amount and type of sex engaged in by young people. While condom use has increased to a degree, those programs aimed at fostering forms of ethical self-reflection (and, hence, self-regulation) pertaining to appropriate ages and circumstances to have sex, numbers of partners, approaches to the opposite sex, and so on, appear to have had little effect. Indeed, in the light of this seeming ineffectuality, one of the central rationales behind formal sex education has remained the indispensability of acquiring legitimate knowledge about sex. This imperative has often been tied to a series of assumptions about the crucial role this knowledge plays in developing the complete and self-fulfilled child. The problems with this formulation have already been dealt with at length in this chapter. These observations have by no means been made with the intention of advocating the removal of sex education from schools. Rather, they have been made as a way of demonstrating the limits of government in relation to self-formation and in relation to reforming the sexual habits of youth. As previously mentioned, programs aimed at constructing the sexually responsible youth must deal with other, much older, forms of conduct in order to achieve their goals. Such programs, like all governmental endeavors, may be characterized in terms of both their considerable achievements and their inherent limitations.

Conclusion

The primary intention of this chapter has been to outline the first half of an alternative approach to youth research, utilizing the concept of governmentality. The central intention has been to provide a conceptual framework for the study of youth that can account for its historical specificity. This alternative framework was then used to more fully explain the relationship between the category of youth and the management of its sex.

The chapter began by outlining the central tenets of governmentality—the conduct of conduct. Previous research had, either explicitly or implicitly, employed a model of power that relied upon the state/civil society dichotomy; however, the focus on governmentality has attempted to dissolve this binary opposition and provide analysts with a more precise set of theoretical tools. The development of governmentality was traced from the time of sovereign power, through the development of the art of government, which expanded the concept of rule yet still employed the rationalities of sovereignty, to the contemporary form of government that takes as its central objective the interests of the population. This chapter also examined how specific analyses of the local effects of governmentality can be conducted utilizing the relationship between governmental programs, the political rationalities that these programs articulate, and the governmental technologies that allow them to be put implemented. It was also argued that within liberal societies, government generally operates, not by direct intervention, but rather at a distance. That is, by employing the expertise of the doctor, the psychologist, the child guidance counselor, and the welfare worker, and by targeting autonomous sites such as the family and the school, various governmental objectives can be achieved. This occurs without compromising the independence or liberty of these sites, upon which governmental success actually relies.

This chapter then addressed the notion of sexuality. Rather than adopting the dominant position that generally locates it as a fundamental drive, an inherent part of human nature outside discourse, it was argued that sexuality is actually created within discourse itself as a form of power-knowledge. Sexuality was, in part, constituted when this new form of government distributed the existing Christian emphasis upon the confession to a wider population. That is, it was argued that sexuality came to be deployed across the social body—augmenting the already existing deployment of alliance—as an ideal apparatus through which a broad range of governmental aspirations could be realized.

Finally, this chapter examined the emergence of youth as a category. It was argued that, like sexuality, youth is historically contingent. It emerged out of existing debates over the child, the juvenile delinquent and the adolescent, and, in particular, debates related to sexuality. Youth came to be constructed as a governmental object at the intersection of a number of legal, educational, medical, and psychological problematizations. It was both produced by, and the focus of, a broad range of expertise that has attempted to align the conduct and aspirations of youth with specific governmental objectives. This has occurred mainly within autonomous domains such as the family, and with varying degrees of success. Also, it was argued that the category of youth has been generated through regulating the relations of time, bodies, and forces, as well as through sorting, classifying, and differentiating individuals as members of classes of person.

CHAPTER 3

Governing the 'At-Risk' Youth

This chapter will exemplify the aforementioned contentions by focusing on the governmental construction of a specific category of person—the at-risk youth. In particular, this chapter will show how the at-risk youth is largely governed at a distance within domains such as the school and the family. Moreover, it will demonstrate how risk is employed as a governmental device for governing youth on the basis of its sex. The at-risk youth appears at the intersection of a variety of knowledges/problematisations, such as education, vocational guidance, youth welfare, family management, and so on. Although in some ways, the at-risk youth simply replaces older characterizations used in the policing of the young, it will also be argued that the preventative policies associated with risk are constituted in terms of factors rather than individuals; that risk permits a greater number of young people to be brought into the field of regulatory strategies; and that prevention is no longer primarily based upon the skill of individual experts, but rather upon the gathering and collation of statistical knowledge. Also, the category of the at-risk youth plays a crucial role in policy documents, such as the Finn Report (1991). In this case, youth is deemed to be at-risk of not making the transition to adulthood successfully. It will be argued that not only is the Finn Report significant in the administrative and cultural shaping of the category of youth, but also, by employing the notion of risk, the Report introduces yet another element of an effective network of governmental intelligibility covering the young. Finally, it will be argued that young women, as a specific example of a risk group, require particular forms of intervention, primarily through changing the vocational aspirations of their parents.

Within the last decade, numerous western countries have tried to commence the process of restructuring education, largely by reorganizing the relationships between school, the workplace, and advanced education. For example, the United Kingdom (The Dearing Report 1996), the United States (National Education Goals Report, 1996), New Zealand (Picot Report, 1988), and Australia (The Finn Report, 1991) have all sought to address such issues as effective and appropriate credentialing, key competencies, educational pathways, recognition of prior learning, coherent national frameworks, target constituencies, and so on.

Within the Australian context, The Finn Report (1991), in combination with the Mayer Report (1992) and the Carmichael Report (1992), is part of a recent attempt to reform postcompulsory education. The overall intention of these reforms has been to construct a single, unified training system. This system would form a connection between the school, the university, the technical college, and the workplace, and is based upon a new type of credentialing that measures key competencies, rather than the duration or title of courses taken. These competencies—which include Language and Communication, Mathematics, Scientific and Technological Understanding, Problem-solving, Cultural Understanding, and Personal and Interpersonal Skills—are intended as pathways across all educational/employment contexts, and will provide a sort of certification lingua franca throughout the country.

The Finn Report extends the aspirations of numerous earlier federal policy initiatives and statements, which were directed not only at establishing a national curriculum and strengthening the connections between education and employment, but also at increasing school retention rates and initiating access and equity programs (Commonwealth Schools Commission, 1987a, 1987b; Dawkins, 1989). Indeed, in the name of equity, the report targets specific categories of youth unlikely to make the transition to adulthood as easily or as successfully as others. Recommendation 7.7 declares: "States and territories [should] examine their information systems with a view to improving their capacity to monitor regional patterns of education and training participation and attainment, especially for 'at-risk' groups." In a paper prepared for the Finn Report (1991) entitled "Dislocated Transitions: Access and Participation for Disadvantaged Young People," John Freeland argues that:

> As is to be expected not all teenagers experience the same probability of being at risk in the transition to adulthood. Those most likely to be at risk tend to be members of households and groups experiencing socio-economic and cultural discrimination and disadvantage...In addition, it should be remembered that young women are relatively more disadvantaged than are young men, a reality which mirrors gender based inequality and discrimination throughout society... (Freeland, 1991:177–179)

Putting aside the matter of gender differences for a moment, two other aspects of this statement are relevant to this chapter. The first is the focus on the transition from being a teenager to being an adult. The second is the notion of being at-risk—in this case, of not making that transition successfully. As Jozefa Sobski (1992) correctly observes in *Pathways to Finn*, these are two familiar themes within youth policy.

First, for the issue of transition, Freeland supports his theoretical framework with James Coleman and Torsten Husen's (1985) *Becoming Adult in a Changing Society*. These authors adopt a familiar position based upon the contention that traditional forms of social organization experienced considerable change at the end of the World War II. Changing patterns of education and employment meant that large numbers of young people decided to remain at school. This resulted in both an increase in the period of parental dependence, as well as an increase in the length of the transition period to adulthood. Whereas they would argue that preadulthood had previously consisted simply of the child and the adolescent, there now emerged the new category of youth, a category fundamentally defined by its transitory status. A great deal of youth research has been done, largely based upon this domain assumption. This is the case whether the transition is to full-time employment, sexual and emotional maturity, or social responsibility (Bowes, 1981; Altman, 1983; Anderson and Blakers, 1984; Wallace and Cross, 1990; Frazer, 1991).

A significant body of literature now exists that records a new set of changes in the labor market, changes as fundamental and far-reaching as those deemed by Coleman and Husen (1985) to have occurred at the end of World War II. This literature suggests that the age grouping of fifteen to nineteen is now extensively engaged in education and training, as opposed to twenty years earlier when most would have been employed (Sweet, 1987;

Ward, 1988; Mass, 1990). This transformation means that one of the central parameters in the transition to adulthood—getting a job—is changing significantly, with the concomitant result that the boundaries of youth (when understood as a function of this transition) are also in a state of flux. It is at this point in the argument that the Finn Report (1991) becomes relevant. Documents such as the Finn, Mayer, and Carmichael Reports can fundamentally reshape and redefine the period of transition from education to employment—the period deemed to be synonymous with the category of youth itself. Consequently, it is within policies derived from such reports that youth becomes operationalized as a category.

The second point of interest in the Freeland quotation is the idea that the transition from teenager to adult is difficult. Moving from teenage dependency to educated, employed adult is by no means a fait accompli. Some social groups can be more at-risk than others of making an unsuccessful transition to employed adulthood. Freeland (1991:177–178) identifies the following "heterogeneous and frequently over-lapping social groups" to be most at-risk. He also notes that in every category on this list, young women are more at-risk than their male counterparts:

- those living in low income circumstances;
- those living in rural and remote and other structurally disadvantaged regions;
- Aborigines and Torres Strait Islanders;
- recently arrived migrant young people from non-English speaking backgrounds;
- early school leavers and those with no postcompulsory qualifications;
- those living in emotionally and physically abusive households;
- those who are without stable and secure accommodation; and
- wards of the State and those living in State institutions.

The Finn Report appears to base its rationale for both defining and dealing with the at-risk youth upon the *Students at Risk Program* (1989). This was part of the measures contained in the Social Justice package for young people as announced in the 1989/90 Budget. Joan Abbott-Chapman and Carol Patterson (1990:1) suggest in turn that the *Students at Risk Program* itself evolved out of preparatory work conducted at the Center for Educational Research and Innovation at the Organization for Economic Co-operation and Development (OECD), for a program entitled *Children and Youth at Risk* (1989).

Such references to at-risk youth are now routine. In "An At-Risk Assessment," Lois Nardini and Richard Antes (1991:56) observe: "By 1987, the buzzword *at-risk* was a commonplace adjective used by the academic community to mean any student who, for one or more reasons, was likely not only to experience failure in school but also to meet with failure in life." The Finn Report, like many other recent documents, also uses the notion of being at-risk extensively. Indeed, a large part of the report (as well as the Freeland [1991] article in appendix 3) concentrates upon a concern for those social categories for whom, statistically speaking, there exists a problematic transition to adulthood.

Since the notion of risk now appears to be an integral feature of the youth research landscape, the questions that occupy the remainder of this chapter are: What precisely is meant by being an at-risk youth? In what contexts is this classification employed? How is risk used in the government of youth? More particularly, how is risk employed as a governmental mechanism for governing youth on the basis of its sex? All of these questions will ultimately be addressed in relation to the specific example of the Finn Report. These questions will be addressed in turn.

The Rhetoric of Risk and the Problem of Youth

In *Risk Society: Towards a New Modernity*, Ulrich Beck (1992) catalogues numerous important changes that have occurred within contemporary society. The most important of these changes, he argues, is that the conflicts and social positions characteristic of a wealth-distributing society are slowly being displaced by those of a risk-distributing society. Indeed, it was the production of wealth that first produced a concomitant set of risks—risks that have now actually supplanted in importance the mechanisms and rationales behind the logic of their original formation. So, whereas until recently the analytical focus fell continually upon the unequal disbursement of social resources, Beck suggests that, since the early 1970s, a new set of variables has become increasingly important—those related to the notion of a society based around risk. Although he concentrates primarily upon what he sees as the by-products of modernization—pollution, deforestation, radioactive fallout—Beck also notes that risk now occupies a far broader and more pervasive discursive position. It has become central to the way in which categories of person are located within the social fabric. Whereas classical sociology describes the contours of an economically stratified society (with its accompanying class positions), Beck stresses the need to focus on the varying relations of risk. That is, although some risks are evenly distributed ("poverty is hierarchic, smog is democratic"), many others cluster in ways peculiar to themselves. As such, social risk positions arise—that is, some people are more at-risk than others of a given outcome. Furthermore, these risk positions do not correlate with specific class positions. They have their own logic and their own momentum.

Although Beck undoubtedly raises some interesting points regarding the evident currency of the concept of risk across various disciplines (Beck himself applies his risk analysis to areas such as gender, the media, biographical patterns, labor, and the work place, and so on), this chapter will follow a somewhat different approach. Rather than adopt Beck's meta-narrative of a totalized risk society replacing an equally totalized class society, this chapter will examine how the notion of risk is deployed within contemporary forms of government, and how it replaced less flexible mechanisms for distributing personhood. Beck was correct in his premise that it is possible for certain social categories to be more at-risk than others. This is certainly true of the way in which youth is now considered. Varieties of at-risk youth now dominate the theoretical landscape across the disciplines and departments dealing with youth issues. The at-risk youth appears at the intersection of various knowledges/problematizations, within law enforcement, the labor market, youth welfare, health, education, and family management. A brief analysis of the use of risk in these areas will illustrate two points. First, risk has become an important component of the grid of governmental intelligibility, through which individuals are differentiated as members of classes of person (such as the at-risk youth). Second, risk is employed as a medium through which youth can be governed at a distance within domains such as the school and the family.

First is the contention that risk becomes an important indicator in a grid of governmental intelligibility. This occurs across a wide range of terrains. It can be demonstrated most easily, however, through an analysis of risk and schooling. Within the general sociological literature on contemporary Western education, it appears to be true that students do not simply and unproblematically fail to achieve. That is, failure is not located within the students themselves. Instead, it resides elsewhere. Most frequently, it resides within society (as, for example, within most Marxist analyses of education). Social influences impinging upon students can be understood in terms of risk factors that endanger the successful completion of an education (Kushman and Kinney, 1989). The logical conclusion of this approach is that failure can eventually become correlated with a range of these risk factors. Such factors may or may not be found within a student's profile. Furthermore, having delineated the risk factors correlated with any given undesirable outcome (delinquency, truancy, poor grades, and so forth), the emphasis is then upon the early observation of such risk factors within specific members of the school population. Evelyn Ogden and Vito Germinario's (1988) *The At-Risk Student* contains a typical chapter for texts of this type, entitled: "Identifying High Risk-Students":

> There is a portion of every school population that consistently shows a lack of the necessary intellectual, emotional and/or social skills to take full advantage of the educational opportunities available to them. Often these students become disadvantaged, and ultimately openly or passively reject school—they are then students-at-high-risk. (Ogden and Germinario, 1988:XVll)

Clearly, Ogden and Germinario identify not only different risk factors, but also different levels of being at-risk. Moreover, these factors change with age and with the type of risk under analysis. Again, Ogden and Germinario roughly delineate three risk age groupings (grades K–4, 5–8, 9–12), which themselves are composed of certain age-specific risk groups, to which they assign particular risks. For example, K–4 risk groups include "family separation children, latch-key children, new students, handicapped children, gifted children and non-English-speaking children." The symptoms of membership of some of these groupings are not always easy to spot. They argue that a "family separation child" can be picked out by such diverse indicators as "changes in the way the child is dressed, outbursts of anger, lateness to school, and complaints of illness, such as headaches or stomachaches" (Ogden and Germinario, 1988:30).

Judy Lehr and Hazel Harris (1988) devote an entire book to one variety of at-risk youth—the at-risk, low-achieving student. It is argued that, within the school, this category of student is treated differently from high-achieving students. Among various other differences, they are "seated further away from the teacher, asked to do less work, given less praise, and given less eye contact." Their own characteristics include "distractibility, short attention span, narrow range of interests and fear of failure" (Lehr and Harris, 1988:10–11). The implication of the book is that a good teacher can begin to spot symptoms such as these, recognize the associated risk grouping, and alter teaching strategies accordingly, with the desired outcome being a student once at-risk of low achievement becoming a high achieving student (who remains at-risk of other things, which need to be addressed as required).

The focus on the youth at-risk of educational failure, however, is not limited to the school. As previously mentioned, when introducing the Finn Report, it also spills over into a set of governmental concerns centered around the transition to employment. After all, some school students are deemed to be at-risk of far more than simply wasting their time in the classroom; their whole future is at-risk:

> [at-risk students] are destined for particular difficulty in our education system. The educational forecast is not good for students who fail subject areas, who are retained, or who are considering dropping out of school. The outlook is dismal for students who come from homes where there has been abuse or neglect or distrust for the schools. The educational prognosis is poor for students who are maladjusted or are substance abusers. At-risk students are heading for failure in school and in life. (Swanson, 1991:3)

In 1979 the Australian (Liberal) Government introduced the *Transition Program* with the aim of improving the preparation of at-risk students for work. This was eventually subsumed by the *Participation and Equity Program* in 1983. Both these programs were aimed at those groups identified as being underrepresented in higher education. Once identified, such at-risk students would then be the target of a number of strategies aimed at greater educational participation and, hence, greater ultimate employability (Frazer, 1991).

The pertinent risk factors in this case are fairly predictable. For example, Ian McAllister (1986:122) concentrates on immigrant youth and contends that they are at greater risk than their Australian-born counterparts of failing to achieve successfully the transition from school to the workplace. He argues that an analysis based upon specific risks permits a far greater degree of policy specificity than one based upon the traditional aggregate measures of unemployment. The conclusion that immigrant youth are disproportionately at-risk for unemployment is supported by the Australian Institute for Multicultural Affairs (1985) report, *Reducing the Risks: Unemployed Migrant Youth and Labour Market Programs*. This finding was the result of a risk-assessment study undertaken by the Commonwealth Employment Service, conducted with the intention of identifying those in greatest need of immediate intervention (Kabala, 1986:37–38). Other risk positions deemed relevant to future unemployment abound: students from poor socio-economic backgrounds (Bowes, 1981), students exhibiting antisocial behavior (Denholm, 1989), students with physical and mental disabilities (Roberts-Yates, 1990), girls in general (Sweet, 1982), and so on. This evidence goes some way toward supporting Beck's (1992) contention that many risks are unevenly distributed, with some people being more at-risk than others of a given outcome. It also supports his conclusion that risk-positions do not correlate directly with class positions (although there are some similarities); rather, they are shaped by factors determined by their own specific context.

Generally then, the notion of risk has become woven into the fabric of the school. As Ogden and Germinario (1988) demonstrate, young people can now be measured against a graded and cumulative set of normal risks, both by their age category, and by the severity of the risk involved. Just as the disciplinary school has become characterized by the minute division of space and time (see chapter 2), risk also has become an important indicator in the grid of governmental, and especially pedagogic, knowledge.

The second point of note regarding risk is that it is employed as a medium through which youth can be governed in various sites at a distance. Even though the at-risk youth has proven to be an excellent mechanism for achieving certain educational ends, this character is by no means solely employed within the confines of the school. The at-risk youth is now firmly located within the risk family, itself a recurrent feature of debates over child and youth welfare. Indeed, Palmo and Palmo argue that the most important common characteristic of the development of an at-risk youth, is a pre-existing dysfunctional family background:

> The at-risk youth is a representative of the family and symbolizes the severity of the difficulties within the family unit. The greater the difficulties demonstrated by the youth, the larger the number of issues that need attention within the family.

> Although there are examples of at-risk youth with pathologies that do not provide an honest picture of the family's difficulties, in most instances the youth's behaviours are an accurate barometer of the family's stability. (Palmo and Palmo, 1989:45)

Not surprisingly, the most common theme when addressing the risk family is that of child abuse—although this preoccupation must be historicized somewhat. The current concern over apparently high levels of child abuse is unlikely to reflect an increase in actual mistreatment; rather, it is more likely to represent the emergence of new thresholds of sensibility, through which once acceptable conduct eventually becomes problematic. Lyn Finch (1993) makes a similar point with the example of incest. Despite of its historical contingency, however, child abuse is currently a major social concern, which is considered to manifest itself in several ways: physical neglect, physical abuse, sexual abuse and/or emotional abuse, deprivation, and neglect (Petrie, 1986). All of these types of abuse have their own specific symptoms to be spotted and acted upon, although the factors that make a child at-risk for these forms of abuse are often common to all. Alan Gilmour (1989:27–30) argues that risk factors for abuse in general include parents who were abused themselves, immature parents, families with marital problems, isolated families, families experiencing specific forms of stress, such as illness, unemployment, or housing difficulties, and so on.

However, specific forms of abuse also have their own risk factors. Kieran O'Hagan (1989:52) argues that the elements that make a child most at-risk of sexual abuse include children with special needs (educational, social, and emotional), inarticulate and socially isolated children, children living in fragmented and seriously deprived families, and mentally handicapped children. The centrality of these risk factors is supported by Beverly Schwartz, Jonathon Horowitz, and Albert Cardarelli (1990:19), to which they added the presence of passive, inadequate fathers, coupled with unhappy mothers, which result in the daughters prematurely assuming the mothering role. Presumably this only applies to the sexual abuse of girls. Conversely, in *Males at Risk: The Other Side of Child Sexual Abuse*, Bolton, Morris, and MacEachron (1990) chart the specificities of the abuse of boys, again tying its prevalence to the existence of a series of distinctive risk factors.

Thus, the risk family is the focus of governmental attention owing to its statistical predisposition to be a significant site of child abuse. However, that abuse is itself regarded as an important risk factor in the forming of a potential delinquent—the archetypal at-risk youth. In *The Child Abuse-Delinquency Connection*, David Sandberg (1989) argues that, of all the characteristics common to the juvenile offender, by far the most frequently found is a history of abuse by their parents and family (whether physical, sexual, or emotional). It follows directly from this observation that, of all the indicators relevant to the process of spotting those at-risk of becoming a delinquent (before then intervening, counseling, and safeguarding them), none is so important as a history of child abuse.

It should not be a surprise that the governmental institutions/agencies associated with crime prevention have such statistics at their disposal. Recent genealogies of contemporary forms of law enforcement have repeatedly emphasized the compilation of extensive documentation on the social body. While pointing in particular to the eventual role of photography, John Tagg argues that:

> Throughout the eighteenth and nineteenth centuries, an immense police text increasingly covered society by means of a complex documentary organisation. But this documentation differed markedly from the traditional methods of judicial or administrative writing. What was registered in it were forms of conduct, attitudes, possibilities, suspicions...(Tagg, 1981:291)

He is not alone in making this kind of observation concerning the rise of the "new" police (Philips, 1980; Emsley, 1982). Indeed, David Garland (1985:112) argues that the development of such forms of documentation, in particular "statistical data, produced by surveys, government institutions and private research," was a crucial condition for the emergence of the discipline of criminology, and it was this new science that initially correlated various physical, social, and psychological factors with criminal activity. Hence, the social factors correlated to juvenile crime have long been common police knowledge.

A further point of interest here involves the continual attention paid to the nexus between the delinquent and its family. In *Problem Children and Familial Relations*, David McCallum (1993:131) cites British Home Office research that regards four of the five main factors for a child's descent into crime to be family related. McCallum argues that this observation serves the political purpose of allocating responsibility for youth unrest to an essentially private sphere—a sphere ostensibly beyond the reach of direct government. However, he notes that insisting upon such a rigorous division between the public and the private is to ignore the role of the family as an effective site for the governance of children. Indeed, McCallum suggests that the contemporary family is in fact "a product of policies designed to reform domestic life," and that the domestic space itself became one of the most important and practical settings for instilling the capacities and attitudes required of a modern population. Yet, despite this knowledge, the conventional dichotomies of humanitarian reform/social control, individual/social, and public/private continue to dominate the conceptual, rhetorical, and governmental landscape:

> Children as young as five and six years will be identified as potential criminals under radical plans being drawn up by the Home Office to stop them drifting into lawlessness in later life... "We want to identify these youngsters who are at risk at an early age so we can help them and their parents...Children with learning difficulties are picked up early in the system and given special help. We want to do the same with children at risk of criminality." (*The Sunday Times*, London, 15 September, 1991:1. Cited in McCallum, 1993:129)

There is a considerable body of literature devoted to the goal of the early recognition of youth at-risk of delinquency. In *Identification of Predelinquents*, Sheldon and Eleanor Glueck (1972) present a range of mechanisms (across a range of ages and cultural backgrounds and so forth— primarily based upon the use of the influential *Glueck Table*), to achieve this end. Not surprisingly, the predominant focus is still upon the family. In fact, all five of their predictive devices involve some element of family functioning. Furthermore, their explanatory model is steadfastly anchored within the discipline of psychology, a feature it shares with the vast majority of the literature on the at-risk youth.

This should not come as any great surprise. Rose (1985:90) has already convincingly argued the efficacy of psychology in the various modalities of (self) government. The psychological influence on the shaping of the at-risk youth extends from the self-evidence of the need for therapeutic intervention and counseling for those affected, to the description of at-risk youth as suffering from a full-blown mental condition. For example, in "Reaching the

Unreachable," Margaret O'Brien (1990:2) argues that social workers should realize that they are dealing with a syndrome when confronted with an at-risk youth. The associated risk behaviors present in some cases fit a specific mental pattern, rather than a collection of discrete activities. This contemporary psychological diagnosis of juvenile pathology has some recognizable antecedents. The central logic does not seem to be that far removed from the one employed in Arthur Manning's (1958) study, *The Bodgie: A Study in Psychological Abnormality*, or even Cyril Burt's (1926), *The Young Delinquent*. This is an interesting point, not simply because it demonstrates the pervasiveness of psychology and its role in defining the pathological, but because in this light, the *at-risk youth* appears to occupy the same discursive position as any number of other, preceding categories of *problem youth*. Whereas the *delinquent* was once the focus of moral concern, then the *socially disadvantaged*, now it is those deemed to be *at-risk* (Bessant, 1993).

However, despite the claim that, in some ways, the social effects of being categorized as an *at-risk youth* differ little from being categorized as, for example, a *delinquent*, it will be argued in the following section of this chapter that several significant differences do exist. That is, the implications of governing through risk are far more extensive than the points raised thus far.

Risk and Government

In "Insurance and Risk," Francois Ewald (1991) charts the parallel and interrelated rise of these two important features of the contemporary social landscape. In this article, Ewald claims that the advent of the insurance/risk coupling in the nineteenth century signaled a crucial epistemological shift. That is, the predictability of the relationship between misfortune and risk formed an integral part of a new laicized society. The destiny of specific individuals was no longer shaped by the unpredictable whims of God or fate; instead, their destiny was tied to the internal functioning of society itself. Accidents or undesirable outcomes were now not simply understood as reflections of God's displeasure. Rather, they became constituted in terms of probability, of rational, calculable, statistical risks that could almost always be prevented.

Indeed, Ewald argues that the calculability of risk is one of its fundamental characteristics. Whereas, taken on an individual basis, accidents often seemingly happen at random, within the context of a given population over a certain length of time, the same accidents appear to be both predictable and calculable. He cites the example of the first industrial statistics from the mid-nineteenth century, where it was first observed that there was a fairly constant level of annual mining accidents: "it follows from this that accidents, just when they may seem to be due to pure chance, are governed by a mysterious law" (Keller, 1889:269, cited in Ewald, 1991:202).

An additional feature of risk, one linked to its calculability, is its collectivity. As such, risk is a property associated with a given population, not with an individual. Ewald (1991:202–203) states that, "Strictly speaking there is no such thing as an individual risk; otherwise insurance would be no more than a wager." Risk only becomes something calculable when spread over a population. Consequently, risk only has meaning when located within a population about which a significant amount of knowledge has been gained. That is, the concept of risk only operates when utilized within a society configured by extensive networks of governmental intelligibility. However, risks are not simply the correlative by-products of the social information available. They are now an important part of the way in which government is deployed.

This final contention is the main focus of Robert Castel's (1991), "From Dangerousness to Risk." He argues that the implications of governing through the notion of risk are far more extensive than a re-labeling of old problem groups. Although he would agree that the *dangerous youth* has now been recategorized as the *at-risk youth*, he suggests that what appears to be a small, semantic change actually signals an important expansion in the possibilities of government. Castel centers his argument around what he considers a vital strategic shift within mental medicine, although he later extends the scope of these changes to all the social work and care professions. He suggests that the original justification for intervention was always around the notion of dangerousness—detecting, diagnosing, confining, and treating dangerous people. Dangerousness was thus viewed as a quality inherent to a given individual who was deemed capable of dangerous actions. Furthermore, dangerousness has also been a capacity recurrently divined within the young (Magarey, 1978:11).

However, an approach founded upon inherent dangerousness had two central problems associated with it. First, it limited any possibility of establishing and maintaining an effective policy of prevention. After all:

> One could only hope to prevent violent acts committed by those whom one had already diagnosed as dangerous. Hence the double limitation arising from the fallibility of such diagnoses on the one hand, and the fact that they can only be carried out on individual patients one by one, on the other. This was why classical psychiatry was only able to make use of the correspondingly crude preventative technologies of confinement and sterilization. (Castel, 1991:283)

The second problem with this approach was that the credibility of psychiatry depended upon factors largely beyond its own control. That is, any system based upon the inherency of danger would always leave the profession vulnerable to criticisms over a lack of predictive consistency. Psychiatrists could not possibly hope to diagnose accurately and effectively neutralize dangerousness in every single case—short of confining massive numbers of people on the smallest suspicion of danger. Furthermore, "Harmless today, they may be dangerous tomorrow" (Doctors Constant, Lunier, and Dumesnil, 1874:67; cited in Castel, 1991:283).

Castel (1991:284) notes that, even in the mid-nineteenth century, psychiatrists such as Morel (who first employed the term *degeneracy*) were well aware of the problems associated with treating dangerousness as an internal quality. Morel suggested, instead, that the focus should fall upon an analysis of the statistical frequency of mental illnesses within specific strata of society. These mental illnesses could then be correlated to particular social circumstances, such as diet, housing, family circumstances, sexual promiscuity, and so on:

> In doing this, Morel was already arguing in terms of *objective* risks: that is to say, statistical correlations between series of phenomena. At the level of practices, he also suggests that the public authorities undertake a special surveillance of those population groups which might by this stage already have been termed "populations at risk." (Castel, 1991:284)

Castel argues that this new approach to social problems, signaled by the shift from dangerousness to risk, has three important implications for the government of populations, all pertinent to the construction of the at-risk youth. First, the preventative policies associated with risk are constituted in terms of factors rather than individuals. Second, risk legitimates increased governmental intervention. Third, prevention is no longer primarily based upon personal expertise but, rather, upon the implementation of a network of governmental intelligibility organized around the notion of risk. While not accepting these three shifts without some qualification, they are still useful.

Considering these shifts in turn, the first involves moving away from focusing on the concrete individual and the notion of the subject, to focusing instead on a combination of risk factors. A prerequisite of employing risk within contemporary government is a necessary disaggregation of the individual—an aggregation that survived within previous forms of analysis (for example, those operating within the logic of dangerousness).

The Dissolution of the Subject

Since the prospect of locating danger within the subject had intrinsic difficulties both in terms of prediction and prevention (as just mentioned), the alternative was to address the factors that appear to be connected with undesirable outcomes or dangers. This circumvention of the inherently dangerous subject solved both problems at once. First, successful prediction became more a matter of statistical likelihood and less a matter of individual ability/credibility. Second, prevention could now be linked to a far wider set of governmental strategies based upon the social distribution of risk factors, rather than upon very limited and fallible individual diagnoses.

One result of this shift is that the factors themselves constitute the object of intervention, and not the concrete individual. Future dangers are now to be found, not hiding within the subject themselves, but within recognizable constellations of relevant risk factors. A child/youth no longer possesses a seed of delinquency, visible to the competent expert; rather, delinquency lies within any number of statistically validated risk factors, such as poverty, abuse, homelessness, and addiction.

The dissolution of the subject into interrelated sets of factors has broad implications. Within medicine, for example, the proliferation of numerous, regular, and diverse health checks has meant that an examination of a patient is now more an examination of a record—a dossier. It is an examination of various, often dispersed, features and factors that, in certain combinations, require intervention. As such, the individualized interview between practitioner and client (is) almost dispensable (Castel, 1991:281). Consequently:

> What the new preventive policies primarily address is no longer individuals but factors, statistical correlations of heterogeneous elements. They deconstruct the concrete subject of intervention, and reconstruct a combination of factors liable to produce risk. Their primary aim is not to confront a concrete dangerous situation, but to anticipate all the possible forms of irruption of danger. (Castel, 1991:288)

This is not merely true of medicine or psychiatry; it is also pertinent to all the disciplines that address social problems and issues. It is certainly the case for those knowledges that shape the category of youth. For example, in "Defining Youth At Risk," Douglas Gross and Dave Capuzzi (1989) attempt to present those factors that best constitute this category. They argue that this is no easy task, as the parameters of the at-risk youth vary, depending upon the risks under scrutiny and the canon of judgment being employed (such as a developmental or an educational perspective). The authors reiterate this point, noting that "the concepts surrounding the student at risk are complex...and filled with tragedy for those individuals who meet the criteria for being at risk" (Gross and Capuzzi, 1989:4). As can be seen from the latter part of this statement, it would appear that the tragedy lies, not within the subject themselves, but in the meeting of certain criteria, in the assemblage of a significant number of undesirable factors.

To extend this point, Gross and Capuzzi (1989:11–12) delineate several sets of factors that permit the definitive charting of the at-risk youth. Two of these are the most relevant. The first predictably identifies the decisive factors relating to the background circumstances of the at-risk youth—dysfunctional family environment, abuse, poverty, low academic ability, lack of coping strategies. The second concerns the factors that should serve as red flags for those who are at risk. This latter list best exemplifies the notion of the at-risk youth as an aggregation of a particular set of identifiable factors. The factors are: a. tardiness; b. absenteeism; c. acting out behaviors; d. lack of motivation; e. poor grades; f. truancy; g. low math and reading score; h.

failing one or more grades; i. lack of identification with school; j. failure to see the relevance of education to life experiences; k. boredom with school; l. rebellious attitude towards authority; m. verbal and language deficiency; n. inability to tolerate structured activities; o. being one or two more graduation credits behind one's age group. It is from such lists that Gross and Capuzzi explicitly assemble the at-risk youth:

> Factors such as these, viewed either individually or in combination, aid the identification process. Young people who, on a consistent basis, demonstrate any of these behaviours or characteristics should be viewed as 'prime' candidates for intervention programs dealing with those at risk. (Gross and Capuzzi, 1991:12)

This is a crucial function of the category of at-risk: it is one of the principal methods for articulating and legitimating the need for intervention of any kind. The at-risk youth, is a youth under scrutiny, and a youth in need of therapeutic intervention. As can be seen in the next section, employing risk rather than dangerousness permits this intervention to be authored and implemented in new and more effective ways.

Increasing the Scope of Government

According to Castel (1991:287), in 1976 there began to be installed in France a nationwide system for detecting childhood abnormalities. Every single infant in France had to undergo a series of examinations. During these inspections, a large amount of data was collected. This covered a myriad of different areas, which was then collated centrally. By correlating various elements of the survey—physical, psychological, and social—certain risk categories emerge.

> The presence of some, or of a certain number, of these factors of risk sets off an automatic alert. That is to say, a specialist, a social worker for example, will be sent to visit the family to confirm or disconfirm the *real* presence of danger, on the basis of the *probabilistic and abstract* existence of risks. One does not *start from* a conflictual situation observable in experience, rather one *deduces* it from a general definition of the dangers one wishes to prevent. (Castel, 1991:287–288)

Castel argues that this new system of preventative healthcare brings with it a new and powerful form of governmental surveillance that no longer even requires the presence of the governed. Whereas more traditional forms of surveillance (such as those associated with the disciplinary institution), require the spatial arrangement of the target population under a central, watchful, panoptic gaze, this new strategy almost entirely avoids the need for such direct scrutiny. As the last section demonstrated, in the first instance, the therapeutic focus falls not upon a given subject but upon a set of abstract factors determined by diverse governmental information gathering techniques. Castel contends that the deployment of risk in this manner permits a virtually limitless augmentation of the possibilities of government, based primarily upon unlimited suspicion. Indeed, Castel argues that:

> "Prevention" in effect promotes suspicion to the dignified scientific rank of a calculus of probability. To be suspected, it is no longer necessary to manifest symptoms of dangerousness or abnormality, it is enough to display whatever characteristics the specialists responsible for the definition of preventative policy have constituted as risk factors. (Castel, 1991:288)

For Ewald (1991:199) "anything *can* be a risk; it all depends upon how one analyses the danger, considers the event." Castel contends that the reach of risk is endless. Nothing remains outside its territory; hence, nothing remains beyond governmental intervention. Because risk can be legitimately found anywhere, there is, therefore, no-one who is not at some risk of something.

There are problems with Castel's analysis at this point. Rather than utilizing a social control model, wherein risk legitimates the limitless imposition of the unwanted forces of government, it is possible instead to regard risk as an effective mechanism for expanding the field of regulatory practices. When premised upon a productive, rather than a coercive, model of power, risk can be viewed as a means of equipping the population with new attributes (or equipping a new, wider population with such attributes). That is, risk can be viewed as simply facilitating the deployment of a form of government which, in a manner that dangerousness could not, expedites (for example) the successful transmission of youth from school to the workplace. Furthermore, while risk does bring more youth into the field of governmental regulation, this is not an infinite process. Indeed, risk is not applied equally across the population; instead, it is generally applied to specifically problematized, targeted populations—for risk to function otherwise would be to lose its central governmental purpose.

The final point to be taken from Castel's work is his contention that the role of the practitioner has become subordinate to the positions of the statistician and the administrator. By this logic, prevention is no longer primarily based upon personal expertise, but rather upon the implementation of a network of governmental intelligibility.

From Practitioner to Administrator

Castel (1991) argues that within the traditional model based upon the notion of inherent dangerousness, the ability to identify and treat any given danger was possessed almost exclusively by the expert concerned. For example, only a trained psychiatrist could satisfactorily recognize the inner mental problems of a delinquent youth. This constituted a domain of specialist knowledge that either marginalized or completely excluded untrained diagnoses. Furthermore, the danger within could only be ascertained via the direct gaze of the professional. This way of understanding danger necessitated a face-to-face relationship between specialist and patient. As such, the whole process was essentially shaped and dominated by the practitioners on the ground, in virtually all key areas—observation, diagnosis, treatment, prevention.

For Castel, however, the shift from dangerousness to risk was marked by a fracturing of the direct relationship between the professional and the client. That is, whereas risk brought with it the benefits of both limiting the culpability of the specialist and of augmenting the possibilities of prevention, it also had the effect of actually subordinating that specialist to the administrator. Because danger was no longer believed to reside in any given person, the face-to-face relationship of the helper and the helped became very much secondary to the much broader governmental establishment of "flows of populations based on the collation of abstract factors deemed liable to produce risk in general" (Castel, 1991:281). Risk lies more in the administrative gathering, arranging, and evaluating of data, rather than in the individual case-files of the professional:

> Administration acquires an almost complete autonomy...The operatives on the ground now become a simple auxiliary to a manager whom he or she supplies with information...These items of information are then stockpiled, processed and distributed along channels completely disconnected from those of professional

practice...The relation which directly connected the fact of possessing a knowledge of a subject and the possibility of intervening...is shattered. (Castel, 1991:293)

There are some problems, however, with simply and unproblematically demarcating the role of practitioner from that of administrator, as Castel has done. It could alternatively be argued that the role of the practitioner is now actually indistinguishable in many ways from that of an administrator. That is, administrative knowledge is now immanent to the therapeutic task of the practitioner. Within this logic, the practitioner can be viewed as merely a conduit between any number of concerns made visible by various techniques of contemporary government and the population as a whole.

Still, whether or not Castel's dichotomizing of the practitioner and the administrator is accepted in its current (mutually exclusive) form, this does not negate the possibility of making some associated observation with regard to the at-risk youth. First, the factors pertinent to spotting an at-risk youth are given to the operatives on the ground second-hand. The at-risk youth is undoubtedly shaped by the accumulation, collation, and correlation of diverse statistical information, and not by the firsthand diagnosis of the specialist. That is, the student is not assessed and dealt with via the direct, therapeutic intervention of the teacher/school counselor whose training permits direct detection of inherent problems. Rather, the expertise of the youth worker lies in a knowledge of the factors indicating risk, and in the various contexts in which risk is mobilized as a governmental category. Within the youth field, the specialists work, for the most part, within the parameters of the classifications given to them through large-scale quantitative research (such as Gross and Capuzzi's [1989] list of important factors in the early identification of an at-risk student).

Second, the shift from the emphasis on the professional/client relationship to a consideration of combinations of factors based upon flows of populations has exponentially broadened the likelihood of detection and prevention. It is no longer only doctors or psychiatrists who are capable of credibly voicing their diagnoses. Risk has democratized the entire process. Teachers are now expected to be aware of the presence of any number of risk factors pertinent to given at-risk groups, be it concerning sexual abuse, drug use, or delinquency. Even parents are now encouraged to look for the presence of risk factors within the confines of the therapeutic family

(Robinson, 1989:338). For example, Ian Watt (1990) delineates ten risk indicators with regard to substance abuse alone (such as mood swings, poor school performance, secretive communication, and so forth) that parents should be aware of in their children.

This last point, concerning the increase in the number of people deemed qualified to look for risk, further supports the point made earlier that the employment of risk has multiplied the possibilities of government. Not only has risk permitted the construction of numerous at-risk positions, but there are also a greater range of experts able to identify risk factors, arrange these factors to a risk grouping and, hence, initiate appropriate intervention—whether this intervention be conducted by themselves, or by someone with even greater expertise.

An Alternative Interpretation of the Finn Report

Almost all of the characteristics of risk, as outlined in the preceding parts of this chapter, are present within the Finn Report. That is, the youth at-risk of not making the transition to adulthood successfully, is both shaped, and operates governmentally, in some fairly predictable ways:

First, the Finn Report identifies a number of graded risk positions. According to the *Students at Risk Program* (1989)—which largely underpins the section of the Finn Report dealing with the at-risk—all students can, under given circumstances, be at-risk of underachievement and eventual unemployment. Certain groups, however, are more vulnerable to this outcome—the archetypal at-risk youth. National statistics estimating the prevalence of this character are most often (although not only) based upon calculations of those who have left school early and yet have not continued with any form of education or training. As previously mentioned, however, a more specific demarcation of the at-risk youth is undertaken for the Finn Report by Freeland (1991). These groups have been identified in part one of this chapter. Going one step further, the Finn Report (1991:134) itself actually ends up by demarcating a smaller subgroup of the at-risk, who require even more rigorous attention and intervention. These groups can be considered to be at-greatest-risk. They include: aboriginal youth, some NESB (non-English speaking backgrounds) young people, some young women, the homeless, the long-term unemployed, those in isolated communities, young offenders, and disabled young people. Thus, although the Finn Report finally delineates a relatively small population as those it considers at-risk (in relation to others operating with the same concept), it would appear as though the report makes this ultimate choice from four basic, incremental levels of risk. As previously mentioned, such a graded system of risk provides an extensive network of governmental intelligibility, within which varying degrees of intervention can be organized, and by which individuals can be practically differentiated as members of classes of person.

Second, and linked to its role in establishing a network of governmental intelligibility, there is another recognizable and important element of the use of risk within the Finn report—that is its calculability. Freeland (1991:178) outlines numerous different ways of reliably calculating the at-risk population, each purporting to arrive at a figure with an accuracy of 0.1 percent. In 1990, the statistics suggested that 15.6 percent of Australian fifteen- to nineteen-year-olds were at-risk. By 1991, this number had increased to 18.3 percent of Australian 15–19 year olds. This exhaustive and meticulous accumulation of data has at least three important implications. First, it is the very mechanism by which knowledge is acquired concerning the social body—that is, it actually permits the construction of such characters as the at-risk youth, and gives those characters numerical and conceptual depth. Second, it provides the very data by which risk is constructed, and it uncovers fluctuations within the risk population, trends that have vital implications for future policy (such as the aforementioned 2.5 percent increase in the at-risk population from 1990 to 1991). Finally, the accurate statistical identification for specific risk groups, as well as their relative size and risk status (low risk, high risk, and so forth) ensures that available resources of government can be directed to their greatest effect. The Finn Report (1991:147) itself makes a series of funding suggestions based upon some of the specific demographics of risk—suggestions grounded in the self-evident credibility of its own statistical calculation.

Third, it can be seen within the Finn Report, as with a good deal of other literature in the field, that the notion of the at-risk youth has largely superseded the preceding notion of the disadvantaged youth which, from the mid-1970s onward, itself eclipsed the problem youth, and the delinquent, and so on (Bessant, 1993). In many parts of the Finn report, however, the two notions are used almost interchangeably. For example, when discussing chapter 7 of the document: "the Review Committee decided that this chapter should focus on a smaller sub-group of the 'at-risk' group identified above—those who would be classified as deeply disadvantaged in relation to their educational training" (Finn Report, 1991:134). It would appear, however, that *disadvantage* seems to be used only in the most general of contexts. Its purpose appears to be the demarcation of a rough area of concern. It lacks the specificity of a risk analysis, either in terms of accurate statistical evaluation, or the flexibility and rigor concomitant with the possibility of layering one set of risks on top of another. Whenever a high degree of theoretical precision is required, *risk* rather than *disadvantage* is employed.

The fourth familiar element in the Finn Report's use of risk, is that risk factors are used rather than any totalized notion of the concrete individual. As just mentioned, the Report occasionally refers to the umbrella concept of disadvantage. However, a further problem exists in that this concept still largely locates the effects of wider structural problems within particular categories of person (although those persons are actually removed from any political blame). This is not true of risk. When the Finn Report employs the term *risk* to address the specificities of a problematic transition to adulthood, it is done in terms of the aggregation of factors. Indeed, the advantage of using an approach based upon the more flexible notion of risk factors, over the more unwieldy and limited idea of disadvantage, is discussed explicitly by Freeland:

> It is more productive to examine the multiplicity of inter-related factors which contribute to the discrimination and inequalities of access and outcome experienced by particular groups of young people rather than to examine broad categories of young people whose "disadvantage" is artificially reduced to...class, race, gender, ethnicity or religion. (Freeland, 1991:4)

Freeland extends this contention even further by arguing that governmental intervention should necessarily avoid any kind of emphasis on *the individual* because, in some ways, this results in a *blame the victim* approach to social problems. Therefore, a satisfactory resolution of this dilemma can be reached only by sidestepping the individual altogether. As an alternative, policy should directly address the factors that constitute the risk situation.

The fifth point concerning risk and the Finn Report also centers around the production and utilization of risk factors. In particular, it involves those arguments detailing their administrative construction. Even when employing the notion of the disadvantaged youth rather than the at-risk youth, there is no suggestion in any of the literature that this is, in some way, an inherent fault within the youth that can be discerned through the face-to-face diagnosis of the highly trained expert. The absence of this assumption is one trait that disadvantage and risk do have in common. Both are indubitably the product of statistical correlation (even though the possibilities with risk are immeasurably greater). The factors constituting the at-risk youth are arrived at, not through firsthand observation followed by insightful extrapolation, but by the accumulation, collation, and correlation of diverse statistical information. The conclusions of this research are then given second-hand to the operatives on the ground, who are trained to recognize the relevant factors and to act appropriately.

For example, in a paper for the Finn Report by John Ainley and Phillip McKenzie (1991:73), the factor regarded as most definitive of the youth at-risk of not making a successful transition from education to adulthood, is the degree of earlier school achievement. Not surprisingly, those who do well at school are more likely to continue in their education. Having ascertained that this is a crucial statistical correlate of risk, they argue that teachers should be trained in the various techniques necessary to identify, diagnose, and assist underachieving students. These would operate within school-based projects, directed at key competencies, but sensitive to risk factors such as the aforementioned one. The *Students at Risk Program*, so highly recommended by the Finn Report, operates on precisely this system. With the same logic, as discussed earlier in this chapter, Lehr and Harris (1988) discuss at length the at-risk, low-achieving student. These writers claim that a good teacher can begin to spot factors associated with this risk grouping, and alter their teaching strategies accordingly. The desired outcome of these new teaching strategies is that students once categorized as low achievers, and hence at-risk, become high-achieving students whose risk rating is much lower.

The role of expertise is not being underestimated here. When arguing that the role of the professional has changed as a result of new statistical and administrative techniques of knowledge acquisition and dissemination, this is not to suggest that professional expertise is now less important, quite the reverse. It is precisely the plausibility and credibility of professional expertise that permits this kind of government to operate effectively, including that employing risk. The vital difference is that the expertise referred to here is not limited simply to the immediate relationship between specialist and client. In the case of risk, expertise largely operates by transforming the professional responsibilities and capacities of teachers, and also by reshaping the practices and the aspirations of the pedagogic family.

Finally, it is the argument regarding the aspirations of parents that constitutes that last noteworthy element of the nexus between risk and the Finn Report. This is particularly pertinent, within the context of this book, as it will be demonstrated that risk has a significant role to play in the government of youth and their sex. That is, it has been argued in the Finn Report that some young women are placed in an at-risk situation owing, to some extent, to the vocational aspirations of their parents. When discussing the issue of calculability, Freeland's (1991:178) figures were cited concerning the percentage of Australian fifteen to nineteen year-olds deemed to be at-risk: 15.6 percent in 1990; 18.3 percent in 1991. Although these two statistics alone reveal an upward trend in youth at-risk, what they do not reveal is the discrepancy between the sexes. Other figures given by Freeland maintain that although the *mean* percentages are 15.8 and 18.3, this actually breaks down into 12.6 percent males—18.8 percent females for 1990, and 16.3 percent males—20.3 percent females for 1991. This is a marked difference.

Freeland argues that there are two central causes for this discrepancy. First, young females are more vulnerable to sexual abuse within the family— a fact that has been well documented. In the New South Wales Government's (1986) report *Girls at Risk*, of the one hundred girls interviewed for the study, thirty-one had been the victims of incest; eighteen had been sexually assaulted. These figures are significantly higher than for equivalent young males (Rea, 1987). Although this is unequivocally an important area of concern, the emphasis will be placed upon the other issue of risk specific to young females. This second difference is owing to "the more rapid demise of female teenage full-time employment" (Freeland, 1991:179). Although in the last twenty-five years the number of young males employed full-time has dropped from 59 percent to 33 percent, the number of young females employed full time has dropped from 58 percent to 23 percent—a far greater decrease (Freeland, 1991:167). The most evident reason for this sex-based discrepancy has been the survival of the apprenticeship system. While many of the other areas of traditional youth employment no longer exist, the apprenticeship system has all but survived intact throughout the recession years. Furthermore, it is a system that is almost exclusively male:

> Over 90 per cent of apprenticeships are held by males, and apprenticeships account for over 50 per cent of teenage male full-time employment. In short, the apprenticeship system has acted as a protected labour market reserve for young males making the transition from school to employment...Gender based labour market segregation means that teenage females have not generally enjoyed the protections offered by the apprenticeship system. (Freeland, 1991:167)

These general inferences are supported by Ainley and McKenzie (1991) who note that in 1989, 27 percent of young males under 19 had been in apprenticeships, as compared with a figure of only 5 percent for the equivalent young females. Therefore, the conclusion is that young females are more vulnerable to unemployment.

Having now demonstrated that young females are more "at-risk" of failing in their transition to adulthood than young males (with respect to unemployment), the question then is: what kind of intervention is appropriate in order to increase the employability of these young females? This question, in combination with a number of other concerns about girls, formed the basis for the Commonwealth Schools Commission's (1987b) *National Policy for the Education of Girls in Australian Schools.* One of the recurrent problem areas mentioned in this, and other, literature, has been the kinds of curriculum choices made by girls within the school, which later hinders their future selection of occupation (sexism in the workplace aside).

Veronica Schwartz (1987) makes some relevant observations in this regard. She, too, contends that girls considerably restrict their post-school educational and employment options by underparticipating in maths, science, and technology. While not directly criticizing the career aspirations of girls, Schwartz points to a need for greater female participation in subjects that will lead to a broader range of job opportunities—such as those associated with traditional apprenticeship schemes. Lesley Parker and Jenny Offer (1987:153) maintain that, although numerous programs have increased the success of girls in maths and science at the lower secondary level, these changes are not reflected at the postcompulsory grades of 11 and 12, let alone in terms of career paths.

Many obstacles, however, stand in the way of the goal to increase job opportunities for young females—many of which are beyond the reach of current educational policy. One area that has been the subject of recent policy initiatives, and is deemed to be within the reach of government, concerns numerous attempts to change the career aspirations of girls away from the apparent reflex predisposition toward the traditional humanities-based subjects. Margaret Powles (1992) notes that with regard to this issue, more young males than females aspire to go to TAFE, an educational route widely associated with the vocational/trades and so forth. Alternatively, more young females than males aspire to go to university. This is a more prestigious location, and the site of caring subjects such as nursing and teaching, but a site currently paying less employment dividends.

Powles records that this trend is even more evident when examining the aspirations of parents. To an even greater extent than their daughters, parents do not want their female children to take a career path involving the kinds of subjects dealt with at TAFE, although the statistics suggest that this leads to jobs. These sorts of perceptions were referred to directly by the then Minister for Education, John Dawkins (1992). Using a set of arguments that infuse the entire Finn Report, he proclaims the need for a reevaluation of the traditional divide between general and vocational education. He also states the need to reexamine the notion of cleverness, extending it beyond the academic, to the technical and the industrial. It is these last two areas that are traditionally dealt with at TAFE, and that least appeal to young females. Dawkins argues that this is where some changes must occur, not only in the broader community attitudes to TAFE, as a poor second choice to university, but also in the career aspirations of girls. It is these aspirations, after all, which place them at-risk. Yet, the responsibility for the career aspirations of young girls is not considered to rest solely, or even predominantly, within themselves. Dawkins, like many others, points to the role of the parents in shaping the choices of their children:

> ANOP (Australian National Opinion Polls) also confirmed the findings of other researchers that parents are the most important influence in young people's career and employment-related decisions. The challenge for the community, then, is to

develop an understanding and appreciation of the full range of education and training options that are available. This is a challenge for young people themselves, and particularly so for parents. (Dawkins, 1992:8)

The *Students at Risk Program* (1989) makes exactly the same point when it claims that parents have a key influence in changing aspirations and intentions. Hence, all school programs dealing with the at-risk student must necessarily incorporate the parent. This is particularly true of young females, as it is their own aspirations which place them at-risk.

Schwartz (1987) also emphasizes the role of the parents in changing the intentions of their daughters, based upon sound facts rather than traditional beliefs about girls' education and employment. She cites the Beazley Report (1984) on education in Western Australia, which stated that curriculum and career choices were generally made as a result of parental pressure related to the roles of females in the community. Furthermore, "much of the reported advice from parents was ill-informed and lacking any real sense of contemporary schooling or the job market..." (Beazley Report, 1984:94; cited in Schwartz, 1987:134). Parker and Offer (1987:153) also argue that the problem for young females appears to lie in their aspirations, and that these can be traced directly to their parents. As such, entrenched stereotypes about jobs among parents need to be changed if girls are not to continue to be at-risk in their transition to employed adulthood.

As mentioned earlier, the at-risk youth is almost always explained in terms of the risk family. The normal rhetoric surrounding this family is one of poverty, abuse, and dysfunction. As mentioned earlier, however, as anything can be a risk, the risk family can take many different forms. In this case, the misplaced career aspirations of parents become an important risk factor, when positioned within the context of the kind of governmental transformations outlined by the Finn Report. This should not be a surprise. As McCallum (1993) observes, the domestic space is one of the most important and practical settings for instilling the capacities and attitudes required of a modern population. In this case, the desired attitudes are inculcated through the rationale of risk.

Furthermore, it is the construction of the risk family that sets up a counterpoint against which the pedagogic family can measure itself. The image of the risk family forms an important part of a strategy aimed at inducing the pedagogic family to reform itself. That is, the notion of risk helps in the formation of families with the ability to problematize their own conduct.

Conclusion

The central aims of *Governing the "At-Risk" Youth* have been as follows. First, this chapter has applied some of the ideas from the previous chapter to a topical field within youth research—the at-risk youth. These ideas permit an analysis of specific formations of youth that accounts for the particular conditions of their emergence and deployment. Thus, the at-risk youth is not to be located within the familiar binary oppositions of normal/delinquent, domination/subordination, or state/civil. Rather, it has been assembled piecemeal as the object of a number of governmental programs. These programs have finite boundaries and limited ambitions, and operate within domains such as the family and the school. Furthermore, these programs organize and direct youth in different ways on the basis of sex.

Second, this chapter has argued that the Finn Report is part of the very process by which youth is formed and re-reformed as a category. In attempting to redefine the period of transition from education to employment, the Finn Report (along with Mayer and Carmichael) forms one of the sites within which the category of youth is given its shape—both administratively and culturally. As has been contended in chapter 2 of this book, youth is not a stage of life, but an artifact of various forms of government. The Finn Report is an element of one such form of government.

Third, within the Finn Report—itself an extensive and effective mechanism of government—the notion of risk operates as an important component of a grid of governmental intelligibility. It allows for an augmentation of the possibilities of governmental regulation (especially of youth), and, in addition, it operates as a productive element of a larger system that records its observation, intervenes strategically, and steers conduct in socially, economically, and morally appropriate directions. The calculability, specificity, and versatility of risk make it a far more efficient tactic than any of its predecessors for describing youth.

A final point, of particular relevance to this book, is that risk is used as a governmental rationale for managing the sex of young people. Young females are constituted as objects of government by different risk factors than their male counterparts. Consequently, the strategies of intervention employed within the various sites of government also differ. Within the Finn Report, social trajectories of young females are regulated by adjusting the career aspirations of the parents. Thus, in effect, the character of the at-risk youth is used as the pretext for modifying and expanding the boundaries, responsibilities, and ambitions of the pedagogic family.

Owing to the importance of the family to contemporary strategies of rule (that is, government at a distance), this is particularly significant. In almost every context in which the at-risk youth is deployed, assumptions are also made about a preexisting risk family. This generally takes the form of the presumption of a causal relationship between the two; that it is the risk family that spawns the at-risk youth (Palmo and Palmo, 1989; Gilmour, 1989). By this reasoning, governmental concerns over such youth frequently translate into governmental programs aimed at the family. The at-risk youth thereby acts as a conduit through which certain kinds of family can be identified and reformed. Again, this is an extension of existing strategies involving the figure of the child, as it was largely concerns over the child that legitimated the family's becoming, not simply the target of governmental scrutiny, but actually saturated with governmental programs and practices of self-reformation.

As has been discussed, however, the flexibility of the notion of risk has also permitted a reorganization of both the ways in which the family can be governed, and ways in which the family can be expected to participate in government. First, as risk expands the field of governmental regulation of youth, given the conclusions reached in the preceding argument, this is also the case for the family. Through the deployment of risk, a greater proportion of family units can now be made intelligible to government. Second, the specificity of risk means that this intelligibility can take new, more precise, and, hence, more effective forms. This includes programs aimed at very particular and intricate aspects of the management of sex. Finally, the family itself becomes enlisted in the processes of risk assessment. It now comes under the purview of responsible parents to check for particular risk indicators within children, as evidence of the existence of specific problems.

The identification of the risk family serves a further useful purpose. Apart from the obvious point that identification is a prerequisite for intervention, it also has a role to play within the logic of Donzelot's regulation of images. After all, the ends of government can be well served through various images of family life, motherhood, and childhood—both positive and negative. As part of a broad set of strategies aimed at enlisting the family in its own self-reformation, images of the good mother are silently defined in relation to those of the bad, just as images of the healthy, ordered, and loving household are counterposed against the risk family. Accordingly, the image of the risk family has an important role to play in the formation of families with the capacity to problematize their own conduct, in that this image provides a visible measure of the central parameters of domestic failure.

The next chapter of this book outlines the second half of an alternative approach to youth research. It will also address youth and sex, but will focus not upon governmentality, but, instead, upon practices of the self. This is not to suggest that governmentality and practices of the self are separate theoretical domains. As will be made perfectly clear, they most certainly are not, and the divide between them is in many ways artificial. However, chapter 4 will examine some of the ways in which the broad governmental programs discussed so far become taken up as practices of self-government. That is, how youth can be understood as the doing of specific types of work on the self.

CHAPTER 4

Sexing the Self

This chapter outlines the second half of an alternative approach to youth research, in that it emphasizes the piecemeal manner in which youthful personae are constructed. In particular, this chapter employs the notion of practices of the self to better explain the relationship between the category of youth and the management of its sex. First, this chapter problematizes the traditional understandings of the self as the inner person. Relevant personages are governmentally distributed to some individuals and, through them, a self is constructed. Second, this chapter argues that the contemporary formation of various types of person can be understood as being related, in part, to the government of populations. Within programs such as those pertinent to the management of sex, governmental technologies structure the practices by which conduct of persons such as youth is patterned, thereby fashioning a kind of youthful habitus. Such management forms part of a general strategy of enrolling the objects of these programs in their own self-reformation. Consequently, youth can be understood as the doing of specific types of work on the self. The final section of the chapter examines some specific ways in which young people fashion a self. This analysis is accomplished by applying Foucault's model of the four aspects of the relationship to one's self (the determination of the ethical substance, the mode of subjectification, practices of the self, and teleology) to the sexual conduct of youth. With a particular focus on young women's magazines, this schema will illustrate how the conduct of youth is targeted and directed, as part of a vocabulary of practices through which a self is formed.

As discussed in chapter 2, there are numerous problems associated with explaining the contemporary exercise of power from within a framework of the state/civil society dichotomy. It was argued instead that diverse programs, taking their target as the population and operating largely at a distance (through domains such as the school and the family, employing the medium of expertise), govern by managing the habits of the population. In this chapter, the strategy of "managing the habits" of the population is to be investigated in terms of a tendency to enlist the population in reforming themselves. It is by specific techniques of self-government, by instilling certain practices of the self within particular target groups, that government operates effectively.

Not surprisingly then, the sexual practices of youth are also the target of governmental intervention through programs that operate by equipping youth to do specific kinds of work on the self. The person of the sexually irresponsible youth is the target of a broad range of programs aimed at enlisting youth in their own sexual self-modification. Such programs are by no means restricted to traditional school-based sex education classes. They also include a range of family planning directives, welfare programs, magazines, and books detailing various aspects of appropriate sexual conduct, schemes operating through youth workers and youth guidance counselors, health policy initiatives, and so on.

Within health policy, for example, the recruitment of youth into their own sexual self-reformation has been particularly evident. Mary Crooks and Marcia Webb (1988) point out that the Youth Policy Development Council of Victoria has attempted numerous initiatives toward improving the health of young people. The first assumption that the Council thought should underpin their programs was that young people should be encouraged and supported in managing their own health (Crooks and Webb, 1988:21). Significantly, of the seven specific categories of concern, five were directly related to sexual conduct (sexuality, being a young parent, contraception, sexually transmitted diseases, and relationships with other people). The message here is clear: sex is the most important youth health issue, and the best way to manage that sex is to encourage self-management.

The central purpose of chapter 4 is to examine some of the mechanisms by which this sexual self-management occurs. The formation of the sexually responsible youth does not occur simply as a result of putting in place governmental programs that target the sexual conduct of young people. It will be argued, instead, that such programs recruit youth into doing particular kinds of work on the self. That is, they encourage and ingrain practices that shape the self in specific ways. In order to employ this theoretical machinery, however, it is first necessary to explain a particular understanding of the "Self" that runs counter to dominant psy-based explanations, and hence much youth research.

The Person, the Individual, and the Self

In *Dialogue with Youth*, Ainslie Mears (1973) expounds a conventional and pervasive understanding of the youth problem, an understanding that betrays a familiar set of domain assumptions concerning the self Covering a wide range of issues, Mears (a psychiatrist) arrives at a number of conclusions on youth: that youthful resistance to both society and parents is natural; that the behavior of youth is more extreme than adult behavior because young people are not yet mature enough to cope adequately with basic human drives, such as the drive for sex; that youth uses the media of clothes, drugs, and sex to express itself; and that youth is a time of trying to find out who one really is. This last claim is a telling one.

In a section entitled, "Do You Ever Wonder, what Is the Real Me?," Mears (1973:262) looks at young people's characteristic search for their inner identity. He argues that the variety of differing contexts within which young people find themselves, and the various social forces that impinge upon them, result in a clouding of the inner self—a distorting of the real. He maintains that, although youths often play a number of different social roles, unless these roles emanate from the natural person within, they will be nothing more than falsehoods. As a consequence, the "'real me' [will be] quite submerged in a flood of psychological turmoil" (Mears, 1973:286). He goes on to say:

> In each of the many spheres in which we live we have to establish our own social identity. At university youth establishes his own characteristics as an individual...The same process evolves at home, and with his girl. However, each of these situations, the university, home life, and the relationship with his girl, are constantly changing. But the inner sense of identity remains unchanged. (Mears, 1973:270)

Indeed, Mears regards the search for the true person within as one of the defining characteristics of youth. This is especially true when addressing sex. Youth is depicted as a time when young people seek to find the truth of their sexuality. Again, this is an inner verity, a component of their true selves. It is only when the sexual conduct of an individual is aligned with their real sexual nature, that an individual can be happy and balanced. If there is a mismatch between the two, the consequences can be dire.

This reasoning also supports most of the literature within a very specific area of youth research, that concerned with anorexia nervosa. As will be shown in chapter 5, the condition of anorexia nervosa is most often explained in terms of a repressed true inner self being locked in a struggle with the external, emaciated false self (Orbach, 1978; Dana, 1987). This thesis will adopt a very different approach to the self to that outlined so far. It will be argued that rather than something that exists inside all individuals—the true inner being—the self is actually a historical contingency, which reflects the inner acquisition of personhood. By demonstrating that the person is a historically variable collection of attributes that human individuals may or may not have, it becomes possible to identify and study the piecemeal manner in which social institutions are implicated in the construction of the self.

In contemporary western societies, there is generally held to be no distinction between the notions of person and individual. This supposition is axiomatic to prevailing conceptions of the self, as the features that constitute the inner self of the human individual also necessarily and intractably fashion the person. In order to support the argument that being an individual does not concomitantly necessitate being a person, however, it is essential to demonstrate that these two concepts have, at some time or in some place, been uncoupled. This task is neither as problematic nor as obscure as it might initially appear, as this division is evident even within a familiar social institution such as the legal system. First, the category of *person* has a technical basis constituted in law by a set of rights and obligations (Frow, 1987:69). These in no way bind personhood to the human individual, but, rather, to the attributes created as artifacts of various forms of knowledge. Second, legal rights are themselves fragmentary, context-bound, and constructed across various legal terrains. Therefore, it is impossible to aggregate all the disparate rights and obligations constitutive of the *person in law* into a coherent entity, let alone something that might be conceived of as corresponding to the individual. Finally, any remaining assumptions concerning person as self can be problematized by noting that the law even allocates personhood to non-human entities that satisfy specific conditions of formation, such as corporations and governmental associations (Wickham, 1990:6).

However, evidence supporting the variable relation between individuals and forms of personhood is not limited to the legal sphere. An essay by Marcel Mauss (1985), entitled "The Category of Mind: The Notion of the Person; the Notion of the Self," and concerning the historical development of the category of person provides disparate examples in defense of this reasoning. The central focus of this work is upon those societies where personhood is externally acquired, such as in societies structured around clan and fraternal loyalties (which principally means ancient Europe and non-European societies), as opposed to societies where it is internally organized. Mauss argues that the contours of personhood are dependent at any given moment upon the social and historical contexts of their formation. Because these are subject to considerable variation, so, too, is the category of person. Paul Hirst and Penny Wooley summarize these arguments by stating:

> The person is not a given entity, concepts of "person" differ between cultures and between periods in our own Graeco-Christian civilisation. And not only concepts, the practices, institutions, and forms of reference which constitute "personalities" also differ, and with them speech, gesture, and conduct. (Hirst and Wooley, 1985:118)

Thus, the person neither has its genesis in some unrefined biological and psychological essence of the individual, nor is it the inevitable outcome of simply being human, as access to this category has at times been restricted along clan and fraternity lines. Rather, personhood should be regarded as a set of statuses, rights, and obligations that may be allocated under certain circumstances. It is a contingent mechanism for publicly organizing the attributes and social relations available to members of the society. Particular persons are special configurations of rights, statuses, capacities, and traits primarily invested in transindividual entities such as names, totems, and masks. Mauss (1985:13) points out that etymology of the word *person* is itself germane to the issue, as it evolved from the Latin *persona*: "a mask, a tragic mask, a ritual mask, and the ancestral mask," in that the attributes of personhood were originally understood as being allocated to that mask and not to its wearer. Consequently, in marked contrast to current western beliefs, the specificities of any particular personage were not invested in the inner self of that individual.

Mauss argues that the inner self came to be axiomatic within contemporary western societies as the result of two main changes in the institutions of law and morality. The first change centered around the belief that the status of person should be available to all eligible individuals. The advent of Roman law resulted in a more general distribution of personhood than had been available through preexisting clan structures. The second change involved attempts by the Stoics to construct a philosophical system based upon individuals becoming responsible for their own conduct. Instead of the attributes of the person being acquired at public ceremonies and rituals, they were now seen as being attached to an inner principle that regulated social behavior. Despite the changes initiated by the Stoics it was, as Mauss (1985:19) points out, the Christians who made a metaphysical entity of the moral person, thereby completing the fusion of personhood and self.

Mauss contends that where this person/individual distinction exists, the society is actually composed of a repertoire or cast list of specific characters, rather than a collection of individuals. These characters constitute the permanence of the clan, and are normally allocated to individuals at public ceremonies. Also, these personages are not necessarily permanent, as individuals can be given several different personages during their lifetime. Likewise, these personages can be forcibly removed and another individual endowed with their characteristics, rights, and honors. In the case of the Kwakiutl of the Pacific Northwest of America, it was possible not only to acquire possessions and prestige through the conquests of war, but it was also possible to accumulate the personages previously attached to other individuals. By killing the previous owner or taking ritual trappings, one could also "inherit his names, his goods, his obligations, his ancestors, his 'person' (personne), in the fullest sense of the word. In this way ranks, goods, personal rights, and things, as well as their particular spirit, are acquired" (Mauss, 1985:8–9).

An outcome of this historical relocation of the person is a concomitant reevaluation of the parameters within which the self can be understood. Gaining the rights, obligations, and capacities of personhood through various private mechanisms of self-shaping (as opposed to through public ritual) does not justify the conclusion that these two processes differ in some fundamental way. That the person has become bonded to the individual does not make this construct any more real, or any less a construct. The modern conception of person, with its attachment to notions of the inner self, has no greater claim to inherent authenticity than do the masks, names, and totems associated with the personages of clan-based societies.

Questioning the legitimacy of current depictions of the self is not limited to discussions on the advent of the moral conscience. Other axes by which the self is granted its singular, essential status have also been found to be dependent upon social factors. For example, Ong (1982) charts the relationship between the advent of writing and the development of contemporary consciousness. He argues not only that modern consciousness is intrinsically different from that which preexisted it, but also that this change was the result of historically identifiable social transformations. While not sharing Ong's viewpoint concerning the unity of consciousness, Hirst and Wooley also consider that:

> Consciousness is not a given datum. Humans' capacities for self-representation and self-reflection depend on definite forms of discourse and definite activities in which they are trained and implicated as agents. These capacities vary. The concept of "person" is intelligible only with reference to a definite substratum of categories, practices, and activities which together give the agent its—complex and differentiated—form. (Hirst and Wooley, 1985:120)

In summary, the source and foundation of personhood is external to the individual. Individuals assume specific personages because they are ascribed bundles of rights and obligations, not simply because they are human beings. The melding of the person into the individual is the result of given historical events. This chapter of the thesis will argue that the formation of youth, as a specific type of person, is not the result of society finally identifying the inner state common to individuals of a certain age. Instead, it will be argued that youth is better understood, in part, through the piecemeal assembly of various practices employed in the government of populations. It will also be argued that youth, as a category of person, is organized in terms of a relation to an inner self—an inner self governed, in particular, through its sex.

Youth and Self-government

As mentioned in the introduction to chapter 1, Forrester (1993) examines some common elements of four working-class subcultures (the Skaters, the Street Machiners, the Graffiti Artists, and the Street Dancers). Although she states that she is reluctant to declare these groups to be intrinsically subcultural, she employs a theoretical framework which, with a few minor variations, closely follows the CCCS position. That is, she focuses her work around the Gramscian notion of hegemony; she argues that groups such as these represent a crisis within that hegemony, she employs the notion of the parent culture, she suggests that such subcultures win space for themselves at the expense of that parent culture, and she emphasizes the notion of style—in this case she is particularly concerned with style as self-expression and personal creativity. It is this final element of subculture theory that is pertinent here. Forrester takes the familiar line that young people are subject to extensive social surveillance and regulation:

> Young People's lives are at present, increasingly marked by social controls being imposed upon them. These range from financial and administrative measures designed to keep them occupied and off the streets, to initiatives designed to regulate their behaviour in the "public sphere" while at the same time putting pressure on them to conform to behavioural norms in their family and school life. (Forrester, 1993:110)

She goes on to argue that the formation of subcultures provides "a means of surviving the assault of the various social and legal authorities on their self-identity" (Forrester, 1993:110). Furthermore, it is within the forms of creative expression specific to each of the four groups that young people find their agency, whether this be through graffiti, or the painstaking construction of a street machine. She argues that traditional forms of artistic expression—sculpture, poetry, drama—are unsuitable for such youth. First, as they are part of the adult world of high culture, they can only be adopted within the context of an oppressive set of power relations: teacher/student, learned/unlearned, dominant/dominated. Second, as such traditional aesthetic forms are saturated with such power relations, they lack the authenticity of youth-generated cultures. That is, they do not have their origins within the unregulated space of young people's subjective experience. Thus, it is only within the realm of subjectivity, a realm quite separate from the external world of social control and regulation, that young people are free to express themselves fully.

> That young people persist in displaying something of themselves through their youth-generated cultures is a testimony to their courage and belief in themselves and their creative potential. In the face of strong opposition from all quarters; society, education, bureaucracy and the state, young people continue to carve out a friendly place in a not so friendly environment. (Forrester, 1993:113)

This chapter will adopt a different understanding of subjectivity from that employed by Forrester. It will now be argued that, far from being a place exempt from external regulation, subjectivity is an attentively and rigorously governed space. Furthermore, this government is central to the formation of specific types of self.

It initially seems counterintuitive to argue that subjectivity, the most important element of theories of the self, is a governed domain. Generally, the machinery of government is obvious and unambiguous—health care programs, case notes, statistics, panopticons, and timetables. That is, the governed domain customarily appears to be that of time, bodies, and forces, external and tangible. This chapter, however, will argue that government works most effectively because it operates within the realm of subjectivity. By steering the desires, aspirations, and feelings of the population, power functions at the level of self-government. Therefore, subjective experience is not a private region, which external powers try to control or exploit (as with much liberal and feminist argument, which takes subjectivity as a given, and then examines the role that society plays in its repression). Subjectivity is not beyond the reach of government—a place of possible retreat. On the contrary, subjectivity is where government is at its most effective.

This contention has been a central focus for Foucault's work. He states that his central objective is to create a history of the various ways in which individuals are made into subjects. In doing so, he, too, rejects the familiar domain assumption of the transcendental subject which, *a priori*, is made up of identical parameters throughout history. Instead, he posits the self as developing as part of the myriad practices by which the human subject is formed (Foucault, 1980). Foucault supports this contention by focusing upon the dual and complementary strategies by which individuals are subjected to, and made the object of, a lattice of governmental technologies. These technologies not only map out types of individual as objects of knowledge, as discussed in chapter 2, they also pattern the conduct of those individuals. That is, through the initial processes of governmentality, various groups of persons within the population are identified. Then, as a result of specific management strategies, their conduct is targeted and directed. It is as a consequence of this intervention that Foucault (1987) can delineate specific modalities of self-formation, such as a certain consciousness of criminality, centering around the way criminals relate to themselves:

> The individual has become an object of knowledge, both to himself and to others, an object who tells the truth about himself in order to know himself and be known, an object who learns to effect changes on himself. These are the techniques which are tied to the scientific discourse in the technologies of the self. (Dreyfus and Rabinow, 1982:174–175)

This is not to suggest that self-evaluation is a novel practice—the product of a governmental society. Doing work on the self was a common practice within certain castes in ancient Greece, where life was understood to be a work of art in need of constant attention and reworking. A more recent example is the seventeenth-century Puritan adoption of medieval casuistry, a technique of evaluation for the complex and often paradoxical moral circumstances of daily life. Hunter (1990) argues that this practice became a significant influence on popular thought and practice in the seventeenth century, as it provided a means of evaluating conduct within a social milieu characterized by radical social change and increasing individuation. Indeed, Hunter (1990:292) proposes that the practice of casuistry played a prominent role in the development of individualism. This provides an example of the way in which existing methods of organizing conduct, such as the techniques of self-evaluation characteristic of casuistry, are later adopted by the machinery of government and distributed to new and wider populations. As discussed in chapter 2, this was also the case with the

Christian confessional practices, which later came to form the basis for the governmental distribution of sexuality.

According to Rose (1990:1), in contrast to these earlier forms of self-management, the contemporary government of the self has three important and distinctive characteristics. First, the subjective capacities of citizens are now integral to the workings of public powers. As he notes, the most conspicuous indication of this concerns the apparatus targeting the welfare of the child—the national importance of the good parent, concerns over schooling, and the high profile of child psychology within the child welfare and justice systems, and so on. Second, it is now an expectation that modern organizations are charged with the task of managing subjectivity. The potential of given institutions to reach their objectives is now often calculated in terms of the capacities of their human resources: their intelligence, motivation, morale, efficiency, or flexibility. Indeed, not only are the academic trajectories of children determined by such criteria within the school, but so are the trajectories of the teachers themselves. Finally, there has emerged a new form of expertise pertaining to subjectivity. This expertise takes many different forms—psychologists, social workers, counselors, therapists, probation officers—"each asserting its virtuosity in respect of the self, in classifying and measuring the psyche, in predicting its vicissitudes, in diagnosing the cause of its troubles and prescribing remedies" (Rose, 1990:2–3). Furthermore, the management of subjectivity has become more important than ever before:

> The multiplying powers of these 'engineers of the soul' seem to manifest something profoundly novel in the relations of authority over the self. These new ways of thinking and acting do not just concern the authorities. They affect each of us, our personal beliefs, wishes and aspirations, in other words, our ethics...Our sense of ourselves has been revolutionised. We have become intensely subjective beings. (Rose, 1990:3)

Effectively then, society is governed through expertise. The image of the good mother, shaped at the intersection of a range of diverse knowledges, provides the impetus for women to remold themselves. Therefore, there now exists a continual process of self-evaluation, to be accomplished according to the criteria provided by experts.

The most important consideration is now to focus upon the ways in which youth itself can be understood in terms of self-government or work on the self. After all, the various problematizations that specify the object youth also have parallel implications for subject-formation. Consequently, youth can be interpreted in terms of specific types of self-formation, including ones bearing on the management of sexual conduct. It is this contention that provides the rationale for the remainder of this chapter.

As stated in chapter 2, one of the central mechanisms of government is the construction of a grid of norms. Young people are defined as normal by modeling their relationships, both to themselves and others, against a complex grid of available governmental manuals. These manuals encompass directions on acceptable approaches to decisions, choices, and judgments, including those concerning the management of their sex. Therefore, as a result of these governmental directives, young people are co-opted into doing work upon themselves, such that an acceptable youthful self is continually fashioned and refashioned. This is precisely what Foucault is referring to when he designates technologies of the self as permitting:

> Individuals to effect by their own means or with the help of others a certain number of operations on their own bodies and souls, thoughts, conduct, and way of being, so as to transform themselves in order to attain a certain state of happiness, purity, wisdom, perfection or immortality. (Foucault, 1988:18)

These technologies form a crucial element in the establishment of a recognizable habitus. Pierre Bourdieu (1977:83) describes habitus as a "matrix of perceptions, appreciations and actions" engendered by objective conditions. It is a set of dispositions that embody the relations, structures, and conventions characteristic of a given group or class. A habitus represents an internalized method of understanding and interacting that is grounded in the body itself, in that it often "function(s) below the level of consciousness and language" (Bourdieu, 1984:466). However, the formation of a particular habitus does not reflect the workings of an inner self. Rather, it is a set of dispositions that are shaped by history, acquired as the result of occupying a particular social position, and modified (to some extent) by each generation. A habitus structures practices and is, in turn, constituted by them.

Thus, the programs that constitute youth as a set of governmental objects, inculcate some of the practices, competencies, and dispositions constitutive of youthful habitus. As Bourdieu points out, these dispositions are the result of programs that are by no means always obvious or overtly relevant, since:

> Nothing seems more ineffable...and, therefore, more precious, than the values given body, made body by the transubstantiation achieved by the hidden persuasion of an implicit pedagogy, capable of instilling a whole cosmology, an ethic, a metaphysic, a political philosophy, through injunctions as insignificant as 'stand up straight' and 'don't hold your knife in your left hand.' (Bourdieu, 1977:94)

Such interventions into conduct, irrespective of their insignificance, are part of the general strategy of enrolling specific categories of individual in their own self-formation. Through this self-formation, these individuals then approximate to designated forms of personhood. This tactic has been especially evident when addressing the child, and, as youth is a reformulation of existing concerns over the child and the adolescent (as mentioned previously), therefore, the same logic applies. Foucault (1976) illustrates this process in his analysis of the pedagogization of children's sex. A specific group of individuals (children) are identified as the target population, and then various sets of knowledges (within sciences such as medicine, education, and psychology) are brought to bear upon this object, with the intention of both modifying its conduct and recruiting persons into their own self-modification. The self of these persons is thereby partially constructed in these terms; consequently, it is this process that correlates to the internal acquisition of personhood.

In summary then, within programs such as those pertinent to the regulation of sex, governmental technologies structure the practices by which conduct is patterned, thereby fashioning a habitus appropriate to a given persona. This forms part of a general strategy of enrolling the object of these programs in its own self-reformation. Consequently, the programs that constitute youth as a governmental object in turn structure the practices through which a youthful habitus is constituted. As these programs target and enlist youth in the formation of its own habitus, youth can, therefore, be appropriately characterized as the doing of specific types of work on the self.

By this reasoning, youth, as a generalized attribute, can also be envisaged as "a locus of experience, one which not only includes a domain of knowledge and a set of rules, [but also] a model of relations to the self" (Foucault, 1987:27).

It has already been argued that youth, as a category of person, is organized in terms of a relation to an inner self. The next section of this chapter examines this relation in more detail, and will also attempt a more specific analysis of some of the practices of self-government constitutive of a youthful habitus. The aim is to demonstrate how youth is shaped by such practices of the self, especially in regards to its sex. This will be accomplished by adapting elements of Foucault's four-part framework for analyzing work on the self, and by focusing chiefly (although not exclusively) upon the role of one particular technology in this process—young women's magazines.

Manuals in Self-management

In *The Media*, Keith Windschuttle (1984:47) contends that, from the mid-1970s to the mid-1980s, there has been a decisive growth in the area of specialist women's magazines. Leaving aside such general titles as *Women's Day* and *New Idea* (whose circulation has remained fairly static), the readership of titles specifically aimed at young women alone has increased by 2500 percent. Magazines such as *Cosmopolitan*, *Cleo* and *Dolly*, along with imports such as *Seventeen*, *Honey* and *Elle*, provide an extensive array of choices for young women. These choices cover a range of ages. For example, *Dolly* and *Seventeen* are primarily aimed at teenagers, *Honey* and *Elle* are directed toward teenagers and women in their early twenties, while both *Cosmopolitan* and *Cleo* are marketed at a range which begins in the late teens and ends in the thirties. As a consequence of the enormous size and range of this market, Windschuttle states that anyone wishing to understand the condition of young women or the relations between the sexes

> needs to come to terms with the contents of women's magazines. Young women buy them in very large numbers...just about every female beyond early childhood in Australia sees one of these magazines regularly. Hence, whatever attitude one takes to them, it must be acknowledged that their influence is pervasive. (Windschuttle, 1984:247)

This pervasive influence has been the subject of considerable discussion. In *The Feminine Mystique*, Betty Friedan (1963) was one of the first to argue that such an influence was almost entirely negative. She claims that these magazines have a significant part to play in reinforcing the subordinate status of women. More specifically, she contends that women are ill-served by magazines that exhort them to value their appearance over their intellects, and that teach them to understand themselves, first and foremost, in terms of their relationship to men.

Friedan is not alone in this analysis. There is a considerable literature that supports this viewpoint (Kaiser, 1979; Wilson, 1981; Sullivan and O'Connor, 1988; Demarest and Garner, 1992). In "A Feminist Theoretical Perspective on the Socialisation of Teenage Girls Through *Seventeen* magazine," Kate Peirce (1990) also argues that the pervasive influence that these magazines have over young women is far from desirable. Like Friedan, she proposes that such magazines are generally most concerned with the promulgation of traditional sex roles—roles that do not operate in women's best interests. That is, she maintains that young women are encouraged to believe that how they look is more important than what they think, that their main goal in life is to find a man, and once found, that she should subordinate herself to him (Peirce, 1990:491). Likewise, in "*Jackie*: An Ideology of Adolescent Femininity," Angela McRobbie (1982) argues that this magazine appears to define success solely in terms of finding (and pleasing) a suitable boyfriend. Indeed, almost all of its articles are focused upon preparing the reader for this outcome. According to Pam Gilbert and Sandra Taylor (1991), a similar set of priorities is evident within *Dolly* magazine. In the book *Fashioning the Feminine: Girls, Popular Culture and Schooling*, they examine an offshoot of *Dolly* magazine, entitled *Dolly Fiction*. Like *Jackie*, this set of short stories also appears to define the lives of young women primarily in terms of getting a boyfriend.

Both the Gilbert and Taylor book and the McRobbie article argue that this form of literature constitutes a significant instrument in the patriarchal repression of young women. According to Gilbert and Taylor (1991:103), the popularity of romantic fiction "necessitates the humiliating and crippling romantic inscription of the body" for young women. This forms part of a broader set of concerns over "the power and ownership of patriarchal consumerism" (Gilbert and Taylor, 1991:74). In a similar vein, McRobbie (1982:268) argues that young women's magazines constitute a highly effective ideological site for the transmission of patriarchal values. Its success lies in the fact that it appears to be a site wherein young women are free from the elements of coercion so obviously in evidence within other terrains, such as the school and the family. Thus, states McRobbie, it is the illusion of freedom that is pursued within the covers of magazines. McRobbie looks forward to the production of a magazine for young women which does not simply, but subtly, "reflect styles created by men to transform them into junior sex-objects" (McRobbie, 1982:282). The production of such a magazine will form one part of a counterhegemonic process whereby young women learn to deconstruct the dominant, oppressive models of femininity, and, in the words of Ann Snitow (1984, cited in Gilbert and Taylor, 1991:103), learn to "project a unique self."

This chapter will propose an alternative understanding of young women's magazines. Rather than locating such texts within an overall model of repression and patriarchal domination, it will be argued here that they can be regarded as practical manuals that enroll young women to do specific kinds of work on themselves. In doing so, they form an effective link between the governmental imperatives aimed at constructing particular personas (such as, for example, "the sexually responsible young person"), and the actual practices whereby these imperatives are operationalized. These manuals do not prevent young women from learning to project a unique self; they constitute a significant source of practices and techniques through which particular types of self are shaped.

This can best be accomplished within the framework described in Foucault's (1987:26–29) *The History of Sexuality, Volume II: The Uses of Pleasure*. He outlines a four-part model that attempts to provide a viable set of theoretical coordinates for analyzing the doing of work on the self. These four elements will be addressed in turn. First is *the determination of the ethical substance*. This involves establishing what constitutes the basis of a particular ethical practice. That is, it involves ascertaining the nature of the domain upon which work is actually to be done. Second is *the mode of subjectification*. This involves an examination of the mechanisms by which targeted populations are enjoined to carry out such work on the self. Third is *forms of elaboration and ethical work*. This is an investigation of some of the ways in which work on the self is done. It is constituted by the mental, physical, and spiritual practices that form an important component of any given habitus. The final element of Foucault's model is *teleology*. This involves an analysis of the kind of person that such practices of the self are directed at producing. It is the idealized result of self-formation. By utilizing this framework, in conjunction with a general (but not exclusive) focus on the role of young women's magazines, the intention is to better explain how the category of youth becomes enlisted in various programs of self-formation, and, in particular, those programs aimed at the management of sex.

Magazines, Sex, and Identity Management

Despite some slight variations, the content of young women's magazines appears to be fairly consistent: men and sex, fashion and beauty, celebrity gossip, and advice (Windschuttle, 1984). Kathryn McMahon (1990) takes this analysis one stage further when she argues that, in effect, these apparently separate areas are simply variations on one central subject—sex. In her article, "The *Cosmopolitan* Ideology and the Management of Desire," she analyzes the content of *Cosmopolitan* magazine over a twelve-year period, from 1976 to 1988. She found that the articles fell into six categories: (1) relationships with men, seventy-seven articles; (2) the lives of celebrities, fifty-one articles; (3) advice about sex, forty-nine articles; (4) beauty, diet, and health, thirty-four articles (5) psychological advice, thirty articles; and (6) work and money, twenty-three articles. She then goes on to say that these categories are actually misleading, since most were actually about sex, anyway.

> For instance, articles in the category of relationships with men and articles about the live of celebrities contained sexually explicit material and dealt with sexual relationships...Those articles in the category of beauty, diet and health were most often prescriptives on how to recreate oneself as a desired object. Those articles in the category of psychological problems and advice...contained advice on depression after a relationship breakup, starting over after an affair, and sexual behaviours. Those articles about work and money eroticised relations of power on the job. (McMahon, 1990:385)

Magazines aimed at the younger end of the market, such as *Jackie* and *Dolly*, have a similar, if more muted, preoccupation with sex and sexuality. Although there is no explicit sex in these stories, the pivotal moment in almost all cases concerns "the kiss"—preparing for it, selecting the right partner for it, and making sure that no other girl gets in first (Gilbert and Taylor, 1991:88).

The question now is—because this is so clearly the central subject matter of young women's magazines, in matters pertaining to sex, what is it that must be addressed in order to be doing relevant work on the self? What is it that forms the basis of a particular ethical practice? The most obvious answer appears to be the notion of sexuality. Reiterating some of the points raised in chapter 2, Sexuality is most commonly framed in terms of a natural faculty that is necessarily possessed by all, in much the same way that all are deemed to possess a personality. In contrast to this approach, it has been argued that sexuality is better located as a historical construct, a mechanism for the policing of populations. Therefore, in matters pertaining to sex, the fundamental material to be worked over by the various practices of self-formation is deemed to be sexuality, an aggregation of discourses.

This has not always been the case, however. Consequently, it is possible to contrast sexuality as the ethical substance of sexual behavior, with previous domains of moral concern. Foucault argues that sexual matters in Ancient Greece were underpinned by the notion of aphrodisia. Although literal translation of aphrodisia is difficult, it roughly refers to sexual relations or carnal acts. Foucault suggests that, for the Greeks, the ethical substance was comprised of the act, linked with pleasure and desire in unity. It was the very nature of this tripartite relationship that actually constituted aphrodisia. He contrasts this with the Christian ethical substance that focused on the eradication of desire and the neutrality of the act—that is, simply producing children, fulfilling conjugal rights. Foucault suggests that *aphrodisia* was eventually replaced by Christian formulations of *the flesh* and *lust*, which were in turn replaced by *sexuality*.

Some further conclusions can be drawn about the nature of sexuality when considered in relation to the mechanisms of self-formation pertinent to the construction of youthful personages. As noted, this current ethical substance differs markedly from its predecessors. It is along one particular axis that the disparities in logic behind sexuality (as opposed to aphrodisia and the flesh) become pertinent to the construction of specific modalities of youth as self—that is, the fashioning of sexuality as a necessarily developmental capacity.

Sexuality is presented in sequential, cumulative, and, most importantly, teleological terms. The influential *Handbook of Human Sexuality*, posits adult sexuality as the end product of various preexisting biological factors such as foetal gonads, pubertal hormones and morphology, neural pathways, and so forth (Wolfman and Money, 1980:4). It is through knowledges such as these that youth (the object at the intersection of these problematizations) has had allocated to it a sexuality that is deemed to be still evolving. One of the implications of this theoretical arrangement is that it formulates a model of youth with sexual capacities that are less developed than those present in mature adulthood. This teleological reasoning has implications for the construction of youth that are not restricted to sexuality alone:

> As with sexual development, moral development is dependent upon the adolescent's cognitive stage. Moral development proceeds by sequential steps...it is therefore difficult to motivate an adolescent to be responsible for his or her sexuality when the concept of responsibility cannot be comprehended. (Smith and Mumford, 1985:14)

It thus should not be surprising that advice given within young women's magazines varies depending upon the age of the general target market for each magazine. For example, in direct correlation with the perceived degree of sexual maturity, magazines such as *Jackie*, *Seventeen* and *Dolly* suggests practices and techniques aimed at how to talk to boys ("Ten Guy Goof-Up You Gotta Avoid"—*Teen*, March 1993), various ways of acquiring a first boyfriend ("Are You a Flirt?" *Dolly*, March 1994), getting him to ask you out ("Making the First Move?"—*Seventeen*, October 1993), managing both the first date ("The First Date: Don't Blow It"—*Dolly*, October 1994) and the first kiss ("Pucker Up"— *Seventeen*, February 1992), and so on. In contrast to this, magazines like *Cosmopolitan* and *Cleo* are aimed at a more mature market, and, consequently, address topics such as how to assess the suitability of a prospective lover ("Weenie or Whopper: Can You Assess His Size without Taking His Clothes Off?"—*Cleo*, February 1994), strategies for picking up men ("How Men Want To Be Seduced"—*Cosmopolitan*, December 1994), specific sexual techniques ("The Seven Things All Men

Love in Bed"—*Cleo*, July, 1994), and for keeping sex interesting in a relationship ("Warm, Wet and Wild"—*Cosmopolitan*, February 1994).

Modes of Persuasion

The question now arises, having once identified and targeted a population—youth—how are members of this category to be persuaded to fulfill their moral obligations? If sexuality forms the material basis of a contemporary moral code in matters of sex, what is it that prompts or induces adherence to that code? Within *Cosmopolitan* magazine, the readers are enjoined to shape themselves sexually in very particular ways. Indeed, much has been written about the persona of the "Cosmo Girl"—"'sexy and wild' but "also romantic and conservative," a good/bad girl, sometimes promiscuous, yet still respectable" (McMahon, 1990:391)— a persona that has been presented as a role model for young women from the mid-1960s onward (Faust, 1980; Dienstfrey, 1988). However, those young women who decide to adopt some (or all) of the practices constitutive of a "Cosmo Girl," including sexual practices, do not make these choices randomly. They are persuaded to adhere to the "Cosmo" sexual code in a variety of different ways. For example, they are persuaded by the promise of being sexually self-fulfilled, by the desire not to be considered abnormal by their peers, by concerns over venereal disease, by worries about being overlooked by men, and so on. Each of these incitements play a part in convincing young women, within the context of the magazines they read, to shape themselves in particular ways. As previously mentioned, these ways differ depending upon the magazine they read. The sexual conduct anticipated within the readership of *Jackie*, is not the same as that expected of someone who reads *Cosmopolitan*.

Before examining some of the specific ways in which contemporary young people are persuaded to do certain kinds of work on themselves, however, there are benefits to be gained from locating such incitements within a broader historical context. Foucault (1984:343) argues that in ancient Greece, noone was compelled to follow a code of sexual ethics. Certainly, these issues were the subject of very limited legal intervention, and the few laws that were directed against sexual misbehavior were not very compelling. Instead, the issue revolved around how one ought to live in order to give that life aesthetic value. Having a beautiful existence and constructing a life as a desirable work of art were far more important in motivating adherence to a sexual ethic than any perceived necessity to follow the scanty moral codes then available. This attitude began to change with the advent of Stoicism, however, with its stress on rationality. Rather than practicing conjugal fidelity simply because of the aesthetic desirability of doing so, Stoics were enjoined to remain faithful to their spouses since, as a member of a community and with responsibilities to that community, this was the rational way to behave. In contrast to both these modes of subjectification, Christianity incited adherence to the given moral code through the compulsion of religious decree. Thus, infidelity was in contravention of divine, and consequently civil, law. Unfortunately, since it would undoubtedly simplify this analysis, the modes of subjectification are no longer as clearly defined:

> Most of us no longer believe that ethics is founded in religion, nor do we want a legal system to intervene in our moral, personal, private life. Recent liberation movements suffer from the fact that they cannot find any new principle on which to base the elaboration of a new ethics. They need an ethics, but they cannot find any other ethics than an ethics founded upon so-called scientific knowledge of what the self is, what desire is, what the unconscious is, and so on. (Foucault, 1984:343)

From this position, Foucault delineates current modes of subjectification as consisting of a tension between a juridical framework (a legacy of religious law), and medical/scientific rationales. This will act as the basis for examining some of the arguments that underpin the various attempts to target and co-opt youth into programs of sexual self-management—particularly those in evidence within young women's magazines. The intention here is not to try to present a comprehensive analysis of all the mechanisms by which contemporary young people are induced to fulfill their moral obligations; rather, it is simply to point out three areas for closer inspection—psychology, medicine, and the law. These will be addressed in turn.

After the first, tentative appearance of the domain of sexuality, it has since become the focus of expert knowledges that demarcate the boundaries between normality and abnormality. While some social norms have a long history and seem relatively stable (that is, prohibitions against homosexuality, concerns over pornography, and so forth), sexual normality is now primarily defined by being counterposed against a myriad of available abnormalities. These abnormalities do not remain merely as undesirable disorders. In many cases, they become personages, such as the homosexual and the pedophiliac, against which the normal can be contrasted. Likewise, this type of scientific pronouncement not only delineates the normal, it also reinforces its own authority. Such statements about sex are by no means limited to psychology, they are made by a number of disciplines claiming expertise in subjectivity. The disciplines in turn construct their own abnormalities. The importance of the normal in determining the conduct of youth has already been discussed in chapter 2. It is the construction of strategic norms that have been instrumental in implementing a pervasive web of governmental intelligibility. This is particularly evident when addressing the management of sex.

However, normality is not solely about comparison. In fact, Rose (1990:130–131) suggests that it has three guises: it is the state that is natural and, therefore, healthy; it is the model against which the actual is compared and found unhealthy; and it is the state that can be achieved through the use of rationalized social programs under the guidance of experts. This schema is relevant to normal youthful sexuality. First, specialist research has, through the compilation of norms, determined what is the natural sexual behavior of their target population—youth. Second, young people are compared against this standard and judged accordingly. Finally, experts pathologize discrepancies and return them to sexual normality. This remodeling does not usually need to take the form of direct external intervention. Rather, those experts enroll particular groups into various programs of self-management. It is by this process that the compilation of norms becomes translated into the fashioning of a *self*.

By detailing the contours of a normal sexuality within an array of governmental manuals, specific moral codes can be promulgated. This strategy is especially evident within those texts both referring to, and used by youth as the sexual norms detailed therein act as a focus for many of the practices of self-formation associated with this category. The desirability of adhering to these norms has become an important mode of subjectification for fulfilling moral obligations.

In January 1980, *Cosmopolitan* magazine conducted an extensive survey of sexual practices among its readership. There were over one hundred thousand replies (as compared to only six thousand in the Kinsey Report

(1953) and only three thousand in the Hite Report (1981)). It was published in the September issue of the magazine as "The Sexual Profile of That *Cosmopolitan* Girl," then later as *The Cosmo Report* (1981). When discussing the various modes of subjectification directed at the sexual conduct of youth, however, it is significant that the report began its introduction with the following *raison-d'etre* for the research:

> ...what about you and me? Are our sexual practices and feelings typical? (Typical of whom?) Are we in tune with the times, or woefully behind or eccentrically ahead of them? (Where do we fit in? Is there some way we can measure ourselves?). (Wolfe, 1981:17)

With chapters entitled, "The Whens, Wheres and How-Oftens of Sex," "Sexual Practices," "Orgasm with a Partner," and "Lovers," the report sets out in precise detail just what constitutes sexual normality for young women. Furthermore, with a chapter on "Sexual Fantasies and Dreams," even the subjectivity of "the Cosmo Girl" can be assessed and normalized. McMahon (1990:390) sums up this process when she states that *Cosmo Report* represents "the construction of the norm as ideal: the *Cosmopolitan Girl*. The reader is expected to compare, which implies judgement, her own sexual experience in relation to this construct." This form of normalizing within *Cosmopolitan* is not only common to most young women's magazines, but also to most other manuals on youth and sex. For example, one book on adolescent sexuality sums up this issue by arguing: "many young people are worried about their sexuality and fear that they have problems simply because they lack information about what is normal" (Collins and Harper, 1978:129).

Of all the normative knowledges specifying youth as their object, two are particularly influential—psychology and medicine. In particular, psychology has a preeminent status in the management of subjectivity. The success of psychology (along with its associated disciplines) is symptomatic, not only of the growth in the knowledges claiming professional expertise within this domain, but also of their value in the government of populations. However, these disciplines should not be understood solely in terms of their immediate regulative utility. They have also become axiomatic to constructing the practices by which a *self* is formed and directed—which includes mechanisms of self-understanding and evaluation, ways of thinking and talking about personal feelings, procedures for managing emotions, and so on (Rose, 1990:3). This also includes supplying a rationale for the foundation of contemporary sexual ethics—a rationale that springs primarily from psychoanalytic theory.

Psychoanalysis propounds a model of the human psyche which, with minor theoretical variations, locates the "biological urge to gain sexual pleasure" within the *id* (Gleitman, 1981:462). This obedience to the pleasure principle is dialectically balanced against the rationally constraining conscience of the *superego*, and it is deemed to be the dictates of this feature of the unconscious that result in the burying of the true sexual self. Such a depiction of lost sexuality, supplemented by arguments about a sexually repressive society, have spawned the belief that a whole, self-fulfilled person can only be achieved by exposing and removing their sexual inhibitions. This model is especially pertinent to the successful creation of a well-balanced adult. Anna Freud sums up the logic of this position by pathologizing children:

> who have built up excessive defences against their drive activities and are now crippled as a result, which acts as barriers against a normal maturation process of phase development. They are perhaps, more than any others, in need of therapeutic help to remove the inner restrictions and clear the path for normal development. (Freud, 1968:14)

Thus, it is increasingly the role of an entire network of experts in subjectivity (not just psychoanalysts, but educational psychologists, guidance counselors, social workers, and so forth) to ensure the normal mental and sexual development of youth. That is, it is the pervasive psy-disciplines that have successfully structured many of the most important practices of self-formation associated with youth. The seeking of sexual fulfillment is now an important mode of subjectification, in that it drives the making of ethical decisions. Likewise, removing sexual repression (judged to be inherent in both the unconscious and society) has also become an important goal of effective self-government.

A concern for normal sexual and mental development of their readers is particularly evident within young women's magazines. Indeed, in "Are Those Sex Articles Really Necessary?" *Cosmopolitan* (October 1993:91) argues that magazines, such as itself, have a crucial role to play in producing an emotionally healthy population. After all, such publications invariably offer psychological advice to help readers overcome their social and sexual problems, and this advice is one of the few sources of information consistently available to young women. In commenting upon the prevalence of psychological advice within magazines like *Cosmopolitan*, Windschuttle (1984:253–254) also makes the link between attempts to remove sexual repression and the adoption of certain practices of (sexual) self-government. He states that within such magazines, psychology has:

> ...clearly been useful in dispelling fears and anxieties that had inhibited sexual relations and personal confidence. However, the sexual revolution as expressed in glossy magazines is far more ambitious than simply wanting to give information and overcome inhibitions. It is a prescription for a whole way of life.

However, there are limits to self-fulfillment. The knowledges of the psy-disciplines are still sexually normative, irrespective of their apparent stance against the structures of social and psychical repression. After all, attaining sexual self-fulfillment may be desirable, but being abnormal is not.

The second mode of subjectification that warrants commentary involves the scientization, and in particular, the medicalization of sex. Magazines such as *Seventeen*, *Dolly*, *Cosmopolitan* and *Cleo* all contain sections that provide medical advice for readers. This advice is most frequently regarding sexual problems. For example, the "problem clinic" in *Cosmopolitan* deals with issues such as concerns over frequency of masturbation, difficulties in having successful sexual intercourse, anatomical questions about genitals, worries about contraception and sexual transmitted diseases, and so on (Windschuttle, 1984:253). Even those parts of young women's magazines that are not specifically addressing medical problems, still adopt a scientific tone when dispensing advice:

> Articles in the sexual advice category share a common tone of address. The author, as expert, addresses the reader with an authority based upon a pseudoscientific tone of objectivity. Though the basis for the expertise of the author is almost never mentioned, sometimes an association is made to "scientific" knowledge by reference to some credentialed person or scientific study. (McMahon, 1990:389)

In general, it can be argued that the sexual self-government of youth is most frequently driven by a scientific emphasis on the consequences of bad management—in particular, unwanted pregnancy and sexually transmitted diseases. The flexibility of risk has meant that it has become an important component in a grid of governmental intelligibility; it also legitimates a broad range of governmental intervention. Although this intervention is by no means only medical, medical discourses provide the central mode of subjectification within this context.

The two most recurrent anxieties over the sex of youth in a medical context involve unwanted pregnancy and sexually transmitted diseases. Greg Logan (1991), in his history of sex education in Queensland, argues that it has been the publication of statistical data for these two social problems that has motivated successive attempts to introduce the subject to the school curriculum. Certainly, these problems occupy a pivotal position within many texts on sex education, in that they locate youth as a category that is inherently at-risk from these misfortunes, yet able to be saved through appropriate instruction (Potter and Smith, 1976; Hyde, 1979). The consequences of being allocated at-risk status, however, do not end simply with the provision of adequate knowledge about the mechanics of sex. Rather, youth has become an object of concern for a network of knowledges, professional groups, strategies, and manuals that advocate and inculcate the practices of self-management necessary to avoid trouble.

This rationale is equally applicable to the processes of self-government necessary to avoid venereal disease. This matter, however, by no means merely revolves around instilling the reflex of using a condom, although it is not irrelevant. The central issue is really the moral problematization of promiscuity. That is, if the mode of subjectification in this context is avoiding sexual trouble, the programs of self-management aimed at youth are more ethical than prophylactic. Even *Cosmopolitan*, which champions the right of single young women to have a sex life, continually stresses the importance of taking measures to prevent sexually transmitted diseases. In addition to this, it also emphasizes the importance of restraint and responsibility when having sex. That is, successful promiscuity (however limited) has to be carefully managed—that is, "sleep with different men, [just] make sure it's safe sex" (*Cosmopolitan*, September 1995:52). More frequently, magazines aimed at a younger market warn against the social and medical consequences of becoming a slag—"flirts or sexually permissive women who flaunt their desire" (Gilbert and Taylor, 1991:82). This is generally accomplished indirectly through articles such as "We Had Sex and then He Dumped Me" (*Girlfriend*, October 1994), "I Had Sex With Him and Now I'm Sorry" (*Teen*, March 1993) and "I Got Drunk and Lost My Virginity" (*Dolly*, October 1994).

It can thus be argued that government can operate in the manner it does, largely because it has found mechanisms of rule that avoid the blunt instruments of sovereign rule—laws, decrees, and regulations. These mechanisms operate, to a great extent, through the expertise provided by disciplines such as psychology and medicine. Furthermore, this expertise works at a distance within domains such as the family and the school. However, this is not to suggest that laws are irrelevant. As the third mode of subjectification to be addressed, the legal system is capable of enforcing certain codes of moral behavior. Directly, this takes several forms. It makes some sex acts illegal (bestiality), some partners illegal (incest), it necessitates consent (rape), it legislates for the privacy of the sex act (indecency), it obstructs the selling of sex (prostitution), it prohibits the circulation of some depictions of sex (pornography), and, crucially, it protects the child from sexual despoilment (pedophilia).

However, the law does not just govern sexual morality directly. A network of legislation exists which, although not directly prohibiting certain forms of sex, impedes, restricts, and marginalizes them. With specific regard to youth, there are laws restricting access to contraception, access to certain films/literature, access to alcohol, laws determining the content of school curricula (debates over sex education), and laws demarcating parental rights. Such legislation not only impinges upon the construction of youth as a governmental object (even if this personage is not necessarily the precise focus of the legislation), it also sets some rough boundaries for the programs of sexual management targeted at youth. Overt forms of government, however, contribute only a very limited amount toward the totality of mechanisms operating to regulate the sexual behavior of the population. There are considerably more effective modes of subjectification operating; hence, the importance of knowledges such as psychology and medicine.

The three modes of subjectification outlined so far are not intended as a comprehensive appraisal of all the ways in which youth is motivated to do work on the self. Neither is the aim to posit them as forces in their own right. They constitute a part of an interrelated vocabulary of incitements, some or all of which may be germane within specific contexts. Rather, the intention has simply been to argue that the governmental programs directed at the sexual self-management of youth, function most effectively at a distance, and to examine those rationales that underpin the practices of the self relevant to the construction of a youthful habitus. These practices will be addressed next.

Practices of the Self

Governmental imperatives aimed at modifying the sexual conduct of the population do not operate simply by the power of decree. Rather, specific categories of person are recruited into programs of self-reformation. For example, the programs that develop from governmental concerns over an issue such as teenage pregnancies, do not simply translate, at some later date, into an improvement in the relevant statistics. Instead, they operate by enlisting youth into doing specific kinds of work on the self—to shape the self, in this case, into the image of the sexually responsible youth. This work takes the form of adopting various practices of the self. That is, youth are persuaded in various ways (the modes of subjectification) to do work on their sexuality (the ethical substance), work that can be understood in terms of an array of different practices.

The case of young women's magazines provides an important example of this process. As mentioned previously, they provide a useful link between specific governmental aspirations and the adoption, by a targeted population, of practices that go some way toward realizing those aspirations. Such magazines provide a medium through which broad governmental programs actually are adopted as practices of self-government by young women. These practices are diverse. They are not restricted to the direct modification of behavior because, as will be demonstrated, they can often include a multiplicity of mental, spiritual, and physical techniques.

Self-interrogation, for example, is now one of the central practices by which self-knowledge is gained. This practice is not a fundamental and inevitable part of what it means to be human, however, any more than is having a moral conscience. Rather, it is a particular historical and cultural attribute. There now seems nothing unusual about the extensive and repetitive self-interrogation that young women's magazines require from their readers. Young women are continually enjoined to scrutinize all aspects of themselves: their sense of fashion, their body shape, their sexual preferences, their libido, their fantasies, their readiness for marriage, their fidelity, and so on. Indeed, the *test yourself* questionnaire is a standard device within most women's magazines. Readers can assess themselves objectively and adjust their conduct/thoughts/aspirations accordingly. In this manner, self-interrogation gains the status of an exercise in scientific inquiry.

Although some part of the magazine appears to be simply informative (sex, celebrities, fashion, advice), even these provide a set of measures—an ideal—against which young women are expected to measure themselves. Ultimately, figures such as "the Cosmo girl" affect the sexual conduct of young women, not simply because they provide a high-visibility role model, but because they cause young women to evaluate themselves in relation to this model, to scrutinize their shortcomings, and then to embark upon various projects of self-modification.

Significantly, these practices of self-interrogation have largely operated in tandem with a second practice—the confession. Like the practice of self-interrogation, the confession also has a significant role within young women's magazines. First, it is common for such magazines to provide a regular forum for readers to write in and share their experiences. Essay-length letters are published detailing everything from birth to bereavement, from sexual experimentation to sexual abuse, and from happy beginnings to unhappy endings. This process is deemed to be therapeutic for the writer, as well as entertaining, informative, and cautionary for the reader. Second, advice within these magazines is most frequently dispensed through direct replies to reader's letters. Features such as the *problem page* and the *doctor's clinic* combine the confessional with the process of government through expertise. Whether the problems are medical, psychological, or ethical, readers confess to experts, who offer advice and guidance, which is then, in turn, translated into self-government. Finally, it can be argued that the phenomenal response to the questionnaire on sexual conduct published in *Cosmopolitan* (which gave rise to the *Cosmo Report*), is an example of the widespread elaboration of confessional practices. Young women were asked to detail the most intimate aspects of their sexuality for the magazine's survey, with which over one hundred thousand complied. Furthermore, within magazines like *Cosmopolitan*, it is often not simply the women who are urged to confess the most intimate details of their sexual practices and fantasies. Readers are also enjoined to persuade their boyfriends, lovers, and husbands to confess their sexual secrets—secrets that have permitted, in turn, the construction of a parallel persona to the "Cosmo Girl": the "Cosmo Man." ("A Survey for Him"—*Cosmopolitan*, September 1995).

Significantly, this willingness to confess not only provides, in this instance, the raw material for the construction of the "Cosmo Girl" (and Man), it also provides, in a broader sense, the raw material by which government can operate effectively. That is, the confession is not only a practice of the self, it is also an important technique of government. Despite the centrality of self-interrogation and incitations to speak as practices of ethical self-management, not all practices of the self constitutive of a youthful habitus are directed at mental or spiritual development. Some are directed at the body itself.

In his lecture "Techniques of the Body," Mauss (1973) suggests that *habitus* should not be understood as merely the soul and its repetitive faculties, but, rather, as the practices of collective and individual practical reason. Such practices are not limited to the most general of cultural practices, nor simply to the practices of self-modification already mentioned, they also include certain socially determined ways of using the body itself, such as walking, sitting, sleeping, and eating. These are not natural and inevitable faculties, independent of social context—with any variation being simply a matter of individual idiosyncrasy. They vary between societies, educations, fashions, statuses, and the sexes. Crucially, there are also differences in practices, dependent upon age.

Mauss (1973:80) exemplifies this final claim when he addresses the issue of (bodily) techniques of adolescence. Irrespective of differences over the pivotal position allocated by Mauss to adolescence (and also some of his domain psychological and ethnological assumptions), a similar point is being made in this chapter. That is, the practices common to specific groups are part of the context-bound processes of person-formation. This is an important contention, as it proposes that a habitus of youth is, in part, assembled through the programs of person-formation associated with acquiring specific techniques of the body. For example, Mauss (1973:74) describes how young girls learn a characteristic way of walking (onioni) as part of the habitus constitutive of a Maori personage. Such gendered bodily practices are important aspects of constructing an acceptable sexual self.

Instructing readers on how to acquire specific bodily practices constitutes an important component of young women's magazines. McRobbie (1982), in her analysis of *Jackie*, contends that the magazine makes it clear that the successful acquisition of femininity (in the style championed by the magazine) is not a *fait accompli* for all teenagers. Rather, becoming the kind of young woman that *Jackie* considers appropriate requires hard work. This work involves, in part, learning to use the body in certain ways:

> Another useful expression though, is the pathetic appealing look, which brings out a boy's protective instinct and has him desperate to get you another drink/help you on with your coat/give you a lift home. It's best done by opening your eyes wide and dropping the mouth open a little looking (hanging your head slightly) directly into the eyes of the boy you're talking to. Practice this. (*Jackie*, cited in McRobbie, 1982:263)

Such techniques of the body are also detailed in magazines like *Cosmopolitan* and *Cleo*. Aside from the wealth of articles on diet and exercise regimen, these magazines also suggest appropriate bodily techniques for matters as specific as "eating while listening intently to a man talking," and as general as "how to be sexy" (Dienstfrey, 1988). Indeed, the techniques of the body associated with sexual conduct are often quite explicit, such as those detailing bodily techniques getting more satisfaction out of sex ("The Orgasm Workout: Clench Your Way to Ecstasy"—*Cleo*, January 1994). Furthermore, articles based around the theme of "What Women Do Wrong in Bed" (*Cosmopolitan*, June 1983) are especially frequent. Detailed instructions are given in a variety of sexual techniques, techniques that then constitute an important part of every "Cosmo Girl's" erotic repertoire ("Drive Him Wild"—*Cleo*, February 1994).

Two points are worthy of emphasis here: the first is to reiterate that young women's magazines are by no means the only manuals that detail ways of constructing an appropriate self through the adoption of specific bodily practices. Such manuals are widespread. For example, Kaye Wellings' (1986) *First Love, First Sex*, (a book endorsed by the Australian Federation of Family Planning Associations), includes advice/directions on dancing, dating, kissing, petting, masturbation, first intercourse, and so forth. It also includes a chapter entitled "Am I normal?" a description of introspective techniques for getting through to the real person underneath, and directions on appropriate bodily gestures and posture.

Second, an emphasis on the importance of acquiring appropriate bodily practices, whether directly sexual or otherwise, is by no means a new phenomenon. For example, during the nineteenth century, school subjects like "Drill" sought to embed specific bodily practices within pupils. David Kirk (1993) argues that from 1850 onward, these forms of instruction began to organize and regulate various aspects of body shape, movement, posture, strength, and flexibility. These bodily practices were not only graded according to age, but also according to sex. Eventually, "Drill" came to be regarded as appropriate for girls, whose bodies were deemed to be better managed through dance, gymnastics, and deportment.

Indeed, the discipline of deportment draws a direct link between bodily practices and sexual self-management. This is particularly evident in an 1896 manual entitled *The Glory of Woman*:

> The arms hang naturally from the shoulders, the hands are in some quiet position, the fingers curve gracefully, with slight parting between the first and second, the third and fourth. There is no stiffness, no uneasy shifting and fidgeting, no moving of fingers or features, but all is rounded and graceful as a statue. It is worth some pains to be a lady of good standing in society. (Allen and McGregor, 1896:447)

Other advice to women on techniques to be rendered habitual include developing a walking style that will not cause the dress to lift, and never sitting with the legs apart. In contrast, men are directed toward the bearing of a soldier, because "the external becomes the internal, and a man becomes really what he endeavours to appear" (Allen and McGregor, 1896:449–450). This is precisely the point. Inculcating specific bodily practices constitutes an important part of the mechanisms involved in the formulation of specific types of personage (and the concomitant regulation of their sex).

Practices of the body associated with variations in posture, mannerism, shape or gait, are not the only way of inscribing habitus onto the body. This can also be accomplished by diverse modes of self-representation (Craik, 1991:6). Although the techniques outlined so far are crucial mechanisms for directing youth into programs of ethical/sexual self-government, they have often lacked the high profile of the stylistic components of habitus. That is, constructing youth as a visible entity in the field of knowledge has very obvious implications for the way in which young people fashion themselves (Bennett, Miller, Swanson, and Tait, 1990/1991:136). The Gulbenkian Inquiry into the role of the arts in young people's lives, outlines a range of informal practices which are significant in this realm:

> music, cultural media (television, video, and the use of microcomputers), magazines, style and fashion, and drinking and fighting...It becomes clear that cultural and media activities are central to the way in which young people live socially and situate themselves within social, economic and personal relations, manifest aspirations and produce responses to their conditions of living. (Willis, 1990:143)

These practices have formed the substance of a great deal of youth research. They have also been interpreted in very different ways. For example, it was ethnographies of such practices that were used to illustrate subculture theory. According to Hebdige (1979:84) the interplay between different social classes constitutes the raw material that then finds its expressive form in youth subcultures. Within this analysis, the notion of the expressive self remains central, as subcultural style is depicted, ultimately, as an expressive response by subcultural members to their material conditions.

This book proposes an understanding of youth style that can be contrasted directly with the understanding of style evidenced within subculture theory. Rather than underpinning the analysis with any notion of the expressive self, the emphasis is instead upon the construction of a particular habitus in terms of clothing and leisure activities, as a crucial component in determining the tenor of any given persona. By making choices from within a vocabulary of available practices, styles, and codes of conduct, work is being done upon the self.

By reinterpreting style in this way, the emphasis on fashion within the medium of young women's magazines becomes all the more significant. In *The Modern Girl*, Lesley Johnson (1993) specifically examines the role of fashion in the construction of youthful femininity. She argues that through the late 1950s and early 1960s, a new persona slowly emerged—*the teenage girl*. This persona was separated from the broader category of *woman*. With the help of manuals that fashioned the teenage girl as consumer, a new persona was constructed. This persona, produced through various forms of self-representation, differs from previous choices available. Furthermore, Johnson (1993:121) argues that the fashion industry plays an important role in the construction of this new persona.

Miller and Rose (1990) also regard the relationship between consumption and self-formation as being of significance. They contend that the private choices of individuals who attempt to maximize the quality of their lives through the artful assembly of a lifestyle put together through the world of goods (Miller and Rose, 1990:25), relocate the modern young consumer as an entrepreneur of the self. Through choosing one form of self-representation over another, by purchasing certain kinds of commodities, by reading particular magazines or listening to specific kinds of music, the youthful self is shaped and reshaped in ways that suit the aspirations of government, business, and the consumer.

> Design, marketing and image construction play a vital role in the transfiguring of goods into desires and vice versa, imbuing each commodity with a "personal" meaning, a glow cast back upon those who purchase it, illuminating the kind of person they are, or want to be. (Miller and Rose, 1990:25)

In summary, techniques of ethical self-formation are central to the management of sexual conduct, as they constitute an integral part of the habitus by which personages such as youth are shaped. Such practices are not restricted to adopting certain stylistic codes. They also include a multiplicity of mental, spiritual, and physical practices, such as self-interrogation, incitements to confession, specific ways of sitting and walking, the regulation of the body through exercise and diet.

Youth, Sex, and Maturity

The last component of Foucault's model of relations to the self argues that all of these sorts of practices of the self are directed at the development of individuals toward particular goals. The focus upon teleology involves asking the question—what kind of person are these practices of self-formation trying to produce?

In the specific case of youth, the notion of teleology is particularly pertinent. The disciplinary control of time has posited youth as a necessarily teleological category, in that youth is produced as a part of the governmental processes of subdividing and ranking time within a linear model. Also, knowledges such as psychology and biology have characterized youth in the teleological terms of development, transition, and maturation. It is the final term of maturity that provides the most important teleology of youth. That is, there is a recurrent emphasis within youth research on the importance of providing the social, moral, and economic circumstances wherein young people can make a successful transition to the full maturity of adulthood. This imperative operates across various terrains.

One that exemplifies the teleology of maturity for youth, is the sexual. Even upon this seemingly unproblematic terrain, however, maturity can still be interpreted in different ways. For example, there is the straightforward biological understanding of what constitutes making the successful transition to full sexual maturity. This is especially evident in education and welfare manuals on youth and sex. In the "Youth Sector Training Program" manual for Queensland youth workers (Crane et al., 1990), the process is even represented diagrammatically, with adolescence shown as evolving into the state of adulthood by processes of self-exploration (self-interrogation). By asking questions such as "Who am I?" the adolescent develops into the mature adult, with self-management skills and a complete identity. Likewise, adolescent sexuality is about experimentation, which leads to the final stage with its established sex role identity. This logic is not restricted to sexuality alone. The categories of physical growth, hormone imbalance, behavior, and identity, all directly associate adolescence/youth with a transition to the finished state of adulthood.

In manuals such as this, the underlying theme is fairly constant. They target the sexuality of youth by various programs of self-management, with the intention of ultimately forging an acceptable finished product—a youth that will make a successful transition to the status of a sexually mature and responsible adult.

However, as previously mentioned, the biological understanding of a successful transition to adulthood is by no means the only option. According to McMahon (1990), *Cosmopolitan* appears to define the successful endpoint of the process of sexual maturity as finding and winning a desirable man. Having accomplished this self-defining task, it only remains for women to make sure that he is kept satisfied—and away from other women. And yet, affluent and contented monogamous heterosexuality is not the only sexual teleology on offer within young women's magazines. According to Gilbert and Taylor (1991), texts such as the *Dolly Fiction* series employ slightly different criteria—perhaps, in this case, owing to the slightly younger age of the readership. Although the emphasis on finding a boyfriend is as strong, if not stronger, than in magazines like *Cosmopolitan*, the teleology is more directed toward the construction of an acceptable feminine (and, hence, romantic) persona, as defined by the literature itself. Consequently, sexual maturity appears to be defined more as a *coming of age*—not in terms of finally having sex, but in terms of having successfully fashioned a persona, and found a suitable partner, such that sex would now be an appropriate possibility.

As these examples demonstrate, the notion of a successful transition to maturity does require close contextualizing, as the criteria that indict a successful transition are by no means self-evident. Neither are they new. It is the enduring images of the good society and the moral persona that largely provide the substance for the contemporary construction of the mature adult. That is, the modern forms of self-government that constitute a significant part of any given habitus (such as that associated with youth) are themselves founded substantially upon a legacy of existing models of self-management, and upon existing norms of conduct.

Conclusion

The central intention of this chapter has been to outline the second half of an alternative approach to the study of youth. This chapter has sought to provide a conceptual framework that can account for the piecemeal formation of the youthful self. This framework was then used to examine how the inner self of youth is governed through its sex.

First, this chapter called into question the dominant understanding of the self as the inner person. It was contended instead that individuals assume specific personages because they are ascribed rights and obligations, not simply because they are human beings. The melding of the person into the individual is actually the result of identifiable historical events, such as the advent of Roman Law and the moral practices of groups such as the Stoics and, later, the Christians. Through various largely internal rituals and practices, personages are assembled within individuals and, through them, a *self* is constructed. It is through contemporary rituals and practices that a *youthful self* is shaped.

Second, it was argued that, within modern western societies, the formation of various types of person (and the concomitant construction of associated subject-positions—selves), is best understood as being related to the government of populations. That is, governmental technologies map out categories of person as objects of knowledge and then pattern the conduct of those persons. Such interventions into subjectivity have become the norm, since far from being a domain beyond government, subjectivity is one of the most heavily governed of all areas. Furthermore, images of appropriate conduct are provided through the medium of expertise, and operate largely within the familiar domains of the school and the family. These images of appropriate conduct provide the impetus for self-analysis and improvement. This self-analysis forms part of a general strategy of enrolling the objects of certain types of governmental programs in their own self-reformation. These arguments are all pertinent to the person of youth. Within programs such as those relevant to the management of sex, governmental technologies structure the practices by which youthful conduct is patterned—thereby fashioning a kind of habitus. Youth, as the object of a broad range of governmental programs, is co-opted into remodeling itself. In general, then, youth can be understood as an example of the piecemeal formation of specific types of person, and as the doing of specific types of work on the self.

Finally, this chapter addressed concern about the manner in which young people learn to construct specific types of relationships with themselves. The analysis of this self-making is accomplished by applying Foucault's four-part model of self-formation, to an examination of the role of manuals such as young women's magazines in the shaping of various aspects of the youthful self. The intention has been to provide a set of tools for approaching the issue of young women's magazines that avoids some of the problems associated with critical theory—a paradigm that translates such magazines almost exclusively in terms of social control. The critical approach neatly delineates the good from the bad, the dominant from the counterhegemonic, and the oppressors from the victims. Such domain assumptions lead to a predictable conclusion: femininity is shaped by domination and repression. In contrast with such an approach, it has been argued here that the reinterpretation of power as productive and organizational opens up research to various conclusions—conclusions that can be reassessed from case to case. This is not to say that the exercise of power cannot still be coercive; however, for the most part, contemporary forms of rule operate by targeting populations, organizing their conduct and capacities, and channeling their aspirations. Young women's magazines play a significant role in this process.

CHAPTER 5

Governing the Body, Governing the Self

This chapter will continue the examination of specific practices of the self associated with the shaping of youth. In particular, it will address the ways in which severe fasting practices have been used by young women as part of the process of governing of the self, achieved through the governing of the body. This will be accomplished by rethinking the dominant contemporary explanation for severe fasting—anorexia nervosa. First, rather than understanding severe fasting as a reflection of problems over the inner self, this chapter will propose that such fasting is one of a piecemeal set of practices used to construct the self in a particular manner. Second, the literature often regards anorexic eating practices as a modern phenomenon, caused by either ove-conformity to, or resistance against, dominant conceptions of femininity. It will be argued instead that, from the thirteenth to the fifteenth century, such practices were also in evidence among pious Christian women. This fasting took place, not within a binary of resistance/conformity to images of femininity, but as one component of a body-centered model of female holiness based upon the theme of imitatio Christi. *The final assumption is that anorexia nervosa is a disease entity which has existed in nature, to be eventually discovered and explained by science. This chapter will argue instead that anorexia nervosa has its origins within an increasing governmental regulation of the population, which included their health and diet. The modern disease took its current shape after numerous boundary struggles, finally emerging as a largely psychologically classified eating disorder. Moreover, these dietary practices have been integrated within a governmental-medical regimen centered on the body.*

Fasting and the Self

The American Anorexia Nervosa Association defines anorexia nervosa as a "serious illness of deliberate self-starvation with profound psychiatric and physical components." It is regarded as a "complex emotional disorder that launches its victims on a course of frenzied dieting in pursuit of excessive thinness" (Neuman and Halvorson, 1983:2). In addition to an *illness* and *disorder*, anorexia nervosa is also commonly referred to as a *disease*, a *sickness*, a *syndrome,* and a *condition*. The point here is obvious: young women lose such large amounts of weight because they are sick, hence titles such as Welbourne and Purgold's (1986) *The Eating Sickness*. Consequently, the fasting practices so evident among young women are now almost always explained in terms of individual pathology, and the name of the pathological state is *anorexia nervosa*. The notion of anorexia nervosa has now superseded all other explanations of why young women fast. It is utilized, fairly unproblematically, at every site and in every context where interest in the issue is expressed.

Feminists have been quick to realize that accepting this paradigm, as it stands, brings with it a lot of undesirable baggage. After all, such a model states that anorectics alone are responsible for their own problems. This explanation places only slight emphasis on the structure of society itself, and certainly does not reveal why it is predominantly women who fast so severely. While some medical and psychological experts have tacked on "socio-cultural influences" at the end of their theories (for example, Vandereycken and Meermann, 1984), this has done little to shift the central focus away from individual pathology. It is precisely this shift that feminists (along with various other social analysts) have attempted. Although their input to the debate has not challenged the use of the medical term *anorexia nervosa*, nor altered the understanding of severe fasting among young women as a *sickness* or an *epidemic*, it has made various attempts to re-define its causes.

Corrigan (1992) suggests that, in their attempts to make links between society and the female body, feminists have taken the notion of anorexia nervosa and reinterpreted it in different ways. One such way, with its roots firmly in the polemics of early 1970s feminism, places the blame squarely upon men. Chernin (1981) argues that the signal feature of patriarchal culture is the subordination of the female body. By preventing women from developing their bodies, patriarchal culture also succeeds in preventing women from developing their powers. In what Corrigan (1992:112) refers to as "stylistic revivalism," Wolf's (1990) *The Beauty Myth* also accuses male-dominated industries such as advertising, fashion, and cosmetics of being responsible for the oppression of women's bodies and, ultimately, for the contemporary epidemic of eating disorders such as anorexia nervosa. She states that in a male-dominated society, the anorectic is the perfect woman—"weak, sexless, and voiceless."

As well as an emphasis upon patriarchy, writers such as Chernin and Wolf have another aspect of their theoretical frameworks in common. They both contend that male domination results in the distortion of women's relationships to themselves. That is, by forcing women to hate their own bodies, women develop a destructive separation between the true inner and the false outer selves. It is this separation that results in anorexia nervosa. Chernin (1986:20) contends that eating disorders such as anorexia nervosa are a reflection of the failure of some women's struggle to find their inner selves. Indeed, anorexia is deemed to be characterized by a lack of a bona fide self—an essence otherwise found within all women. She also equates the *self* with the most fundamental of all essences, the *soul* (or, more explicitly, the collective soul of womanhood)—arguing that anorexia nervosa is the most obvious expression of the ongoing struggle being waged for that soul (Chernin, 1983:196). While other writers may read the psychoanalytic terrain slightly differently, they still base their theories on a foundation of the authentic inner person (Bruch, 1974; Palazzoli, 1974; Dana, 1987; Garrett, 1992). Each individual is deemed to contain an inner person that constitutes the real self. Moreover, anorexia nervosa is somehow tied to this self.

It is at this point that the first set of criticisms can be raised about literature addressing anorexia nervosa, as it is precisely this understanding of the self that has been problematized in chapter 4. By detailing the effects of the specific changes within ancient Greek, Roman, and early Christian societies, Mauss (1985) was able to argue that the inner self is not the fundamental human essence, but is, instead, the internal acquisition of personhood. This form of historicizing is also useful when addressing the issue of severe fasting practices. After all, food asceticism is not new.

Voluntary starvation has a well-documented history. There are recorded cases of fasting to death in ancient Greek and early Christian times (Brown, 1988). An analysis of the dietary asceticism of certain castes within ancient Greece permits a reevaluation of the relationship between the self and the adoption of severe fasting practices.

Cultivating a Self: The Dietetics of Antiquity

In ancient Greece, members of certain elite castes made specific choices about how best to care for themselves, not just in the physical sense, but also in order to cultivate themselves as moral persons. In choosing one possibility over another, this gave their lives a certain value and tenor—and status. Life was understood as a work of art. Moreover, it was a work of art that required constant attention. The construction of a satisfactory self required the constant and rigorous application of a multitude of practices of self-government. Foucault (1987:10–11) refers to the arts of existence, which were:

> those intentional and voluntary actions by which men not only set themselves rules of conduct, but also seek to transform themselves, to change themselves in their singular being and to make their life into an *oeuvre* that carries certain aesthetic values and meets certain stylistic criteria. (Foucault, 1987:10–11)

However, utilizing the arts of existence to fashion a suitable self was not an easy task. First, it was a set of practices restricted to specific castes. To a slave or commoner, excessive concern over forming a beautiful self would have been a fairly pointless. It was only in those circles regarded as being the "bearers of culture," that such aesthetic practices could have meaning (Foucault, 1990:45).

Second, the notion of personal austerity was pivotal to cultivating the self. To attain an acceptable self involved struggle. The individual who refused to submit to their own desires (be it lust, gluttony, ambition, and so forth) was highly valued. After all, the individual who could not govern themselves, certainly could not govern the state. Indeed, governing oneself, managing one's estate, and participating in the running of one's city were deemed to be analogous practices (Foucault, 1987:76). Furthermore, it was important that this kind of self-mastery be continually rehearsed, as inherent within the arts of existence was an anticipation of usage. In this manner, ascetic denial became an essential part of the fabric from which the moderate and cultured personage was fashioned. It also became a crucial criterion in distinguishing a virtuous life from the life of one deemed less worthy.

Although the arts of existence encompassed a diverse range of practices of self-management, they were normally codified within specific regimens—regimens that covered various areas. Hippocrates, in Book VI of the *Epidemics,* stated that there were five areas that required measurement: sexual relations, exercise, sleep, drink, and (of pertinence to this chapter), food (Foucault, 1987:101). In *A Regimen for Health*, Hippocrates set out a basic dietary regimen by which the ordinary man could live as he should (Jones, 1923b:45). However, this was not to be utilized verbatim by those who were not ordinary men. As Ludwig Edelstein (1967) points out in *The Dietetics of Antiquity*, individual variations to dietary regimens were considered essential and even the earliest Hippocratic regimen took into consideration sex and age when advocating specific eating practices:

> A man is not even the same at all times of life; his age is a factor which must be considered in selecting food...In addition, the regulation is different according to sex: the rules which are valid for men do not apply to women. The physician, with his insight into the nature of health, must therefore demand that people regulated their nourishment...in accordance with...these factors. (Edelstein, 1967:304)

Therefore, the dietary practices by which a man constructed an acceptable self differed from the corresponding practices deemed fitting for women, just as the dietary practices of youth differed from other stages of life. Consequently (and of direct relevance to this chapter), there existed specific eating practices associated with young women, compliance with which had not only physical but moral implications. Although only a comparatively small amount was written concerning suitable dietary regimens for young women, its central themes involved notions of delicacy, menstruation, and pregnancy (especially since menstruation was attributed to the nature of women's delicate "spongy" flesh, which soaked up blood only to periodically release it) (Dean-Jones, 1991:111). For instance, Hippocrates stressed the suitability of dry food owing to the softness of their flesh and advised less diluted drink to facilitate pregnancy (Jones, 1923b:53). Rufus of Ephesus supported this contention, maintaining that if pregnancy was the desired end of coitus, then men should eat well but women consume proportionately less, after all, "it is necessary that the one give and the other receive" (Foucault, 1990:131). In Hippocrates' *The Diseases of Women,* it was suggested that unsuitable food, whether sharp or bitter, may even be responsible for premature birth and still-born babies (Phillips, 1973:113). Hippocrates also gave advice on the role and importance of fasting as part of a dietary regimen. He declared that, although fasting became easier with age, youths did not bear fasting easily. He stated that the body should not be permitted to attain extreme thinness, since this condition was treacherous (Jones, 1923c:101).

Nevertheless, fasting also had a more direct role to play in forming a self in ancient Greece than simply being one element of living as one should. Individuals systematically declined nourishment as a part of the exercises of self-mastery mentioned earlier. Ascetic denial of food was utilized as a mechanism of self-testing. By being able to govern the desire for food, not only could fitness to govern be demonstrated, but also the quality of self being cultivated could be enhanced. Foucault (1990:20–21) points to ancient Greek heroes who had such mastery of themselves as to be able to turn away from all temptation, and then to almost identical figures within Christian lore. Indeed, he argues that the first Christian doctrines owe much to the moral philosophy of antiquity (Foucault, 1987:14–15). So, too, fasting became a mechanism by which early Christians constructed the self in a holy manner (through the medium of the body). Peter Brown argues that the ideal self of the desert hermit involved an emaciated body-image. The logic of such self-starvation involved the belief that under conditions of perfect purity, the body would need virtually no sustenance.

Significantly, the dietary practices of the early Christians cannot be understood as a single corpus of ideas or practices. While there does appear to be a trend during the first few centuries toward increasing the importance placed upon sexual morality (alongside a commensurate reduction in the importance of food), this occurs in a piecemeal and contingent manner. Certainly, there was no consensus amongst Christians on precisely why fasting and specific food taboos were important within holy life (Simoons, 1961). For example, some Christians (such as the Encratites—followers of Tatian, second century A.D.) believed that abstentions in general were valued as they separated men from beasts (Brown, 1988:92–93). Other Christian groups, (including the Manichaeans of the third to fifth century A.D.)

considered that immoderate eating was a catalyst for the manifestation of the sexual desires through which the kingdom of darkness gained influence. A further variation in understanding the importance of fasting related it directly to the notion of charity. According to Augustine of Hippo, "The hungry Christ will receive that from which the fasting Christian abstains" (Bynum, 1987:35). All of these early Christian rationalizations of fasting (and more) had currency at certain times and among certain groups. To complicate the picture further, the notion of fasting itself was also flexibly interpreted. It could mean going without food altogether, as in the case of one of the desert fathers, Simeon Stylites, who ate nothing for the whole of lent (Arbesmann, cited in Bynum, 1987:321). Usually, however, it referred to refusing certain foods, to eating only one meal each day, or going without food on specific days. Consequently, the practices of not eating and/or refusing certain foods have tended to fuse into a single concept—fasting.

Differences also existed concerning gender, although information on the fasting practices specifically relating to women during this time is scarce. Brown (1988:269) has some observations on the gendering of religious ascetic practices. He suggests that, although there was some overlap between men and women in their use of austerity, there also appear to have been discernible differences. For example, women ascetics already had a reputation for their ability to endure exceptionally long fasts. Certainly, if they wished to demonstrate their piety through asceticism, their choice of terrain may have been considerably more restricted than that of equivalent men, for as Brown points out:

> Deprived of the clear boundary of the desert, their energies less drained by hard physical labor and unable to expose themselves far from their place of residence for fear of sexual violence, women frequently defined themselves as separate from the world through exceptionally rigid control of their diet. (Brown, 1988:269)

Such a limitation on the piety of women is reflected in the stories told of their religiosity. Whereas the holiest of men were depicted as knowing nothing about women or money, the equivalent women were said to have grown up not knowing what an apple looked like. As will be discussed in the next section of this chapter, one thousand years later, in medieval Europe, there was still deemed to exist a distinctive relationship between adopting severe fasting practices and female piety.

So far, chapter 5 has made three main points. First, by regulating their diet in the correct manner (which normally involved fasting), some ancient Greek castes constructed a life "lived as one should." Such practices both demonstrated the ability to govern their own desires, and established their right to govern others. Thus, fasting did not reflect problems over the self, as with contemporary theories of anorexia nervosa. Rather, it constituted one of the most important mechanisms by which an acceptable self was formed—a self shaped in part through a rigorous government of the body.

Second, dietary asceticism acted as mechanisms of both social distinction and social differentiation. To shape the self in a way deemed desirable by a particular caste was also to become elevated in the ranks of that caste. Therefore, following difficult dietary regimen (which generally included fasting), could result in considerable status. However, such ethical practices were not deemed fitting for everyone under all circumstances. Adjustments were to be made to the dietary regimen according to a number of factors, including age and sex. Particular eating habits thereby became a mechanism of social differentiation. According to this logic, young women would have been encouraged to shape themselves, and their bodies, by eating in a certain manner (although, at this stage, such practices of self-shaping were restricted to an elite few). This leads to the final point concerning the autonomy of ethical practices.

Once ascetic dietary practices have been brought into existence, even within such restricted circles, they can then act as a model for later societies to follow. Even though they may subsequently have been cut off from their original belief systems, they can still act to pattern the conduct of ensuing social groups. Furthermore, although these ethical practices may have had their genesis in elite and restricted circles, as was the case in ancient Greece, and although they may only resurface in dispersed locations at various intervals, they can continue to act as a model for human conduct. In addition, the potential is always there for those practices to be distributed to the wider community. Dietary asceticism is one example of such an occurrence.

The next section of this chapter examines the contention within the literature on anorexia nervosa that the broad distribution of such severe fasting practices is a modern phenomenon, and one best tied to the coercive effects of contemporary gender roles. In the influential *The Golden Cage,* Bruch (1978:8) is making precisely this claim when she states that "new

Diseases are rare, and a disease that selectively befalls the young, rich and beautiful is practically unheard of. But such a disease is affecting the daughters of well-to-do, educated, and successful families."

Historicizing Fasting

As mentioned earlier, Corrigan (1992) argues that feminists have attempted to explain anorexia nervosa in different ways. The first way has depicted the anorectic as the ultimate product of patriarchal fashioning—a victim of male design. An alternative, however, and more subtle, body of literature exists that situates anorexia nervosa as a symptom/manifestation of the way in which contemporary society socializes women. While still employing a model that emphasizes a struggle over the inner self, most feminist literature on anorexia nervosa does not seek to explain such fasting simply in terms of something that men do to women. Rather, the focus is shifted from the institutions of patriarchy, to the complex relationships that are deemed to exist between women, their bodies, and food. Anorexia nervosa is thereby placed within the binary response of resistance/conformity to contemporary notions of femininity.

Orbach (1978) states that it is obvious why women, rather than men, become anorectics in such large numbers, after all, "bird-like eating is a reflection of a culture that praises thinness and fragility in women." The logic here is that the anorectic assumes such cultural expectations and surpasses them. She supports these claims by stating that the central aspect of a women's existence is her appearance, and that women are socialized into a preoccupation with constructing a self-image that others will find pleasing, an image that is almost exclusively thin. Therefore, anorexia nervosa is *hyperfemininity*.

Edwards (1987:71) disagrees, describing it instead as a form of rebellion, an opting-out, a protest. Although she locates normal slimming in terms of conformity, she argues that anorectics are attempting to gain autonomy, not only from society but from their own denigrated female bodies. That is, they use fasting as a mechanism of retreating from femininity altogether. Reflecting this theoretical shift, *hyperfemininity* has now become *antifemininity*. Bordo (1988) expands on this analysis. She states that the concept of resistance in anorexia nervosa can be understood to operate at two levels of meaning. The first is a rejection of traditional female roles, since many anorectics express dismay at the prospect of ending up in the same social and physical circumstances as their mothers. The second operates at a much deeper level, suggesting that anorectics have an intense fear of "The Female." This archetype is constructed as being "hungering, voracious, all-needing, and all-wanting," especially in the areas of sex and food.

Although Bordo's work employs some aspects of previous research, such as a variation on the inner self theme, she does not limit her analysis of anorexia nervosa to the binary of resistance/conformity to contemporary images of femininity. In the paper "The Body and the Reproduction of Femininity: A Feminist Appropriation of Foucault," Bordo (1989) suggests that anorexia nervosa may well have its origins in various normalizing practices and techniques of self-formation and self-discipline. This observation opens up a new field of possibilities that will now be addressed. It will now be argued that the current prevalence of severe fasting practices within the population of young, middle-class girls is neither a new phenomenon, nor is it necessarily best explained from within the binary of resistance/conformity. As with the last section of this chapter (where the notion of the self was placed in historical context), these new possibilities can be best explored by historicizing severe fasting. This historicizing will be accomplished by examining the dietary asceticism of medieval Christian women who, from the thirteenth to the fifteenth century, adopted fasting practices similar to those now associated with anorexia nervosa.

Women, Piety, and Fasting

In *Holy Anorexia*, a study of medieval dietary asceticism, Rudolph Bell (1985) examines the histories of Christian women who starved themselves in the name of piety, some achieving canonization as well as simply their own deaths. Individuals like Hadewijch, Beatrice of Nazareth, Angela of Foligno, and Catherine of Siena all voluntarily fasted to extreme lengths, became emaciated, amenorrheic, and ultimately died—classic signs, in the contemporary context, of anorexia nervosa. Of the 261 women upon whom he focuses his study: "about one-third of this number the historical record is so meagre that nothing of consequence can be concluded about them for my purposes. Of the remaining 170 or so, more than half displayed clear signs of anorexia" (Bell, 1985:3).

The prevalence of severe fasting practices among young women from the thirteenth to the fifteenth century rebuts the second assumption common to research into anorexia nervosa—that severe fasting is a contemporary phenomenon, and that these practices are, in some way, caused by the social expectations now placed upon young women. However, medieval fasting also raises two questions—first, why did some medieval women choose to fast to extreme lengths as a way of demonstrating their piety, second, to what extent is the modern category of anorexia nervosa useful in describing medieval fasting?

In *Holy Feast, Holy Fast,* Caroline Bynum (1987) answers the question of why some medieval women chose to adopt severe fasting practices as a form of self-shaping in a number of ways, three of which will be addressed here. First, changes in the way in which the Eucharist was interpreted had the effect of making some religious practices more extreme. Second, food was an available mechanism through which women could manipulate their own circumstances. Finally, in medieval female religiosity, severe fasting formed an important component within the motifs of service and suffering—all stemming from the notion of *Imitatio Christi*.

First, the Eucharist, where God became bread and wine, was as crucial to medieval piety as was the fast. In fact, the two sets of practices were originally seen to spring from the same underpinning logic, in that they tied Christians to one another, to the rhythm of nature, and to God. Thus, it was not simply feast/fast that provided text for religious metaphor. The notion of "God as food" was considered equally important. Medieval authors such as John Tauler spoke of "eating and being eaten by God." Similarly, Romanos considered Jesus to be the "celestial bread" that hell "cannot digest" (Bynum, 1987:32,40). In early Christianity the commensalism of holy communion signaled an expansion of community. The sharing of the single loaf acted to enhance the "internal coherence, unity and equality of the Christian group." It was above all else a corporate practice. The question of precisely how Christ came to be present during the Eucharist was of little interest to early Christians (Bynum, 1987:49).

However, Bynum (1987:53) argues that the context of the Eucharist was in the process of transformation throughout the Middle Ages, which, in turn, had quite dramatic effects upon the fasting practices of some devout Christians—women in particular. A series of theological debates had begun to rage. Did God exist in the whole wafer or in each separate crumb? Could God be hurt by chewing? Was God present in the bread before the wine was consecrated? These debates over transubstantiation and concomitance signaled a fundamental shift in the notion of communion: the Eucharist itself had slowly become an object of adoration. This transition was completed late in the thirteenth century, by which time the consecrated bread and wine had become objects of awe and wonderment. Eucharistic miracles abounded. God, formerly intangible and ethereal, was now manifest and visible at the moment of communion. It thereby became possible to experience God directly and personally. In part as a consequence of this, the corporate nature of early Christian eucharistic piety started to disappear. Fasting practices reflected this shift from the communal to the personal and the practice of some individuals was increasingly idiosyncratic and extreme. It was in this religious context that the ascetic fasting practices, deemed by Bell (1985) to be early examples of anorexia nervosa, had their genesis.

Bynum's second point was that food constituted an available mechanism through which women could manipulate their own circumstances. Since women's primary role (other than childbirth) involved the preparation of food, fasting was the most obvious and culturally acceptable form of asceticism. It merely acted to emphasize what women did in their daily lives—to prepare, rather than to consume, food. As Bynum states:

> Fasting and charitable food distribution, and their miraculous counterparts—surviving on the Eucharist alone, food multiplication miracles, the female body that exudes food or curing liquid—were thus, in one sense, religious expressions of social facts. They manifested in religious behaviour the sexual division of labour. (Bynum, 1987:192–193)

Therefore, just as men often renounced the things over which they had control (money and possessions), women's renunciation tended to focus upon that which they regulated—food. Unlike equivalent men, women were not in a position to renounce their property, largely because they actually had very little control over it. Bynum (1984:24) gives several examples of how women were actively prohibited from giving their possessions away, such as Mary of Oignies and Clare of Assisi. Likewise, it was not a simple matter for women to embrace chastity suddenly, if they were already married. Women such as Margaret of Cortona and Angela of Foligno had to wait for their husbands to die before they could act upon their calling. As a consequence of these restrictions, fasting practices and other food-related demonstrations of piety could occur fairly unproblematically within a framework of institutions or economic supports shaped and governed by others.

However, female fasting did not always blend in to daily life without any difficulties. Bynum (1987:193) argues that the extreme fasting practices of some young women actually did affect the running of their households, and this disruption permitted them some form of leverage over their conditions and their future. Furthermore, in a more directly theological way, fasting permitted them to bypass the mediating male influence of the priest on their religious experiences. Whereas the female was normally characterized as the passive recipient of spiritual favor (such as in the Eucharist), ascetic fasting became part of a vocabulary of food-related practices that allowed women more active and direct access to their God.

Finally, Bynum argues, in medieval female religiosity, severe fasting formed an important component within the motifs of service and suffering— all stemming from the notion of *imitatio Christi*. This formed an important component of a model of female piety that differed markedly from the model characteristic of equivalent men. According to Weinstein and Bell (1982:220) there exists a specific set of practices characteristic of male saints, whose typical habitus might include deeds such as brave missionary work, championing public morality, and passionate oratory. In contrast, the female model for holy conduct features mysticism, charity, and penitential asceticism. They suggest that women saints were less institutionalized than men, that mystical communication with God played a greater role in women's piety, that their religious calling developed more steadily than men's, that their piety was more body centered than men's, and that it emphasized the notion of service and suffering.

Service and suffering was also a central component within the spiritual theme of *imitatio Christi*. Before the thirteenth century, *imitatio Christi* was understood in a largely symbolic manner. It was applied to conduct such as using Christ as a role model, or observing dietary restrictions during Lent in order to simulate Christ's forty days of fasting in the desert. However, just as the "body and blood of Christ" came to be taken literally in the Eucharist, so, too, *imitatio Christi* took on a literal meaning concerning Christ's suffering in this world. The female body itself thereby became the primary site for extravagant exhibitions of piety to be written. Women were far more likely than equivalent men to take vows of chastity, to torture themselves with devices such as hair shirts and chain girdles, and to whip and starve themselves (Weinstein and Bell, 1982:234). Through the piecemeal employment of practices such as these, medieval women shaped a self in *imitatio Christi*. It is within this context that the severe fasting of those women must be considered.

Setting Limits to Anorexia Nervosa

From the arguments raised so far, it is understandable that food—particularly fasting—became a ready site for medieval women to demonstrate their holiness. The question can now be asked, however, Were women such as St. Catherine of Siena suffering from anorexia nervosa? Bell (1985:20–21) has few doubts about this. After all, as medieval people faced other illnesses that still exist today (such as bubonic plague), there is no reason that the same assumptions cannot be made about anorexia nervosa—that is, it is a physiological and psychological ailment that has always been most prevalent among young women. Bell argues that medieval fasting women were suffering from a mental state that he considered psychologically analogous to that found in contemporary anorectics. He supports this contention by noting several symptomatic similarities, other than the fact that medieval dietary ascetics were also predominantly young and female, became very thin, and often died.

Yet the situation is considerably more complex than Bell's analysis might suggest. First, the fasting practices of medieval holy women do not fit the criteria used most frequently to diagnose anorexia nervosa. As will be discussed in the next section, the *Feighner-Criteria for Anorexia Nervosa* require, for a positive diagnosis, an intense fear of becoming obese and a disturbance of body image—for example, claiming to feel fat even when emaciated. These features were not present in medieval fasting women, as weight or body size was not pertinent in any way to their dietary practices. In fact, all but missing, too, was the *raison d'etre* for most contemporary fasting—the notion of dieting for health. As Henisch (1976:16) points out when discussing medieval attitudes toward the seven deadly sins: "Rigorous diets when endured merely for the sake of health received as little sympathy from sharp-eyed commentators on gluttony as (did) ostentatious dinner parties. Dieting for fashion had not yet been invented."

On these grounds alone, it would appear that the modern concept of anorexia nervosa is unsuitable for retrospective application to women of the thirteenth century. Other arguments, however, lend additional weight to the rejection of such hypothetical links. Brumberg (1988) states that the evidence linking the two phenomena is exceedingly weak and is primarily based upon interpretive acts of faith or upon flimsy medical evidence, like hyperactivity, amenorrhea or lanugo. Although there are clearly secular cases where medieval women stopped eating (that is, they made no claims to piety), this does not, therefore, imply the existence of anorexia nervosa. There are feasible emotional or organic conditions/circumstances that manifest this symptom. Brumberg also points out that, although both the modern anorectic and the medieval holy woman may share similar physical experiences upon starving, the routes into their respective fasting practices are very different, and this, therefore, negates the possibility of any real comparison. Bynum does not so much argue against medieval ascetics having anorexia nervosa, as argue that it is not a particularly helpful line of inquiry. She rightly points out that:

> "Medieval anorexia" is not quite the right topic for historical investigation. We should not isolate the rather rare phenomenon called by contemporaries "miraculous abstinence" or "fasting girls" from the broader phenomenon of the overpowering concern with food—with feast as well as fast—that characterizes the lives and writings of medieval women. (Bynum, 1987:206)

In the light of these arguments, it would appear that the broad distribution of severe fasting practices among young women is not simply a contemporary phenomenon. Some medieval women engaged in ascetic practices that also involved severe fasting. However, explanations for fasting cannot be found within the binary of resistance/conformity to dominant images of femininity. Rather, the fasting of medieval women can only be understood when placed in its religious historical context, which is very different from that which was later to give rise to anorexia nervosa. This understanding requires a knowledge of religious conventions based upon the dual and supplementary dietary imperatives of feast and fast, and of an increasingly extreme interpretation of Christian doctrine. It requires a knowledge of the role that food played in women's piety, as part of the theme of *imitatio Christi*.

As discussed in the last section, ethical practices can act as models for conduct, even when separated from their original belief systems. Although dietary asceticism may have had its genesis in antiquity and been associated with living as one should, it survived in restricted Christian circles only to resurface in medieval times as a set of predominantly female practices linked to piety and penitence. However, severe ascetic fasting among young women did not cease with the death of St. Catherine of Siena. On the contrary, her life story (and others like her—Clare of Assisi, Angela of Foligno, Margaret of Cortona) was retold to audiences as a form of religious inspiration for centuries afterward (Bell, 1985:152). Her own writings and those of her biographer, Raymond of Capua, were also used as exemplary texts for others who wished to duplicate her dietary practices and, hence, her piety. Even as late as the 1880s, the *vitae* of medieval fasting women such as St. Catherine were being used as models for the conduct of young women (Brumberg, 1988:184). The circumstances, however, that had given rise to the spectacular individualism of the thirteenth and fourteenth centuries had long since devolved into a less individually challenging religiosity that marginalized the laity, frowned upon severe asceticism, and cast the role of the holy women as that of do-gooder. Thus, those young women who still chose to shape their spiritual practices in the tradition of the medieval ascetics, came to be regarded as increasingly anachronistic.

Government and the Invention of Anorexia Nervosa

Anorexia nervosa now has a well-documented and often-quoted history, which traces how we came to grasp what it "really is." Once discovered, in 1873, this new disease was not only used to explain why some contemporary women fast severely, it was also retrospectively allocated to earlier fasting women. However, it was not until 1962 when some specific diagnostic criteria were established for the disease (Bruch, 1962). These included a disturbance of body image, a disturbance in the accuracy of perception of internal stimuli (that is, nutritional need), and a paralyzing sense of ineffectiveness (also Bruch, 1966). Groundbreaking though they were, these criteria were still considered somewhat vague. In 1972, an attempt was made to rectify this problem by Feighner et al. They proposed the widely used *Feighner-Criteria for Anorexia Nervosa* (Feighner, Robins, Guze, Woodruff, Winokur, and Munoz, 1972:57–63). This, in turn, was refined by the American Psychiatric Association in 1980, with the *DSM-111 Criteria for Anorexia Nervosa*:

A. Intense fear of becoming obese, which does not diminish as weight loss progresses.
B. Disturbance of body image, e.g., claiming to "feel fat" even when emaciated.
C. Weight loss of at least 25% of original body weight; or, if under 18 years of age, weight loss from original body weight plus projected weight gain expected from growth charts may be combined to make the 25%.
D. Refusal to maintain body weight over a minimal normal weight for age and height.
E. No known physical illness that would account for the weight loss.

Although these characteristics now give shape to the notion of anorexia nervosa, there are numerous divisions in the scientific community over precisely what causes anorexia nervosa. While almost all agree that the answer to this question has several components, the dominant (medical) explanations appear most comfortable when clustered around the disciplines of physiology and psychology. Indeed, the *International Journal of Eating Disorders* states that it will consider only articles from within these disciplines. Irrespective of these minor divisions, this research shares a common assumption—that anorexia nervosa exists in nature. This chapter adopts a different approach, suggesting that when new canons of judgment are employed—such as those associated with science—new realities emerge. Anorexia nervosa is only one such reality. The remainder of this chapter will trace how this reality emerged.

In *Fasting Girls*, Brumberg (1988) illustrates the changing interpretations given to women's fasting practices owing to the rise of several new important canons of judgment. She states that in the eighteenth century, although severe fasting was no longer conducted within the medieval context of feast/fast—hunger and starvation were no longer commonplace (Arnold, 1988)—"miraculous maids" excited both religious and secular interest. The fact that young women could exist without food for years in the manner of the fourteenth century saints was still taken as a sign of holiness. Nonetheless, the claim that any particular young woman ate nothing now required some form of proof (as the possibility of existing without nourishment was still considered possible, just rather unlikely). Then, having once established that no food was being eaten, the authorities were perfectly happy to designate such fasting "miraculous." As the tests became increasingly rigorous, however, and owing to a number of well-publicized frauds, there emerged a trend towards skepticism and later pathologization. This trend was already evident in the comments of the English philosopher Thomas Hobbes. Upon witnessing the physique of an emaciated young girl who apparently ate nothing and who was consequently regarded by locals as holy, he described her instead as "manifestly sick" (Brumberg, 1988:50).

Government, Health, and Diet

Significantly, such illnesses were now part of a governmental concern for the health of the population. Foucault (1984b:227) argues that, in medieval times, power exercised two main functions—war, in terms of the hard-won monopoly of arms and peace, through the arbitration of lawsuits and the punishment of crimes. At the end of the middle ages, there was added to these roles both the maintenance of order and the organization of enrichment. Finally, in the eighteenth century, a further function emerged—that of providing a social milieu that promised physical well-being, health, and optimum longevity. Foucault argues that, before the end of the seventeenth century, those institutions that attended to the needy also sufficed as a generalized mechanism for dealing with disease. That is, medicine per se was not distinguished from various other mechanisms that provided assistance to the sick poor. Moreover, this service came largely from charitable organizations. It did not differentiate illness from an assortment of other incapacities. These included old age, abandonment, unemployment, and destitution. A mix of all these factors existed within the "necessitous pauper." However, by the eighteenth century, this nebulous character began to be subdivided. For example, the *pauper* gave way to a series of well-delimited categories based upon perceptions of their relative idleness (*good poor, bad poor, wilfully idle, involuntarily unemployed*) (Foucault, 1984b:276). This disaggregation of the objects of charity, like the pauper, was a result of an increased ability to discriminate within a population that was becoming more and more a concern of government. It was also, in part, driven by the imperatives associated with first demarcating, and then maintaining, a productive and able-bodied workforce.

Thus, concern over the health of the population became one of the central objectives of political power. As Foucault (1984b:277) states: "The imperative of health: at once the duty of each and the objective of all." Rather than simply offering philanthropic support for the needy, the concern shifted to raising the health of the social body in its entirety. As a result of the accelerating demographic processes of surveying, classifying, and organizing, the problems of health that these new techniques of government discerned within the population were then tackled with ever greater acuity. Consequently:

> The "body"—the body of individuals and the body of populations—appears as the bearer of new variables, not merely between the scarce and the numerous, the submissive and the restive, rich and poor, healthy and sick, strong and weak, but also between the more or less utilisable, more or less amenable to profitable investment, those with greater or lesser prospects of survival, death, and illness, and with more or less capacity for being usefully trained. The biological traits of a population become relevant factors in economic management. (Foucault, 1984b:279)

An early symptom of the increasing concern for health was the popularity of treatises on dietetic management during the seventeenth and eighteenth centuries. Turner (1982a;1982b), in "The Government of the Body: Medical Regimens and the Rationalisation of Diet," and "The Discourse of Diet," examines the influence of the Scottish doctor and writer George Cheyne (d. 1743). Cheyne was influenced by Rousseau in that he held that ill-health was blamed upon man's flight from nature into civilization. In *An Essay of Health and Long Life* (1724), *An Essay on Regimen* (1740), and *The Natural Method of Cureing Diseases of the Body* (1742), Cheyne argued that the illnesses that beset society were the diseases of abundance (Turner, 1982a:260). He considered that the diversity and quantity of food that had recently become available to the population had resulted in a widespread disruption of the body's natural equilibrium. Having reduced his own weight from 448 pounds through a strict dietary regimen, he embarked upon a campaign to persuade others to share his newfound good health. As others would do fifty years later, he advocated a largely vegetarian diet as well as regular exercise and sleep. Furthermore, he individualized his recommendations based on criteria such as age, size, occupation, and sex (Turner, 1982a:264–265).

As appears to be the case with many ethical practices, it should be noted that Cheyne's ideas were popular only within a specific social stratum. It was among the affluent, urban, and educated that such practices were adopted. As Turner points out, Cheyne's regimen was largely irrelevant to the working classes whose diet of cereals was determined far more by cost and availability than by choice—although it has been suggested that Cheyne's views were popularized to a limited extent through the support of John Wesley, whose own religious asceticism he found echoed in a dietary regimen that propounded temperance and moderation (Turner, 1982a:265).

The important issue here, however, is that a direct link was drawn between diet and health. This link was expanded in the nineteenth century into the science of dietetics. This science arose not directly out of the regimen of doctors such as Cheyne, but rather more out of debates over urban management, industrial efficiency, and costs of incarceration (Turner, 1982b:166–167). Examples of these connections can be detected in the studies of Rowntree at the end of the nineteenth century (Rowntree, cited in Turner, 1982b:267). In his study of the working classes of York, he sought to obtain accurate calorific data for the energy requirement of workers. He concluded that servants were overfed, that artisans had enough food, if they were careful, and that the largest proportion of the population, the laboring classes, were seriously underfed. Turner (1982a:266) also argues that not only does Rowntree's research demonstrate an understanding of the body-as-machine, whose food efficiency can be empirically tested, it also locates such dietary concerns within broader moral, eugenic, and nationalistic rationalities.

In summary, the ascetic dietary programs that first began to appear in the seventeenth century were directed at, and adopted by, aristocratic and professional elites. These practices had their origins not only in an increasing emphasis on dietary delicacy and self-control, and in a Rousseauian belief that poor health was a measure of humankind's alienation from both nature and a natural diet, they were also prompted by the first stirrings of a wider governmental concern for health. These practices did not really migrate to the wider community until toward the end of the nineteenth century, where they then proliferated:

> Contemporary anxieties about obesity and dieting, slimming and anorexia, eating and allergy are part of the extension of rational calculation over the body...We can claim, therefore, that the dietary practices of the eighteenth-century professional classes have gradually percolated through the social system to embrace all social groups in a framework of organised eating, drinking and physical training. (Turner, 1982a:266)

Consequently, it is within the context of a concern for health, diet, and the body that the fasting practices of young women must now be placed. This concern is particularly evident within medicine. The medical model has a complex and important role to play in shaping contemporary explanations of severe fasting practices. It is necessary to be cautious, however, when discussing the rise of the medical model. This model is, by its very nature, a piecemeal collection of different disciplines and knowledges that are by no means unitary in their domain assumptions, methodologies, constituencies, or objectives. The rather haphazard and contingent assembly of the notion of anorexia nervosa furnishes a good example of this heterogeneity. Despite this proviso, however, some general trends are present and worth comment.

Medicine, Nosology, Hysteria

Foucault (1973), in *The Birth of the Clinic*, charts an important shift that occurred at the beginning of the eighteenth century, from the old classificatory medicine to the new anatomo-clinical method. The old system was centered around the construction of a taxonomy of diseases, which were organized into a variety of families, genera, and subspecies. These diseases could only be known in their purest form when all the obscuring and mediating characteristics of the patient themselves had been removed—such as predispositions, age, way of life, and so forth (Foucault, 1973:8). It was believed that taking a patient to hospital complicated the situation, as it changed the individual's natural disposition, thereby further disguising the illness. Hospital doctors would, therefore, see only "distorted, altered diseases" (Foucault, 1973:17). The rise of the new medicine, based upon clinical observation and the compilation of medical norms, did not signal a complete rejection of all old methods. Both can still be characterized by their extensive use of taxonomies. Nevertheless, by the early nineteenth century, doctors had begun to adopt a new way of seeing—both their patients and their diseases. This new vision did not come about as a result of a single scientific discovery nor moment of individual inspiration; instead, it came about as a result of a complex of more or less unconnected social, technical, and theoretical shifts. That is, as a consequence of numerous anxieties concerning the urban, working-class population (overcrowding, contagion, immorality), hospitalization was made a prerequisite for those who, while being supported by charitable agencies within the community, sought medical treatment. Consequently, doctors could now follow the progress of any number of examples of a particular illness. Furthermore, statistical analyses not only enabled the construction of life histories of each complaint (and, hence, new and more comprehensive nosologies), they also permitted the compilation of medical norms for a large number of examples. These reorganizations were, in part, responsible for the emergence of the pivotal notion of "the case":

> the unique intersection between a body and a life history, as the proper object for medical knowledge and for the practice of the cure. The case was unique but intelligible, for its individuality could be charted in terms of conformity to, or deviation from, the general standards of functioning which were now available for comparison. (Rose, 1985:32)

Foucault (1977) expands on such individuation/normalization in *Discipline and Punish*, where he also demonstrates how modern institutions, such as the hospital, are apparatuses of observation, classification, and pedagogy. Through these roles, the hospital forms an important site for the policing of the social body.

The hospital is by no means the only such location, however. Arguably of equal importance is the family. The dual and supplementary governmental concerns over health and public order now meant that it was no longer just a matter of producing the right number of children, it also meant producing the right kind of children (Foucault, 1984b:279). There would, henceforth, be definite parental obligations to their children—care, hygiene, diet, exercise, to name but a few. As discussed in chapter 2, the family is no longer simply a kinship network, it becomes a "dense, saturated, permanent" pedagogic apparatus. As such, it also becomes the most constant and effective agent of medicalization (Foucault, 1984b:280). Hence, when young Victorian women fasted, a degree of culpability was frequently apportioned to the family for failing in the duty of care—healthy families do not produce fasting children.

The concern for health did not stop with simply policing the external manifestations of abnormality within the urban population, such as illness, malnutrition, deformity, or unfitness. As Rose (1985, 1990) contends, the health of the mind was now to be subject to governmental intervention and regulation. The rise of the psy-disciplines (psychology, psychiatry, psychoanalysis) denotes the emergence of a new rationale of government targeting human individuality. The conduct of citizens was now to be directed by investigating, cataloguing, interpreting, and modifying their mental capacities and predispositions:

> One fruitful way of thinking about the mode of functioning of the psychological sciences...might therefore be to understand them as *techniques for the disciplining of human difference*: individualising humans through classifying them, calibrating their capacities and conducts, inscribing and recording their attributes and deficiencies, managing and utilising their individuality and variability. (Rose, 1988:187)

Just as the pauper became subdivided into more precise and workable categories, so, too, were the mental faculties of the population, beginning with the young. A concern over the notion of the feeble-minded, combined with the newfound psychometric techniques of mental measurement, resulted in the burgeoning of the taxonomies that set out the problems of the mind. Within the realm of *educational handicap* alone, there were only two classifications prior to 1890—*idiot* and *imbecile*. This had swelled to eight by 1913 (including divisions such as *moral imbecile*, and *mental defective*) and on to twelve in 1945 (with *severely subnormal, maladjusted*, and *delicate*). Currently, the possible choices of educational handicap are enormous (Tomlinson, 1982).

It is not surprising, then, that young women who fasted severely were subject to close medical and psychological scrutiny. Conveniently, these disciplines could utilize as the centerpiece of their explanatory models an already existing, well-defined pathological category—the hysterical woman. Indeed, Foucault (1976:104) argues that a crucial characteristic of the government of eighteenth- and nineteenth-century society was the hysterization of women's bodies. This was the process whereby the female body was integrated into the sphere of medical practice, whereupon it was analyzed, qualified, and disqualified owing to its saturation with sexuality. At this time, female behavior was generally understood as being an extension of their reproductive capacities (hence, hysteria—*hysteros,* Greek for uterus). In practice, hysteria became a conveniently ambiguous term that covered all those forms of mental and physical stress not covered more precisely within the boundaries of other complaints. Furthermore, the rather vague nosology of hysteria meant that it could be applied to virtually anyone, if the subject were female, and generally from the affluent middle classes. Arguably, the emergence of the hysterical young woman was closely linked to a shift within Victorian society that saw the child becoming more central to the bourgeois family.

Therefore, having finally rejected the notion of anorexia mirabilis as a satisfactory explanation of severe fasting among young women, it should not be surprising that science produced a new nosological grouping to cover what was now almost exclusively regarded as some form of sickness—anorexia hysterica. In 1873, Sir William Gull presented a paper to the Clinical Society in London entitled "Anorexia Hysterica," which was published soon afterward as "Anorexia Nervosa (Apepsia Hysterica, Anorexia Hysterica)." He did not have the field entirely to himself, however. Also in 1873, a Paris neurologist, Dr. Charles Lasague published a paper entitled "L'anorexie hysterique." Gull soon ceased using the term *hysterica*, (owing partly to its imprecision, partly to the fact that some young men manifested the condition, and partly as a way of separating his own findings from those of Lasague), although he did not really seek to move his new classification—*anorexia nervosa*—from the general terrain of hysteria. That is, sufferers from the newly delineated condition of anorexia nervosa were still largely regarded as being hysterical (Brumberg, 1988:118–119).

Shaping Anorexia Nervosa as a Disease Entity

By the end of the nineteenth century, severe fasting among young women was no longer directly related to religious piety—although some, such as Mollie Fancher "the Brooklyn Enigma," incorporated spiritualism into their fasting (and arguably some notions of purity were still a feature of the belief systems underpinning these dietary practices). Instead, the wealthy young women who were the main constituency for self-starvation were slowly cemented in, and cementing, their role as patient. As previously mentioned, the initial diagnosis pointed to hysterical women, whose hysteria became manifest through the symptoms of inedia. Eventually, their fasting practices were extracted from this nebulous nosological space and given an adjacent branch all to themselves. Brumberg (1988) points to the influence of three factors responsible for this change—American asylums, French psychiatry, and elite British medicine.

Within the American asylums, many patients refused to eat. Consequently, it was necessary to develop techniques for keeping such individuals alive (most based simply upon forced feeding), techniques that then accorded the asylums a relative expertise in the fasting field. Whereas this refusal had been seen merely as a symptom of their derangement, by the mid-nineteenth century, as the asylums began to exchange their role of dumping ground for that of therapeutic institution, more specificity was required. It now became clear that people refused food for different reasons. Certainly the well-educated young women, whose only quirk seemed to be the desire to starve themselves to death, could not be properly classified with complete lunatics. Additional motivation for an interest in fasting came from the visibility of such fasting to the general population:

> For American asylum superintendents, who were accountable to the public, the spectre of death by starvation was particularly frightening. Mortality statistics from public asylums were published in professional journals and also abstracted in newspapers. A high death rate within the asylum was a serious indication of failure...In both England and the United States alienists paid close attention to anorexia. As a result, the first crude classifications for what we now call eating disorders emerged. (Brumberg, 1988:102–103)

The second major influence on the delineation of anorexia nervosa as a discreet disease entity came from French psychiatry, in particular from Charles Lasague. As previously mentioned, the bourgeois family of the nineteenth century underwent significant changes—especially in regard to the status of the child. It was psychiatry that first made the link between family dysfunction and fasting practices. Lasague put this succinctly when he stated that: "We should acquire an erroneous idea of the disease by confining ourselves to an examination of the patient" (Lasague, cited in Brumberg, 1988:128). He suggested that emotional conflicts between the young woman and her parents were the root cause of *l'anorexie hysterique*.

He also produced a rough, three-stage description of the normal development of the disease: it begins with general comments by the young woman of a certain anxiety after eating, which develops into fasting amid conflict with her parents. Then, as fasting intensifies, her dietary habits become the preoccupation of the entire family and friends. She becomes the center of attention, and exhibits pathological contentment. Finally, physical deterioration is evident and medical/therapeutic intervention is necessary. Brumberg (1988:135) suggests that pressure from the parents to marry may, in part, have been behind this fasting. If this is the case, just as medieval women used food as a mechanism of matrimonial leverage, so, too, did the young women of Lasague's middle-class France. Consequently, although these actions were no longer connected to the same belief system, they continued to act as a model for conduct and they continued, to a limited extent, to allow young women some control over their own circumstances.

The final component of the complex of knowledges/influences that manufactured anorexia nervosa as a discreet entity, involves the consultants of elite British medicine—such as Sir William Gull. In the nineteenth century, considerable social stigma still attached to asylums. For wealthy families with fasting daughters, these institutions were the very last resort. Consequently, specialists in private practice provided a viable and welcome alternative—and soon claimed expertise in the area. It was Gull who first distinguished anorexia nervosa from other illnesses, both mental and physical, which manifested the same symptoms. More specifically, his basic conclusion was that, if the fasting patient were neither a) a bona fide lunatic, or b) suffering from a disease that produces protracted loss of appetite, then the patient suffered from a particular ailment—anorexia nervosa (Brumberg, 1988). The shaping of anorexia nervosa in this way suited all concerned. Medical science had now concluded that the young women were not insane enough for incarceration (much to the relief of their families), but definitely in need of specialist medical treatment (much to the relief of the specialists):

> When the modern disease entity anorexia nervosa was named and identified, it recommended itself to physicians (and to families) precisely because it was a medical diagnosis that conformed to (their) clinical and social requirements. (Brumberg, 1988:110)

Consequently, the truth of anorexia nervosa finally emerged from all other obscuring and misleading diagnoses. This occurred as a result of the classificatory imperatives associated with asylum management, the psychological explanations of some apparent dysfunctions within the French bourgeois family, and the efforts by British consultants and parents to keep young fasting women out of mental institutions. However, having once produced a discreet disease entity, these initial knowledges/influences were not alone in giving it its current shape.

However, the shaping of what actually constituted anorexia nervosa was not as cut and dried as might first appear. It only took on its present form after a variety of different knowledges struggled over its authorship. Mainstream medicine, neurology, psychiatry, psychoanalysis, and even the bourgeois family itself, have all had a say in the shaping of the anorectic. Lucas (1981) contends that the discovery of anorexia nervosa occurred in five teleological stages. He first observed a descriptive era (ending in 1914), where the disease was identified but not satisfactorily explained. This era would include the efforts of Gull and Lasague—individuals who observed the disease, but did not understand it. The descriptive era was superseded first by the pituitary era (ending in 1940); research into anorexia nervosa in the first part of the twentieth century was dominated by endocrinology. For a while, Simmonds Disease was in danger of returning the newly discovered anorexia nervosa back to its old status of being merely a symptom of another underlying organic illness. Additional research and a certain taxonomic flexibility, however, permitted the retention of both as separate disease entities. Lucas states that, effectively, the influence of endocrinology ended here. This is not entirely accurate, however. It still continues to inform discourse on anorexia nervosa, albeit in a more limited way. Some recent medical research now points to a malfunctioning hypothalamus (Vandereycken and Meermann, 1984:51).

Despite ongoing physiological research, from the 1930s onward, a new body of knowledge informed debates on this problem. Psychosomatic medicine advocated the use of psychotherapy in the treatment of anorectics. The procedure soon became routine among general practitioners. Essentially, it actually involved only an early form of counseling. That is, it was believed that anorexic behavior patterns could be challenged and then modified by determining their real cause through carefully managed conversation and analysis. Upon comparing the texts of numerous conversations between therapists and anorectics, details of the normal anorectic's personality began to be delineated—introverted, reserved, insecure, self-denying, and so forth (Strober, 1986:238). These traits are still considered valid.

In Lucas's model, the 1930s notion of the anorexic personality was complicated by the rise of psychoanalysis, which predictably pointed the causal finger at sex. However, the numerous psychoanalytic interpretations that were produced from the beginning of the 1940s to the end of the 1960s varied considerably. For example, refusal to eat was linked directly to sexual repression—anorectics were depicted as cold, puritanical, and sexually maladjusted. It was also argued that the refusal to eat was a defense against promiscuity and probable prostitution, or that the force feeding that anorectics would inevitably face was part of a fellatio fantasy. Often, anorexia nervosa was explained in terms of sexual conflict manifested in terms of a fear of oral impregnation, except for one analyst who claimed success after finally getting his patient to admit her fantasy of eating his penis (Brumberg, 1988:224).

Irrespective of these contradictions, psychoanalysis was instrumental in shaping anorexia nervosa until the beginning of the 1970s (Lucas's "modern era"), when the illness was rigorously quantified through the *Feighner-Criteria* and co-opted into mainstream psychology. In addition to having firmly positioned such fasting in terms of a mental affliction, psychology has further reinforced its own expertise in the area (as well as the self-evidence of the pathological nature of the problem), by delineating in anorectics some common personality traits. However, not only does anorexia nervosa normally appear within a pathological personality, psychological research suggests that this personality then exists within a similarly pathological family (Beattie, 1988; Kog and Vandereycken, 1989). Thus, not only has psychology succeeded in staking the greatest claim to explaining the reason some young women fast, but it has also delineated one of the central targets for therapeutic intervention and rehabilitation—the family. Anorexia nervosa, however, is not now explained solely in psychological terms. Upon close inspection, the influence of disciplines such as physiology, psychoanalysis, and medicine can all still be discerned within the literature.

Conclusion

Significant numbers of young women are currently engaged in severe ascetic fasting practices. Almost all explanations of this behavior, as exemplified by texts such as Bruch's (1974) *Eating Disorders: Obesity, Anorexia Nervosa and the Person Within*, center around the disease entity anorexia nervosa. Bruch argues that the origins of the modern disease anorexia nervosa can be traced to struggles/contradictions between the authentic, inner self and the wider expectations of contemporary culture. Furthermore, it was only through scientific tenacity and clear-sightedness that the reality of the illness became apparent.

This chapter has adopted a different approach. Practices such as ascetic fasting are not expressions of the struggle between the authentic and the inauthentic self, or even between the authentic self and the external world, they are the very practices by which a self is formed. When St. Catherine of Siena refused food, this was her attempt to shape herself in certain ways. She was doing specific work on herself, and one of the central techniques that she used was severe fasting. This logic still applies. Contemporary anorectics are also shaping themselves, not only physically—through the rigorous government of their diet, and, hence, their bodies—but also ethically, through what Liz Eckerman (1987) refers to as a quest for secular sainthood achieved through the transcendence of the body. The crucial difference, however, lies in the emergence of scientific canons of judgment at the end of the eighteenth century that reinterpreted the ascetic dietary practices of young women in terms of pathological illness.

With these facts in mind, it has been argued here that contemporary images of femininity have not been the genesis of severe fasting practices among young women (whether as resistance or conformity). Rather, these practices have a certain autonomy, and in acting as modes of conduct, they can migrate from one context to another and from one era to the next (through, for example, mediums such as exemplary texts). The same practices that once signified piety and penitence, five hundred years later can now signify anything from asceticism to aestheticism. Certainly, the beliefs attached to these practices (both by those who employ them and by those who see them being employed) reflect an array of social and governmental imperatives. Such beliefs, however, should not be placed in a causal relation to these practices, rather they are simply part of the belief system that supports them. Fear of fatness does not cause, in an absolute way, the employment of severe fasting practices, it simply directs choices from existing repertoires of human conduct.

All the evidence suggests that severe fasting practices are largely characteristic of a specific social category—young women. This is the result of identifiable historical reasons, however, rather than the result of some feature of the essential nature of the inner female. Young women are fashioned, and fashion themselves, in particular ways. It is not only their chronological age and sex organs that distinguish them from other groups, it is also their mode of living. It would appear from the evidence that fasting has been one of a vocabulary of practices that have repeatedly featured in the habitus of young women. Consequently, fasting has been one of the ways in which young women shape themselves, and are shaped, as young women. It has not been the intention of this chapter to suggest that any research that adopts the premise of anorexia nervosa is missing the point. As was stated earlier, within current canons of judgment, young fasting women are anorectics. Much good work can be done from this starting point. Neither has it been the intention to suggest that the common explanatory landmarks of anorexia nervosa—media images of women, fad dieting, healthism, women's roles—are irrelevant, far from it. These constitute the most important features of the belief system that supports contemporary fasting practices. Instead, this chapter has raised a question concerning the degree to which ancient practices of social distinction can be seen as surviving within modern practices of personal stylization. Furthermore, it has illustrated how these practices have been integrated within a governmental-medical regimen centered on the body—all of which leads to a continuum of possible understandings of contemporary fasting. Finally, the intention has been simply to take a fresh look at anorexia nervosa, and, in doing so, to shed some new light upon one of the processes by which, through the government of the body, young people manage their sex and have their sex managed.

CONCLUSION

Youth, Government, and Culture

This book began by pointing out that youth research generally functions within some familiar frames of reference. Even those inquiries into youth that do not utilize subculture theory directly, often adopt its domain assumptions and operate across the same conceptual terrain. Within this position, the category of youth is located within the binary oppositions of domination/subordination and resistance/submission. It is also largely defined by its struggle with adult culture, and by some of its specific forms of conduct and ways of representing itself. Young people:

> are alienated from society in a range of ways. They lack control over their lives economically and politically. For the majority of young people, choice in direction of their life is severely limited by the conditions they live in. Young people are constantly confronted and directly affected by decisions, events and processes that are out of their control. (Moysey, 1993:13)

It was argued, however, that theoretical foundations of subculture theory have been problematized within the wider field of social debate. A rejection of the social control model of power, in combination with a concomitant rejection of totalizing forms of cultural analysis, has left a considerable percentage of contemporary youth researchers bereft of a convincing theoretical framework around which to structure their work.

This book went on to propose an alternative approach, based upon the work of Foucault, Mauss, and Rose, and focusing upon youth and the management of sex. First, the contemporary exercise of power was depicted as no longer being founded primarily upon coercion, but rather upon the notion of governmentality—the conduct of conduct (Gordon, 1991:2). This form of rule augmented the previous structures of sovereignty, and had as its target and *raison d'etre* the population—and, in particular, problem populations. In fact, it is the identification and resolution of social problems that underpin all governmental activity. One such problem area has involved the relationship between the category of youth and its sex, both in terms of governing various target populations on the basis of sex, and also in terms of regulating sexual conduct.

In this latter case, however, problematic sexual conduct was not explained in terms of the mismatch between desires of an inherent sexuality and the strictures of modern convention. Rather, sexuality is a historically contingent mechanism of rule, which emerged from the elaboration of Christian confessional practices, and which has been deployed across the social body. Sexuality provided an ideal apparatus through which a broad range of governmental aspirations could be realized. Seen in this light, the relationship between youth and sexual conduct appears very different, especially when it is considered that sexuality is one of the most effective mechanisms of government, and that youth is one of the most densely governed of all social categories.

Furthermore, the government of youth should not be understood as the external imposition of a set of organizing imperatives on a fixed and self-evident object. Youth is not a fact in itself—a transhistoric stage of life. Instead, it has been formed and reformed by the very governmental mechanisms that seek to administer its conduct. Not only did youth evolve out of previous problem populations, such as the adolescent and the juvenile delinquent, but youth also emerged as an object at the intersection of a diverse collection of legal, educational, medical, and psychological problematizations.

Second, it was noted that governmental programs do not simply and directly translate into a modified and regulated population. The process of translation primarily occurs through enrolling target groups in their own self-reformation. For example, programs aimed at altering the problematic sexual conduct of youth in an era of HIV/AIDS, operate by convincing the members of this category to reshape their conduct in more appropriate ways—to do work on themselves. This occurs not through direct state intervention, but at a distance through the medium of expertise. That is, young people are persuaded into particular modes of self-modification through the learned voice of a relevant expert. A sexually responsible self is engineered via the doctor, the Human Relationship Education teacher, the school counselor, the social worker, and even the responsible parent.

Implicit in this characterization of self-government is an understanding of the self that has been removed from the psy-based essentialism of the person within. The self is not to be found by introspection and reflection; rather, these are two of the very practices by which a certain type of self is constructed. Because youth is a particular category of person, and the modern self is the internalization of personhood, youth can therefore be understood as a form of personhood anchored in the self—although this self is a piecemeal and discontinuous one, as all selves must necessarily be. Furthermore, this youthful self is constructed by the employment of a number of specific practices of self-formation—Foucault's practices of the self. By certain forms of bodily conduct, by continual self-interrogation and analysis, through speaking about themselves to others, and by the adoption of specific codes of dress, young people form and re-form a habitus constitutive of youth. Thus, youth is the doing of specific types of work on the self.

Having outlined a new approach to youth research, it is not the intention to imply that the large body of existing youth work is without virtue, nor to imply that those youth practitioners who operate using its domain assumptions are wasting their time. Subculture theory proved to be a significant conceptual advance. It not only provided the first new conceptual framework for the study of youth since the Chicago School's delinquency model in the 1930s, it also challenged existing reductionist theories of ideology within Marxism. Also, research such as the Burdekin Report (1991) serves an important social function. It is informed by expert knowledges, it assembles a range of information from sites as disparate as the children's court, the school, the police, welfare agencies, voluntary organizations, the Bureau of Statistics, the hospitals, and the family. Such work is crucial to the continued functioning of government. Likewise, studies on the specificities and peculiarities of youth conduct (such as those associated with subcultural research), irrespective of their theoretical motivation, also provide information that feeds back into the governmental machinery.

A criticism that should be made of such existing youth research, however, is of the view it has of itself. It does not simply describe the real life of young people, whether in subcultures or otherwise. It is not a neutral observer of what society does to its youth. This research does not stand outside government and record its efforts. As objectionable as it might be to those researchers and practitioners who utilize this paradigm, their efforts are an integral part of government's successful operation. It is an important part of the processes by which youth has itself become an object of knowledge, constructed via a curious combination of strategies, knowledges, and forms of analysis. That is, youth research does not simply chart, in a detached and objective manner, the unfortunate plight of youth in contemporary society; rather, it is one of the mechanisms by which youth is formed and re-formed as a category. Furthermore, many of the studies that have attempted to liberate youth from its sexual repression—through interviews, surveys, ethnographies, and the like—have succeeded only in charting the space by which government is able to operate more effectively, thus regulating conduct more closely. It is this research that has apportioned to youth many of the capacities now deemed inherent to the category, and it is this research that remakes both youth and society in new ways.

Another problem with much existing youth research is the use of a unitary understanding of power that translates its exercise solely in terms of social control. The Marxist approach neatly delineates the state from the civil, the dominant from the counterhegemonic, and the oppressors from the victims. Such a conceptualization predisposes all forms of youth research to the same ultimate conclusions—that youth is shaped by domination and repression. It follows from this that the history of youth and sex becomes a history of restriction, compulsion, and sublimation.

In contrast to such an approach, this book has argued that the reinterpretation of power as productive and organizational opens up research to a variety of conclusions—conclusions that can be re-assessed from case to case. This is not to say that contemporary forms of the exercise of power cannot still be coercive; however, governmentality operates primarily by targeting populations, organizing their capacities, and channeling their aspirations. For example, the at-risk youth category should not simply be regarded as a new and more effective mechanism of increased governmental control and surveillance. The approach proposed in this book contends that the at-risk youth has its own specific history. Likewise, the at-risk youth is not merely another example of a label used to dominate young people. It can better be understood as a useful governmental tactic for identifying problem groups with the intention of facilitating desirable social ends. It seems more appropriate to applaud the identification of young women as a category likely to struggle in finding employment than to decry it. The fact that such a limited percentage of the youth population is deemed to be at-risk speaks to the success of government over the last two hundred years in equipping its citizenry with the required capacities, aspirations, and forms of conduct. Even where the government falls short of its objectives, feedback loops back into new and diverse governmental programs ensuring that government can continue to operate—to redistribute resources, to create new populations, to engender new aspirations, to forge new links between agencies, to form new capacities, and to target new problems.

This new theoretical approach to research has implication for youth practitioners in three ways. First, youth need no longer necessarily be positioned, *a priori*, as the inevitable and recurrent focus of the coercive power of adult/state institutions, just as resistance to this power need no longer be positioned as the driving force behind all youth culture and conduct. While not wishing to understate any of the difficulties faced by young people, this book argues for a more complex understanding of power relations than one which simply locates youth as victim. It argues, instead, for an approach that recognizes that power is not a singular relation, and that young people simultaneously undergo and exercise power. That is, it argues for a greater contextualization of power relations when dealing with youth issues.

The second implication for practitioners is that the self-evidence and coherence of many of the youth categories delineated by subculture theory, categories which, in turn, have acted as sites of intervention (Denholm, Horniblow, and Smalley, 1992:25), have now been called into question. The notion that members of specific subcultures can have their conduct decoded in a relatively unproblematic or unambiguous manner, is not viable. Young people are enjoined to shape themselves in various ways, some of which they may share with their peers. The aggregation of these practices, attitudes, and forms of self-representation into discrete subcultures is often a fairly arbitrary process. Furthermore, it neglects factors such as varying degrees of affiliation to group membership, local variations in subcultural forms, and broad differences in the meanings assigned to participation in specific subcultural activities.

The final implication of this book for youth practitioners is the necessity to recognize the non-unified nature of the category of youth. Youth is the focus of various governmental programs, policy documents, initiatives, and projects—all shaped across a range of social sites and problematizations. As such, it is an object configured in a variety of different ways—ways contingent upon these contextual specificities. Consequently, some of the current familiar assumptions that inform youth practitioners—that young people possess a number of essential characteristics which bind them together as a category (resistance to authority, innate creativity, a time of storm and stress, and so forth)—must be abandoned.

The significance of the arguments detailed in this book are not limited to youth practitioners. They also have implications for academic researchers within the field of youth studies. Again, there are three points of note, points that have some similarities to those outlined above. First, research cannot approach the topic of youth as if it were a unitary object. Youth does not possess a conceptual essence that can be readily and easily transported from one theoretical context to another. Rather, categories of youth are differentially constructed, in part as artifacts of government at the intersection of various problematizations and bodies of knowledge. In the final analysis then, the notion of youth is constituted by a set of social classifications that are simply aggregations of information, diverse sets of data that specify youth as their object.

The second implication for research within youth studies is that a greater degree of specificity is required. This book has argued that it is inadequate to operate with a domain assumption that presupposes that the category of youth has the same fundamental form, irrespective of the research context. That is, it is inadequate to presuppose that the notion of youth is deployed identically within sites as diverse as education policy documents and medical texts, or welfare reports and marketing analyses, or psychometric profiles and legal discourse. Each of these contexts is likely to operate with its own version of what constitutes youth. Therefore, if research in the field of youth studies is to avoid accusations of reductionism, it is important to realize that different formations of youth have their own specific histories.

The final implication for youth studies, and one central to the structure of this book, is that the use of subculture theory should now be regarded as problematic. In addition to the totalizing manner in which youth is utilized within subculture theory, as was discussed at length in chapter 1, there are also significant difficulties associated with subculture theory's reliance upon the concepts of hegemony, consciousness, and culture. If this theoretical apparatus is severely flawed, however, as has been argued, how then might the conceptual approach outlined in this book be used specifically to reinterpret the set of social formations that have constituted the object of subculture research? That is, if subcultures are not counterhegemonic responses to the dominant order, how might they be understood and investigated by researchers within the field of youth studies? This question will now be addressed.

In the Denholm, Horniblow, and Smalley (1992) article introduced in chapter 1, "The Times They Are Still a' Changing: Characteristics of Tasmanian Adolescent Peer Groups," the authors outline the central characteristics of twelve contemporary youth subcultures, including such groups as Bogans, Skeggs, Hippies, Tecs, and Gothics. It is this final group—the Gothics—that can be used to exemplify the difference between traditional subculture theory and the approach advocated by this book. Accompanied by a sketch, Denholm, Horniblow, and Smalley list the defining characteristics of a Gothic:

> **Dress and Appearance**: All black including hair, Doc Marten shoes or boots, black stockings, short skirts, big coats, white make-up, dyed or weirdly cut hair, heaps of eyeliner, rings and upside down cross around their necks...
> **Key activities and behaviour**: Against the church, slouch around, smoking pot and raging out, generally just talk together, criticise other people, keep to themselves, seances, meditating, loud concerts, visit grave yards at night, shopping at flea markets.
> **Relationships with adults**: Rebellious, avoid and hate adults, don't get along at all, usually don't live with parents, adults dislike them. (Denholm, Horniblow, and Smalley, 1992:23)

As with all the groups listed by Denholm, Horniblow, and Smalley (1992:18), Gothics are placed within the familiar subcultural context of unemployment, poverty, and homelessness. Furthermore, as can be seen from the comments about their relationships with adults, Gothics are constructed primarily as an oppositional group. Like the Skinheads, Teddy Boys, and Punks who preceded them, Gothics are depicted as engaging in a struggle against the existing social order. Indeed, Denholm, Horniblow, and Smalley (1992:25) discuss the problems that youth practitioners face dealing with subcultures such as Gothics, as they often have the perception that they are dealing with another part of the establishment.

These writers are by no means alone in their delineation of a Gothic subculture. In "Youth Tribes of Australia," Caroline Lees (1988) sets out to describe the most significant youth subcultures of the late 1980s. Alongside such groups as Skateboarders, Hip-hoppers and Surfies, she addresses the Gothics—painting a very similar portrait to that proffered by Denholm, Horniblow, and Smalley:

> They wear black: black clothes, long back-combed hair, black lipstick, eye make-up and nail varnish. Faces are as pale as possible. Perhaps the most famous gothic was Dracula: his jet black hair, blood red satin coffin lining and the been-dead-for-a-thousand-years look...A more recent role model is Morticia from the TV series *The Addams Family*. (Lees, 1988:7)

Lees argues that Gothics are best understood as a Bohemian offshoot of the Punk movement. She claims, however, that whereas the Punks had a political agenda—anarchy—the Gothics do not. Their statement is simply the way they look. That is, the Gothic subculture is primarily based upon the making of specific fashion choices. It is not about an involvement in any kind of struggle, ritualized or otherwise. This claim problematizes the use of subculture theory for analyzing the Gothics.

The Gothic choice of dress also presents further difficulties for the unproblematic utilization of subculture theory. In Hall and Jeffeson's (1976) "Resistance Through Rituals," it is claimed that the lifestyles and fashions of subculture members are mediated versions of the parent culture. For example, it is argued that the stylish Mods and the boot-and-braces Skinheads, respectively, reflected the upwardly and downwardly mobile sections of the fragmented, post-war British working class. Stressing the centrality of a link to the parent culture, however, appears inappropriate for the Gothics. Their choice of wearing thick black clothes and heavy wooden crucifixes seems unrelated to the dominant working class Australian culture, particularly in a climate as hot as Brisbane—"their stronghold" (Lees, 1988:7).

Given such difficulties, subculture theory appears to provide an unsuitable conceptual foundation for explaining groups such as the Gothics.

In contrast, the approach to youth detailed within this book promises to provide a more flexible and historically specific explanatory framework. Thus, rather than examining the Gothics in terms of resistance and a mediated parent culture, a more fruitful approach might involve an examination of five particular areas: first, the relationship between Gothics and the music and fashion industries; second, the forms of self-fashioning associated with the Gothic persona; third, a historical contextualizing of the Gothic; fourth, the differentiating logic and forms of government that give rise to categories such as Gothics; and, finally, the ways in which the Gothics are reported upon and analyzed in the media. Taking these in turn:

The Lees (1988) article states that the appearance and continuation of groups such as Gothics often hinge upon the success of an associated musical style. One Gothic is quoted as saying, "If there's no music, there's no fad because the music creates the fad" (Lees, 1998:8). The success enjoyed by bands such as Siousie and the Banshees, The Cure, The Sisters of Mercy, Dead or Alive, The Jesus and Mary Chain, and the Mission—bands most generally associated with the Gothics—have ensured that subcultural affiliation, however loosely defined, remains high. Indeed, in an article by Sue Widdicombe and Rob Wooffitt (1990:268–269), entitled "'Being' Versus 'Doing' Punk: On Achieving Authenticity as a Member," a Gothic interviewee makes this very point: "Well, there's been The Mission that's just started, and it's a lot more popular, especially with younger people...it's become really trendy to be a gothic."

While the Gothics are, in part, undoubtedly the cultural by-product of particular changes in the music industry, the lineage of these changes has been a subject for debate. As previously mentioned, Lees (1988) regards Gothics simply as a Bohemian offshoot of the Punk movement. Widdicombe and Wooffitt (1990:275) disagree, stating that "Gothics are partly a synthesis of the hippy and punk cultures." This assessment is, in turn, challenged by Leigh Krenske (1993) who contends, using a model derived from Larkin's (1992) *The Guiness Who's Who of Heavy Metal*, that Gothic has its origins partly in the Punk movement, but also in what she refers to as Speed/Thrash/Alternative music.

An analysis of the music industry and its associated tastes, however, provides only one part of the picture. As a grouping most easily defined by its appearance, the Gothics are also the by-product of the marketing practices, stylistic conventions, and global trends associated with the fashion industry. For example, it has been argued that the Punk style originally developed, not as a spontaneous cultural response to social and economic disenchantment among the young, but rather out of a series of fashion statements by Vivienne Westwood, an avant-garde British clothes designer, in the early 1970s (Nordquist, 1991:75). With hindsight, by the end of the 1970s, several aspects of Punk fashion, particular those styles adopted by women, were already heading towards those more readily associated with the Gothic. The following description of Nancy Spungen (the girlfriend of Sid Vicious, the "Sex Pistols" bass player) already sounds more Gothic than Punk.

> Nancy and her friends wore black clothing also, the gloves, leather jackets, belts and neckbands corresponding to the male clothing but instead of jeans the females wore tight, short skirts in black leather or fabric with fishnet stockings and high heels. The women whitened their skin and used heavy makeup to outline and highlight their eyes and lips. (Nordquist, 1991:76)

Wearing black clothes at this time was not a choice restricted to Punks and the early Gothics; indeed, it was a staple of the fashion industry throughout the late seventies and early eighties (LeBlanc, 1991:64). Undoubtedly, then, the frequency with which black clothing was being worn within the wider community played a significant role in informing the fashion choices that came to be made by such youth groups (and vice-versa). Again, the point being made here is that Gothic codes of dress do not originate from an inner wellspring of youthful creativity and resistance, but are, instead, related, in part, to broader trends, innovations, and marketing strategies within the fashion industry.

Yet, it can also be argued that the notion of fashion has broader implications for an analysis of the Gothics than simply the choice of specific clothes and make-up—a claim that leads to the second possible area of investigation—the forms of self-fashioning associated with developing a Gothic persona. As has been discussed extensively throughout this book, a particular persona is not adopted as a reflection of the inner self; instead, it is actively acquired through various practices of self-shaping. While the use of fashion is central to this process—"the artful assembly of a lifestyle put together through the world of goods" (Miller and Rose, 1990:25)—a persona is also constructed through the adoption of particular techniques of the body (dances, postures, ways of walking, forms of bodily adornment); obedience to specific codes of conduct (social and personal habits, forms of recreation, relations to authority and each other); the cultivation of certain tastes (musical, artistic, narcotic), and so on. All of these practices, techniques, and behaviors constitute active ways of doing work on the self. They are the mechanisms by which a given persona is shaped.

The Gothic persona is no exception; it, too, requires considerable work. Whereas the Skinhead persona is generally characterized in terms of its overtly belligerent self-confidence, its high level of physicality combined with frequent displays of aggression (Cashmore, 1984:63–76), the Gothic persona is much more restrained. With their slow gait and melancholic forms of dance (involving little more than swaying), Gothics are customarily represented as quiet, reflective, and somber to the point of morbidity (Shuker, 1989:12). This form of self-shaping is precisely what is meant by the romantic fashioning of personality. Indeed, as the next possible area of investigation will demonstrate, significant links exist between the Romantic Movement of the eighteenth and nineteenth centuries and the Gothics.

Many of the specific practices of self-fashioning widely identified with the Gothics have a history dating back well before the end of the 1970s, when the current youth culture gained momentum. Although the actual Goths were a Germanic people who lived in Europe between the third and fifth century A.D., the notion of "the Gothic" began over one thousand years later, in the classically influenced renaissance, when the term was used (primarily within the context of architecture) as a disparaging way of referring to buildings constructed in the "barbaric" styles of the Middle Ages (Germann, 1972:181–182). It was not until the "Gothic Revival," which is associated with the late eighteenth and nineteenth centuries, that contemporary understandings of the Gothic began to take shape. During this period, many of the stylistic features characteristic of medieval architecture were repopularized and integrated into building design. However, as Kenneth Clarke points out, this must be placed in a wider context.

> From the first the new taste for Gothic architecture was no more than a symptom of a great change of ideas which we now call the Romantic Movement. No one can define this change; but any definition must suggest that the Middle Ages took the place of classical times as an ideal in art and letters. (Clarke, 1978:66)

Hence, as with the Romantic Movement, the influence of Gothic Revival has been deemed to extend beyond the architectural to include the literary. Clarke (1978:28) argues that early in the eighteenth century, the Gothic Mood began to inform poetry. This mood was soon evidenced within the new and increasingly popular literary form—the novel—such that by the nineteenth century, augmented by the distributive possibilities associated with the cheap mass production of books, the Gothic constituted a prominent element of most Victorian writers thematic vocabulary. Just what constituted the Gothic mood is the subject of considerable debate. Some writers link it back directly to the perceived emotional properties of Gothic architecture, "to the sombre, mysterious and awesome atmosphere of medieval churches" (Germann, 1972:182–183). Other writers point to the recurrence of specific topics and motifs within literature: young women in isolated settings, a man with a sinister secret, repressed desire, incest, and so on (Masse, 1990:679). Other writers still are more general in their analysis, regarding the Gothic as constituted by "horror, violence, perverted sexuality, the grotesque" (Goddu, 1995:58).

Having pointed to some specific motifs in nineteenth century architecture and literature, the intention is not to assert the existence of an unbroken link with a late twentieth century subculture. As has just been discussed, not only is deciding what constitutes the Gothic a point of debate, but the Gothic Revival itself is also widely considered to have petered out over a century ago. Instead, the intention is simply to suggest that in the hundred years since the end of the Gothic Revival, Gothic themes have repeatedly reemerged and been popularized at various different times, and within various contexts, such as within architecture (Clarke, 1978), literature (Western and Ruggiero, 1978), cinema (Toumey, 1992), television (Ledwon, 1993), music (Goddu, 1995) fashion (Lees, 1988), and even cuisine (Jakobson, 1988).

Again, linking the Romantic Movement, the Gothic Revival, and contemporary Gothics would be possible only as the result of detailed analysis. One point of departure for such a study, however, might involve an examination of the nexus between gender and the Gothic. Contemporary feminist literature has made a number of significant points: it has illustrated the preeminence of women writers within Gothic literature (such as Mary

Shelley and Jane Austen); it has highlighted the pivotal role played by women within the structure of the Gothic novel (although generally from a psychoanalytic perspective); and it has suggested that the readership of such novels was primarily female (Ruggiero and Western, 1977; Mussell, 1983; Restuccia, 1986; Masse, 1990). It is, therefore, conceivable that some convincing links can be made between these feminist claims, and the fact that the contemporary Gothics are predominantly female—to the extent that subculture members are also referred to as "Witches"—(Denholm, Horniblow, and Smalley, 1992:23).

The fourth area of investigation might involve an examination of the differentiating logic that gives rise to categories such as the Gothics. As was discussed in chapter 1, by arranging and codifying individuals along an increasing number of axes, it becomes possible to create a more comprehensive domain of government. That is, through the construction of an extensive vocabulary of social categories, governmental programs can be shaped, targeted, and implemented most effectively. Furthermore, in a system largely based around the dual and supplementary processes of individuation and normalization, it is those who do not conform to given social norms that are the subject of greatest attention.

The case of problem youth exemplifies this. Denholm, Horniblow, and Smalley (1992:25) stress how important it is for youth practitioners to be able to keep abreast of how youth is categorized (and categorizes itself) at any given moment. As previously mentioned, they provide profiles of twelve separate youth subcultures, detailing how each is likely to respond in its contact with adults. Presumably then, youth practitioners can modify their own expectations and conduct depending upon the particular characteristics of the group concerned.

These researchers are by no means alone in the practice of subdividing the category of youth into smaller and more manageable components. They cite examples of subculture from both Canada (Bangers, Preps, Skinheads, Bopps) and Great Britain (Metal heads, Punkers, Posers, Mods) to support their argument (Denholm, Horniblow, and Smalley, 1992:18). Even the category of Gothic itself is subject to further subdivision. Widdicome and Wooffitt (1990) contend that a distinction can be made between Gothics, New Gothics, and MiniGothics. This differentiation is based upon criteria such as age, various specificities of dress, the length of time an individual has been a Gothic, and the perceived degree of affiliation to the subculture.

A final area of investigation into the Gothics might involve an analysis of how the media choose to report youth issues. The relationship between youth and the media has been the subject of extensive comment. One common viewpoint is advanced by Muncie (1984) in *What's the Matter With Kids Today*, in which he argues that the media have sought to blame youth for many social contemporary ills. This process, he contends, has been so effective and thorough, that the very category of youth itself has become inexorably linked to social transgression and delinquency (Muncie, 1984:9).

In *Hooligan: A History of Respectable Fears*, however, Geoffrey Pearson (1983) suggests that this is nothing new. Instead, he argues that moral panics over the young have occurred on a regular basis since the days of Merrie England. In what he refers to as "history lessons without dates," Pearson (1983:10) details the rhetoric that mourns the loss of a previous "golden age" of youthful obedience, which is utilized as a contrasting backdrop to what is perceived as the existing chaos and violence. He goes on to argue that previous eras all had their own folk devils—be they Garrotters, Hooligans, Teddy boys or Muggers—through which they all perceived their own decline (Pearson,1983:209).

Such youth folk devils have also existed in Australia. In "Bodgies and Widgies: Folk Devils of the Fifties," John Braithwaite and Bob Barker (1978) outline the rise and fall of the Bodgie panic. They chart the positioning of the benign bodgie as the locus for concerns generated by the rapidly changing social relations of the time. They contend that by persistently and emotively exaggerating Bodgie conduct, the media successfully set an adverse agenda for the ensuing discourse on youth. And yet, as in the article "Bodgies and Widgies: Just Working-class Kids Doing Working-class Things," Jon Stratton states that:

> The construction of bodgies and widgies was that of the dominant, by which I mean middle-class, culture. Bodgies and Widgies were constructed by the media as a threat to Australian (middle-class) culture. In an important sense, however, there were never any real bodgies and widgies. The terms were developed and adopted by some young people as a way of describing a person with a certain set of interests. Bodgies and widgies were, in many respects, just ordinary young people—just as were the much later punks or goths. (Stratton, 1993:88)

Similarities between the way in which the media addressed the Bodgies, and the way it now addresses the Gothics, is the subject of a paper by Roy Shuker (1989), entitled "From Bodgies to Gothics: Pop Culture and Moral Panic in New Zealand." He examines the manner in which the suicide of three Gothics in 1988 was dealt with by elements of the New Zealand press, contending that, as with the Bodgies thirty years earlier, the press "fastened on and sensationalised a youth subculture, presenting the Gothic cultists in a stylized and stereotyped way" (Shuker, 1989:15). In support of this argument, Shuker cites numerous newspaper headlines and commentaries, such as "Gothic Cult Suicides" (*Dominion*, 25 September 1988), "Gothic Lifestyle Puts Young at Risk—Doctor" (*Dominion*, 27 September 1988), and "Gothic Music Preaches a Message of Despondency Wrapped in the Mysticism of Death" (*Dominion*, 23 September 1988).

Upon closer examination of the evidence, however, not only did all of the suicides turn out to be family related, but Shuker also suggests that there is even reason to doubt that the Gothic subculture exists in any collective way at all, other than as a loose affiliation of musical tastes and fashion conventions. As he points out, the media's "attempt to create an identifiable symbol, the Gothic Cultist, was found wanting when subjected to closer scrutiny" (Shuker, 1989:13).

These elements of Shuker's argument stem from the influential *Folk Devils and Moral Panics*, in which Stanley Cohen (1973) describes the virtual media invention of Mods and Rockers—folk devils of the sixties. Two points are important: first—and in keeping with tenor of this book—if the complexities of the field are not to be lost, the folk devil/moral panic nexus is one that requires specific and detailed historical research to be useful (see, for example, Mark Finnane's (1989) analysis of the 1950s campaign against children's comics). Second, while hardly constituting a convincing social threat (the Gothic panic did not last long), like Cohen, Shuker underscores the influential role played by the media in constructing a given subcultural persona, and in distributing that persona within sections of the population. In this way, the media did not only report the (mis)conduct of subcultures, they had a significant role in their construction. The media have not merely described the Gothics, they have been instrumental in their creation as a coherent social group. Thus, it can be argued, in cases like this, that the media feed on their own inventions, as they continue to identify, catalogue, and explain each new youth subculture.

The same can be said for youth subculture theory itself. As was discussed in chapter 1, not only have youth subcultures provided academics with much-sought-after sites of resistance to the dominant order to study (McRobbie, 1980), but subculture theory itself has provided a ready conceptual framework for the analysis of successive waves of post-war so-called problem youth. Thus, it is through the logic of subculture theory that homeless young people have been transformed into Streetkids. Likewise, some young people, who happen to share a nebulous cluster of musical and fashion tastes, have been transformed into Gothics. After all, subculture theory needs subcultures to investigate.

In summary then, this book has argued that subcultural social formations, such as the Gothics, did not evolve as resistance to a dominant culture. Instead, they are a response to the governmental construction of youth as an object of knowledge, or rather, they are the by-product of particular forms of government, generated by specific power/knowledge relations. As Carrington (1993:105) observes, youth subcultures do not defy government, "On the contrary, they could be said to entail forms of governance which operate through the medium of youth culture and teenage consumerism."

Accordingly, attempts to account for the phenomenon of subcultures should begin, not with notions of a shared, resistant class/generational consciousness, but, rather, with detailed investigations of specific forms of government, such as those involving conventions and customs within the fashion and music industries, the distribution of technologies of marketing and consumption, the adoption of various techniques of self-shaping, the prevalence of different journalistic practices, routines of policing, and so on. Subcultural style is not an expression of relationship between a given social class, its material conditions, and its economic and cultural aspirations. Rather, it constitutes the construction of particular habitus, shaped by fashion and leisure activities, through which certain youthful personae are given their form.

To conclude, this book has sought to provide an approach to the study of youth that can offer a greater degree of contextual flexibility and historical rigor than has previously been the case. Central to this approach is the proposition that the existence of the category of youth is not an inevitable part of the human growth process; rather, it is better understood as a cluster of social classifications, positionalities, and sites of intervention. Furthermore, this cluster has been closely managed. That is, youth has been constituted as a governmental object at the intersection of a number of problematizations, and, as a part of this process, youth has been shaped by knowledges that have attempted to align the conduct and aspirations of youth with specific governmental objectives. This form of management largely operates by recruiting young people into various programs of self-regulation, often within domains such as the school and the family.

In examining some of the ways in which this management occurs, this book has focused on sex. This is because it is argued that sex constitutes an effective medium through which the population can be governed. That is, the careful management of the domain of sex provides an important mechanism through which a broad range of governmental aspirations can be realized. This management is by no means restricted to sexual conduct. Rather, it also includes an analysis of some of the ways in which youthful conduct, attitudes, and practices of self-shaping are managed according to sex. Thus, in this book, the management of sex has incorporated areas as diverse as an examination of the effects of young women's magazines, an analysis of governmental programs that target parental aspirations for their daughters, and a historical contextualization of young women's ascetic dietary practices.

In addressing youth in this manner, the two central advantages of the approach advocated in *Youth, Sex, and Government* are clearly exemplified. First, particular formations of youth have their own specific histories, histories that cannot simply be subsumed within broad and amorphous depictions of youth as a stage of life or youth as resistance. Therefore, utilizing information, ideas, and arguments drawn from governmental imperatives associated with the management of sex, it is suggested that youth is best understood as a set of interrelated categories that evolved out of earlier governmental objects, was shaped by particular historical circumstances, and must be placed in a precise context to be meaningful.

Second, as it is a set of interrelated categories, youth cannot be studied as a unitary object. The piecemeal approach suggested here describes formations of youth as specific amalgams of data, which are accumulated from diverse sites and problematizations—such as, for example, those associated with the management of sex. Furthermore, the resulting formations of youth are both shaped, and enjoined to shape themselves, through the application of diverse sets of practices that also have their own histories.

It is hoped that by proposing a new conceptual framework and a new set of analytical resources for studying youth, not only will it be possible to approach youth research with a sensitivity to the specificity of formations of youth, but it will also be possible to reinvigorate what has become a rather stale field of research.

BIBLIOGRAPHY

Abbott-Chapman, J. and C. Patterson. 1990. *The Students at Risk Program: An Evaluation of Projects in Tasmanian Schools*, (Report 1). Youth Education Studies Centre: University of Tasmania.

Ainley, J. and D. McKenzie. 1991. Participation by Disadvantaged Young People in Post-compulsory Education and Training, Appendix 3. In B. Finn, (Chair), *Young People's Participation in Post-compulsory Education and Training: Report of the Australian Education Council Review Committee*. Canberra: AGPS.

Allen, M. and A. McGregor. 1896. *The Glory of Woman: Or Love, Marriage, and Maternity*. Sydney: Hayes.

Althusser, L. 1971. *Lenin and Philosophy and Other Essays*. New York: Monthly Review.

Altman, S. 1983. Transforming Transed, *Radical Education Dossier*. 20:12–15.

Anderson, D. and C. Blakers. 1984. *Youth in Transition: An Annotated Bibliography*. AGPS: Canberra.

Appleby, J. 1992. *Liberalism and Republicanism in the Historical Imagination*. Cambridge: Harvard University Press.

Aries, P. 1960. *Centuries of Childhood*. Harmondsworth: Penguin.

Arnett, J. 1996. *Metalheads*. Boulder: Westview Press.

Arnold, D. 1988. *Famine: Social Crisis and Historical Change*. Oxford: Blackwell.

Australian Institute for Multicultural Affairs. 1985. *Reducing the Risks: Unemployed Migrant Youth and Labour Market Programs*. Canberra: AGPS.

Australian, The. Editorial. 1989. Apple Isle Follows Its Youth Down the Drain. (April 8):1.

Beattie, H. 1988. Eating Disorders and the Mother-Daughter Relationship, *The International Journal of Eating Disorders*. 7(4):453–460.

Beck, U. 1992. *Risk Society: Towards a New Modernity*. London: Sage.

Bell, R. 1985. *Holy Anorexia.* Chicago: University of Chicago Press.

Bell, R. 1987. *Changing Bodies, Changing Lives.* New York: Random House.

Bell, V. 1993. Governing Childhood: Neo-liberalism and the Law. *Economy and Society.* 22(3):390–405.

Benjamin, H. and R. Masters. 1964. *Prostitution and Morality.* New York: Julien Press.

Bennett, T., T. Miller, G. Swanson and G. Tait. 1990/1991. Youth Cultures and Arts Policies. *Culture and Policy.* (2:2/3:1):136–165.

Bennett, T. 1991. *Outside Literature.* London: Routledge.

Bessant, B. (ed.). 1988. *Mother State and Her Little Ones: Children and Youth in Australia 1980s—1930s.* Melbourne: Centre for Youth and Community Studies.

Bessant, J. 1993. Contesting Models of Policy: Problem Setting and the Australian Experience. Paper presented to the School of Cultural and Policy Studies, Queensland University of Technology (Kelvin Grove), September.

Bolton, F. L. Morris and A. MacEachron. 1990. *Males at Risk: The Other Side of Child Sexual Abuse.* London: Sage.

Bordo, S. 1988. Anorexia Nervosa: Psychopathology as the Crystallization of Culture. In I. Diamond and L. Quinby (eds.), *Feminism and Foucault: Reflections on Resistance.* Boston: Northeastern University Press.

Bordo, S. 1989. The Body and the Reproduction of Femininity: A Feminist Appropriation of Foucault. In A. Jagger and S. Bordo (eds.), *Gender/Body/Knowledge: Feminist Reconstructions of Being and Knowing.* New Brunswick: Rutgers University Press.

Bourdieu, P. 1977. *Outline of a Theory of Practice.* Cambridge: Cambridge University Press.

Bourdieu, P. 1984. *Distinction: A Social Critique of the Judgement of Taste,* London: Routledge and Kegan Paul.

Bowes, J. 1981. *Transition Education Programs for the ACT: Issues of Policy and Research.* Canberra: Department of Education.

Braithwaite, J. and M. Barker. 1978. Bodgies and Widgies: Folk Devils of the Fifties. In P. Wilson and J. Braithwaite (eds.), *The Two Faces of Deviance.* St Lucia: University of Queensland Press.

Brake, M. 1985. *Comparative Youth Culture: The Sociology of Youth Culture and Youth Subculture in America, Britain and Canada.* London: Routledge and Kegan Paul.

Brenton, M. 1978. *The Runaways.* New York: Penguin.

Brown, P. 1988. *The Body and Society: Men, Women, and Sexual Renunciation in Early Christianity.* New York: Columbia University Press.

Bruch, H. 1962. Perceptual and Conceptual Disturbances in Anorexia Nervosa. *Psychosomatic Medicine.* 24(2):187–194.

Bruch, H. 1966. Anorexia Nervosa and Its Differential Diagnosis, *The Journal of Nervous and Mental Disease.* 141(5):555–566.

Bruch, H. 1974. *Eating Disorders: Obesity, Anorexia Nervosa and the Person Within.* New York: Penguin

Bruch, H. 1978. *The Golden Cage: The Enigma of Anorexia Nervosa.* London: Open Books.

Brumberg, J. 1988. *Fasting Girls: The Emergence of Anorexia Nervosa as a Modern Disease.* Cambridge: Harvard University Press.

Burchell, G. 1991. Peculiar Interests: Civil Society and Governing "The System of Natural Liberty." In G. Burchell, C. Gordon and P. Miller (eds.), *The Foucault Effect: Studies in Governmentality.* London: Harvester Wheatsheaf.

Burchell, G. 1993. Liberal Government and Techniques of the Self. *Economy and Society.* 22(3):267–283.

Burdekin, B. (Chair). 1989. *Our Homeless Children.* Human Rights and Equal Opportunity Commission, Report of the National Inquiry into Homeless Children. AGPS: Canberra.

Burt, C. 1926. *The Young Delinquent.* London: London University Press.

Bynum, C. 1984. Women's Stories, Women's Symbols: A Critique of Victor Turner's Theory of Liminality. In F. Reynolds and R. Moore (eds.), *Anthropology and the Study of Religion.* Chicago: Centre for the Scientific Study of Religion.

Bynum, C. 1987. *Holy Feast and Holy Fast: The Religious Significance of Food to Medieval Women.* Berkley: University of California Press.

Calderstone, M. 1981. From Then to Now—and Where Next? In L. Brown (ed.), *Sex Education in the Eighties: The Challenge of Healthy Sexual Revolution.* New York: Plenum Press.

Carmichael, L. (Chair). 1992. *The Australian Vocational Certificate Training System*. Employment and Skills Formation Council, National Board of Employment, Education and Training. Canberra: AGPS.

Carrington, K. 1993. *Offending Girls: Sex, Youth and Justice*. Sydney:Allen and Unwin.

Cashmore, E. 1979. *Rastaman*. London: Allen and Unwin.

Cashmore, E. 1984. *No Future: Youth and Society*. London: Heinemann.

Castel, R. 1991. From Dangerousness to Risk. In G. Burchell, C. Gordon and P. Miller (eds.), *The Foucault Effect: Studies in Governmentality*. London: Harvester/Wheatsheaf.

Centre for Educational Research and Innovation. 1989. *Children and Youth at Risk*. Paris: OECD.

Chernin, K. 1981. *The Obsession: Reflections on the Tyranny of Slenderness*. New York: Harper and Row.

Chernin, K. 1983. *Womansize: The Tyranny of Slenderness*. London: Woman's Press.

Chernin, K. 1986. *The Hungry Self: Women, Eating and Identity*. London: Virago Press.

Chesser, E. 1971. *Human Aspects of Sexual Deviance*. London: Jarrolds.

Cimbolic, P. and D. Jobes. 1990. *Youth Suicide: Issues, Assessment and Intervention*. Springfield: Thomas.

Clark, K. 1978. *The Gothic Revival*. London: John Murray.

Clarke, G. 1982. Defending Ski-jumpers: A Critique of Theories of Youth Subcultures. Occasional Paper. Birmingham: CCCS.

Clarke, J. 1975. The Skinheads and the Magical Recovery of Working Class Community. *Cultural Studies*. (7/8):99–102.

Clarke, J., S. Hall, T. Jefferson and B. Roberts. 1976. Subcultures, Cultures and Class. In S. Hall and T. Jefferson (eds.), *Resistance through Rituals*. London: Hutchinson.

Cleo. 1994. The Orgasm Workout: Clench Your Way to Ecstasy. (January): 64–68.

Cleo. 1994. Weenie or Whopper: Can You Assess His Size Without Taking His Clothes Off? (February):56–60.

Cleo. 1994. Drive Him Wild: Foreplay Is Something to Be Savoured, Not Rushed. (February):104.

Cleo. 1994. The Seven Things All Men Love in Bed. (July):86–88.

Cloward, R. and L. Ohlin. 1960. *Delinquency and Opportunity: A Theory of Delinquent Gangs*. New York: Free Press.

Coffield, F., C. Borrill, and S. Marshall. 1986. *Growing Up at the Margins*. Milton Keynes: Open University Press.

Cohen, A. 1955. *Delinquent Boys: The Culture of the Gang*. Chicago: Free Press.

Cohen, M. 1991. Changing to Safer Sex: Personality, Logic and Habit. In P. Aggleton, G. Hart and P. Davies (eds.). *AIDS: Responses, Interventions and Care*. London: Falmer.

Cohen, P. 1972. Sub-cultural Conflict and Working Class Community. *Working Papers in Cultural Studies No.2*, CCCS.

Cohen, S. 1973. *Folk Devils and Moral Panics: The Creation of the Mods and Rockers*. Oxford: Blackwell.

Coleman, J. and T. Husen. 1985. *Becoming Adult in a Changing Society*. Centre for Educational Research and Innovation. Paris: OECD.

Collins, J. and J. Harper. 1978. *The Adolescent Boy: An Australian Analysis*. Australia: Cassell.

Committee of Inquiry into Homelessness and Inadequate Housing in the ACT and Surrounding Regions. 1984. Canberra: AGPS.

Commonwealth Schools Commission. 1987a. *In the National Interest: Secondary Education and Youth Policy in Australia*. Canberra: AGPS.

Commonwealth Schools Commission. 1987b. *The National Policy for the Education of Girls in Australian Schools*. Canberra: AGPS.

Connell, R., D. Ashenden, S. Kessler, and G. Dowsett. 1982. *Making the Difference: Schools, Families and Social Division*. Sydney: Allen and Unwin.

Connell, W., D. Stroobant, K. Sinclair, R. Connell, and K. Rogers. 1975. *12 to 20: Studies of City Youth*. Sydney: Hicks Smith and Sons.

Corrigan, A. 1992. Fashion, Beauty and Feminism. *Meanjin*. 51(1):107–122.

Cosmopolitan. 1993. What Women Do Wrong In Bed. (June):50–51.

Cosmopolitan. 1993. Are Those Sex Articles Really Necessary? (October): 90–96.

Cosmopolitan. 1994. Warm, Wet and Wild. (February):10–11.

Cosmopolitan. 1994. How Men Want to Be Seduced. (December):76–82.

Cosmopolitan. 1995. It's OK to Be a Bitch! (September):52.

Cosmopolitan. 1995. A Survey For Him. (September):184–186.

Counihan, T. 1982. Minding the Family: Donzelot and His Critics. *Local Consumption.* 3:19–48.

Cousins, M. and A. Hussain. 1986. The Question of Ideology: Althusser, Pecheux and Foucault. In J. Law (ed.), *Power, Belief, Action: A New Sociology of Knowledge.* London: Routledge and Kegan Paul.

Coward, R. 1977. Class, Culture and the Social Formation. *Screen.* (17):75–105.

Craik, J. 1991. Accounting for Fashion: Cultural Studies and Ephemera. Paper presented to Dismantle Freemantle Cultural Studies Conference, Freemantle, Western Australia, June.

Crane, P., G. Embelton, S. Harris, and M. Stokes. 1990. *Participants Manual Youth Sector Training Program.* Queensland: Division of Youth.

Criminal Justice Commission. 1991. *Regulating Morality? An Inquiry into Prostitution in Queensland.* Brisbane: Go Print.

Dana, M. 1987. Boundaries: One Way Mirror to the Self. In M. Lawrence (ed.), *Fed Up and Hungry: Women, Oppression and Food.* London: Women's Press.

Davis, J. and J. Sandoval. 1991. *Suicidal Youth: School-based Intervention and Prevention.* San Francisco: Jossey-Bass.

Dawkins, J. 1989. *Strengthening Australia's Schools.* Canberra: AGPS.

Dawkins, J. 1992. Post-compulsory Education and Training: The National Challenge. *Unicorn.* 18(1):6–12.

Dean-Jones, L. 1991. The Cultural Construction of the Female Body in Classical Greek Science. In S. Pomeroy (ed.), *Women's History and Ancient History.* Chapel Hill: University of North Carolina Press.

Demarest, J. and J. Garner. 1992. The Representation of Women's Roles in Women's Magazines Over the Past 30 Years. *The Journal of Psychology.* 126(4):357–369.

Denholm, C. 1989. School Based Child and Youth Care Services in Canadian Schools. *Youth Studies.* 8(4):44–77.

Denholm, C., T. Horniblow, and R. Smalley. 1992. The Times They Are Still a' Changing: Characteristics of Tasmanian Adolescent Peer Groups. *Youth Studies Australia.* 11(2):18–25.

Department of Education, Employment, and Training. 1989. *Students at Risk Program.* Canberra: AGPS.

Derrida, J. 1979. *Spurs: Nietzsche's Styles*. Chicago: University of Chicago Press.
Derrida, J. 1981. *Dissemination*. London: Althlone Press.
Dienstfrey, H. 1988. That Cosmopolitan Girl. *The Antioch Review*. 118(2): 430–436.
Dolly. 1994. Are You a Flirt? (March):46.
Dolly. 1994. I Got Drunk and Lost My Virginity. (October):108.
Dolly. 1994. The First Date: Don't Blow It. (October):76–80.
Donnelly, F. 1987. *The Youth Link Story*. Wellington: Allen and Unwin.
Donzelot, J. 1979. *The Policing of Families*. New York: Pantheon Books.
Dorn, N. 1983. *Alcohol, Youth and the State*. Canberra: Croom Helm.
Downes, D. 1966. *The Delinquent Solution*. London: Routledge and Kegan Paul.
Dreyfus, H. and P. Rabinow. 1982. *Michel Foucault: Beyond Structuralism and Hermeneutics*. Brighton: Harvester.
Eckermann, I. 1987. Selfhood versus Sainthood: Towards a Social Conception of Anorexia Nervosa. In S. Abraham and D. Llewellyn-Jones (eds.), *Eating Disorders and Disordered Eating*. Sydney: Ashwood House.
Edelstein, L. 1967. The Dietetics of Antiquity. In O. Temkin and C. Temkin (eds.), *Ancient Medicine: Selected Paper's of Ludwig Edelstein*. Baltimore: Johns Hopkins University Press.
Edwards, G. 1987. Anorexia and the Family. In M. Lawrence (ed.), *Fed Up and Hungry: Women, Oppression and Food*. London: Women's Press.
Elias, N. 1978. *The Civilising Process, Volume One: The History of Manners*. Oxford: Blackwell.
Ellis, H. 1946. *Studies in the Psychology of Sex*. London: Heinemann.
Embling, J. 1986. *Fragmented Lives: A Darker Side of Australian Life*. Ringwood: Penguin.
Emsley, C. 1982. *Crime and Society in England, 1750–1900*. London: Longman.
Ewald, F. 1991. Insurance and Risk. In G. Burchell, C. Gordon and P. Miller (eds.), *The Foucault Effect: Studies in Governmentality*. London: Harvester/Wheatsheaf.
Faust, B. 1980. *Women, Sex and Pornography*. Harmondsworth: Penguin.

Feighner, J., E. Robins, S. Guze, R. Woodruff, G. Winokur, and R. Munoz. 1972. Diagnostic Criteria for Use in Psychiatric Research. *Archives of General Psychiatry.* (26):57–63.

Finch, L. 1993. *The Classing Gaze: Sexuality, Class and Surveillance.* Sydney: Allen and Unwin.

Finn, B. (Chair). 1991. *Young People's Participation in Post-Compulsory Education and Training: Report of the Australian Education Council Review Committee.* Canberra: AGPS.

Finnane, M. 1989. Censorship and the Child: Explaining the Comics Campaign. *Australian Historical Studies.* 23(92):220–240.

Fopp, R. 1983. Youth Homelessness: Transition to Where? *Newsletter; National Clearinghouse for Youth Studies*, Part 1. 2(2):30–50.

Fopp, R. 1989. Homeless Young People in Australia: Estimating Numbers and Incidence. In Human Rights and Equal Opportunity Commission, (Chairman B. Burdekin), *Our Homeless Children.* Report of the National Inquiry into Homeless Children. Canberra: AGPS.

Forrester, L. 1993. Youth-Generated Cultures in Western Sydney. In R. White (ed.), *Youth Subcultures: Theory, History and the Australian Experience.* Hobart: National Clearinghouse for Youth Studies.

Foucault, M. 1965. *Madness and Civilisation.* London: Tavistock.

Foucault, M. 1972. *The Archaeology of Knowledge.* New York: Pantheon.

Foucault, M. 1973. *The Birth of the Clinic: An Archaeology of Medical Perception.* London: Tavistock.

Foucault, M. 1976. *The History of Sexuality, Volume 1: An Introduction.* Harmondsworth: Penguin.

Foucault, M. 1977. *Discipline and Punish: The Birth of the Prison.* Harmondsworth: Penguin.

Foucault, M. 1980. Truth and Power. In C. Gordon (ed.), *Selected Interviews and Other Writings 1972–1977 by Michel Foucault.* Brighton: Harvester Press.

Foucault, M. 1984a. On the Genealogy of Ethics: An Overview of Work in Progress. In P. Rabinow (ed.), *The Foucault Reader.* Harmondsworth: Penguin.

Foucault, M. 1984b. The Politics of Health in the Eighteenth Century. In P. Rabinow (ed.), *The Foucault Reader.* Harmondsworth: Penguin.

Foucault, M. 1984c. Space, Knowledge, Power. In P. Rabinow (ed.), *The Foucault Reader.* Harmondsworth: Penguin.

Foucault, M. 1987. *The History of Sexuality, Volume II: The Uses of Pleasure*. Harmondsworth: Penguin.

Foucault, M. 1988. Technologies of the Self. In L. Martin, H. Gutman, and P. Hutton (eds.), *Technologies of the Self*. Amherst: University of Massachusetts Press.

Foucault, M. 1989. *Resume Descours, 1970–1982*. Paris: Julliard.

Foucault, M. 1990. *The History of Sexuality, Volume III: The Care of the Self*. Harmondsworth: Penguin.

Foucault, M. 1991. Governmentality. In G. Burchell, C. Gordon and P. Miller (eds.), *The Foucault Effect: Studies in Governmentality*. London: Harvester Wheatsheaf.

Frazer, B. 1991. Alternatives to Unemployment: Some Outcomes of the Transition Education Program. *Youth Studies*. 10(3):50–53.

Freeland, J. 1991. Dislocated Transitions: Access and Participation for Disadvantaged Young People, Appendix 3. In B. Finn, (Chair), *Young People's Participation in Post-Compulsory Education and Training: Report of the Australian Education Council Review Committee. Canberra:* AGPS.

Freud, A. 1968. Adolescence. In A. Winder and D. Angus (eds.), *Adolescence: Contemporary Studies*. New York: American Books.

Friedan, B. 1963. *The Feminine Mystique*. New York: Dell.

Frow, J. 1987. The Subject of Law. In G. Wickham (ed.), *Social Theory and Legal Politic*. Sydney: Local Consumption.

Gagnon, J. and W. Simon. 1973. *Sexual Conduct*. Chicago: Aldine Publishing Co.

Garland, D. 1985. The Criminal and His Science. *British Journal of Criminology*. 25(2):109–113.

Garrett, C. 1992. *Anorexia Nervosa as Personal and Social Ritual*. Working Papers in Women's Studies, 6. University of Western Sydney.

Germann, G. 1972. *Gothic Revival in Europe and Britain: Sources, Influences and Ideas*. London: Lund Humphries.

Gilbert, P. and S. Taylor. 1991. *Fashioning the Feminine: Girls, Popular Culture and Schooling*. Sydney: Allen and Unwin.

Gilmour, A. 1989. *Innocent Victims: The Question of Child Abuse*. London: Michael Joseph.

Girlfriend. 1994. We Had Sex and Then He Dumped Me. (October):74–77.

Gleitman, H. 1981. *Psychology*. New York: Norton.

Glueck, S. and E. Glueck. (Eds.). 1972. *Identification of Predelinquents: Validation Studies and Some Suggested Uses of Glueck Table.* New York: Intercontinental Medical Book Corporation.

Goddu, T. 1995. Bloody Daggers and Lonesome Graveyards: The Gothic and Country Music. *The South Atlantic Quarterly.* (94):57–80.

Gokhale, S. 1987. Homeless Youth and Streetkids: Problems and Programs. *The Bulletin of the National Clearinghouse of Youth Studies.* 6(4):15–20.

Gordon, C. 1986. The Soul of the Citizen: Max Weber and Michel Foucault on Rationality and Government. In S. Lash and S. Whimster (eds.), *Max Weber, Rationality and Modernity.* London: Allen and Unwin.

Gordon, C. 1991. Governmental Rationality: An Introduction. In G. Burchell, C. Gordon and P. Miller (eds.), *The Foucault Effect: Studies in Governmentality.* London: Harvester Wheatsheaf.

Gramsci, A. 1957. *The Modern Prince, and Other Writings.* New York: International Publishers.

Gross, D. and D. Capuzzi. 1989. Defining Youth at Risk. In D. Capuzzi and D. Gross (eds.), *Youth at Risk:A Resource for Counselors, Teachers and Parents.* Alexandria: American Association for counseling and Development.

Hall, G. 1904. *Adolescence: Its Psychology, and Its Relation to Physiology, Anthropology, Sociology, Sex Crimes, Religion and Education.* 2 Volumes. New York: Appleton and Co.

Hall, S. and T. Jefferson. (eds.). 1976. *Resistance through Rituals.* London: Hutchinson.

Hamm, M. and W. Chambliss. 1994. *American Skinheads: The Criminology of Control and Hate Crime.* Westport: Praeger Publishers.

Hebdige, D. 1976. The Meaning of Mod. In S. Hall and T. Jefferson (eds.), *Resistance Through Rituals. London:* Hutchinson.

Hebdige, D. 1976. Reggae, Rudies and Rastas. In S. Hall and T. Jefferson (eds.), *Resistance through Rituals.* London:Hutchinson.

Hebdige, D. 1979. *Subculture:The Meaning of Style.* London: Methuen.

Hebdige, D. 1988. *Hiding in the Light.* London: Routledge.

Henisch, B. 1976. *Fast and Feast: Food in Medieval Society.* University Park: Pennsylvania State University Press.

Hindess, B. 1986. "Interests" in Political Analysis. In J. Law (ed.), *Power, Action Belief: A New Sociology of Knowledge*. London: Routledge and Kegan Paul.

Hirst, P. 1979. *On Law and Ideology*. New Jersey: Humanities Press.

Hirst, P. and P. Wooley. 1985. *Social Relations and Human Attributes*. London: Tavistock.

Hite, S. 1981. *The Hite Report*. New York: Dell.

Holland, J., C. Ramazanglu, S. Scott, S. Sharpe, and R. Thomson. 1991. Between Embarrassment and Trust: Young Women and Diversity of Condom Use. In P. Aggleton, G. Hart and P. Davies (eds.), *AIDS: Responses, Interventions and Care*. London: Falmer.

Homans, H. and P. Aggleton. 1988. Health Education, HIV Infection and AIDS. In P. Aggleton and H. Homans (eds.), *Social Aspects of AIDS*. London: Falmer.

Hunter, I. 1984. Laughter and Warmth: Sex Education in Victorian Secondary Schools. *Sex, Politics and Representation*. Sydney: Local Consumption.

Hunter, I. 1988a. Setting Limits to Culture. *New Formations*. 4, (Spring):103–121.

Hunter, I. 1988b. *Culture and Government: The Emergence of Literary Education*. London: MacMillan.

Hunter, I. 1990. Body Building and Self-Shaping: Mauss's Exemplary Sociology of Human Attributes. Paper presented at the Fifth Annual Meeting of the International Association for Philosophy and Literature, University of California.

Hunter, I. 1993a. The Pastoral Bureaucracy: Towards a Less Principled Understanding of State Schooling. In D. Meredyth and D. Tyler (eds.), *Child and Citizen: Genealogies of Schooling and Subjectivity*. Griffith University: Institute For Cultural Policy Studies.

Hunter, I. 1993b. Culture, Bureaucracy and the History of Popular Education. In D. Meredyth and D. Tyler (eds.), *Child and Citizen: Genealogies of Schooling and Subjectivity*. Griffith University: Institute For Cultural Policy Studies.

Hunter, I. 1993c. In What Sense Is Liberal Government "Liberal." Paper presented at the Governmentality Conference, Australian National University, Canberra, February.

Hyde, J. 1979. *Understanding Human Sexuality*. New York: McGraw Hill

Ingham, R., A. Woodcock, and K. Stenner. 1992. The Limitations of Rational Decision-making Models as Applied to Young People's Sexual Behaviour. In P. Aggleton, P. Davies and G. Hart (eds.), *AIDS: Rights, Risk and Reason*. London: Falmer.

Inquiry into Prostitution. 1985. *Final Report*. Government of Victoria.

Jackson, M. 1984. Sexology and the Social Construction of Male Sexuality. In L. Coveney, M. Jackson, S. Jeffreys, L. Kaye and P. Mahony (eds.), *The Sexuality Papers: Male Sexuality and the Social Control of Women*. London: Hutchinson.

Jakobson, R. 1988. Pike Polish Style: Le Brochet a la Polonaise. *Societies*. (19):11–16.

James, J. and J. Meyerding 1977. Early Sexual Experiences and Prostitution. *American Journal of Psychiatry*. 134(12):1381–1385.

Jefferson, S. 1976. Cultural Responses of the Teds. In S. Hall and T. Jefferson (eds.), *Resistance through Rituals*. London: Hutchinson.

Jenkins, R. 1983. *Lads, Citizens and Ordinary Kids: Working-Class Youth Life-styles in Belfast*. London: Routledge and Kegan Paul.

Johnson, L. 1993. *The Modern Girl: Girlhood and Growing Up*. Sydney: Allen and Unwin.

Jones, W. 1923a. Ancient Medicine. *Hippocrates*. Loeb Edition. Vol. I. London: Heinemann.

Jones, W. 1923b. Regimen in Health. *Hippocrates*.. Loeb Edition. Vol. IV. London: Heinemann.

Jones, W. 1923c. Aphorisms. *Hippocrates*. Loeb Edition, Vol. IV. London: Heinemann.

Kabala, M. 1986. The Labour Market Experience of Immigrant Youth. *Youth Studies*. 5(1):36–39.

Kaiser, K. 1979. The New Women's Magazines: It's the Same Old Story. *Frontiers*. (4):14–17.

Kamens, D. 1985. Youth and the State: A Cross-National Analysis of The Changing Status of Adolescence. *Comparative Political Studies*. 18(1):3–36.

Kessler, S., D. Ashenden, R. Connell and G. Dowsett. 1982. *Ockers and Disco-maniacs*. Sydney: Inner City Education Centre.

King, K. 1988. Youth Subcultures: A Search For Style. North Central Sociological Association, Association Paper.

Kinsey, A. 1953. *Sexual Behaviour in the Human Female.* Philadelphia: Saunders.

Kirk, D. 1993. *The Body, Schooling and Culture.* Geelong: Deakin University.

Kissane, K. 1985. Runaways. *The National Times.* May, p. 8.

Kog, E. and W. Vandereycken. 1989. The Facts: A Review of Research Data on Eating Disorder Families. In W. Vandereycken, E. Kog and J. Vanderlinden (eds.), *The Family Approach to Eating Disorders: Assessment and Treatment of Anorexia Nervosa and Bulimia.* New York: PMA.

Krenske, L. 1993. Boys Keep Swinging: The Social Construction of Corporeality and Gender Differences in Heavy Metal Music. Unpublished Honours Thesis, Department of Anthropology and Sociology, University of Queensland.

Kushman, J. and P. Kinney. 1989. Understanding and Preventing School Dropout. In D. Capuzzi and D. Gross (eds.), *Youth at Risk: A Resource for Counselors, Teachers and Parents.* Alexandria: American Association for Counseling and Development.

Laclau, E. and C. Mouffe. 1985. *Hegemony and Socialist Strategy: Towards a Radical Democratic Politics.* London: Verso.

LeBlanc, A. 1991. All Part of the Act: A Hundred Years of Costume in Anglo-American Popular Music. In P. Cunningham and S. Voso Lab (eds.), *Dress and Popular Culture.* Ohio: Bowling Green State University Popular Press.

Ledwon, L. 1993. Twin Peaks and the Television Gothic. *Literature/Film Quarterly.* 21(4):260–270.

Lees, C. 1988. Youth Tribes of Australia. *The Bulletin.* June 14:7–13.

Lehr, J. and H. Harris. 1988. *At-Risk, Low Achieving Student in the Classroom,* National Education Association: Washington D.C.

Locher, D. 1995. The Death of a Subculture: Youth, Music, and the Failure to Develop Group Identity. American Sociological Association, Association Paper.

Logan, G. 1991. *Sex Education in Queensland: A History of the Debate 1900–1980.* Queensland: Department of Education.

Lucas, A. 1981. Towards the Understanding of Anorexia Nervosa as a Disease Entity. *Mayo Clinic Proceedings.* (56):254–264.

Magarey, S. 1978. The Invention of Juvenile Delinquency in Early Nineteenth Century England. *Labour History.* (340):11–25.

Manning, A. 1958. *The Bodgie: A Study of Psychological Abnormality*, Sydney: Angus and Robertson.

Marx, K. 1964. *The German Ideology.* Moscow: Progress Publishers.

Marx, K. 1951. The Eighteenth Brumaire. In *Marx-Engles: Selected Works*, Vol. 1. London: Lawrence and Wishart.

Marx , K. and F. Engels. 1955. *The Communist Manifesto.* New York: Appleton.

Mason, G. 1990. *Youth Suicide in Australia: Prevention Strategies.* Department of Employment, Education and Training. Canberra: AGPS.

Mass, F. 1990. Becoming Adult: The Effects of Prolonged Dependence on Young People. *Youth Studies.* 9(1):24–29.

Masse, M. 1990. Gothic Repetition: Husbands, Horrors, and Things That Go Bump in the Night. *Signs.* 15(4):679–709.

Matza, D. and G. Sykes. 1961. Juvenile Delinquency and Subterranian Values. *American Sociological Review.* (26):712–19.

Mauss, M. 1973. Techniques of the Body. *Economy and Society.* 2(1):70–87.

Mauss, M. 1985. A Category of Human Mind: The Notion of the Person; the Notion of the Self. In M. Carrithers, S. Collins and S. Lukes (eds.), *The Category of the Person: Anthropology, Philosophy, History.* Cambridge: Cambridge University Press.

Mayer, E. (Chair) 1992. *Putting General Education to Work: The Key Competencies Report.* Canberra: Australian Education Council.

McAllister, I. 1986. Explaining Unemployment: Australian and Immigrant Youth Compared. *Search.* 17(5–6):122–125.

McCallum, D. 1993. Problem Children and Familial Relations. In D. Meredyth and D. Tyler (eds.), *Child and Citizen: Genealogies of Schooling and Subjectivity.* Griffith University: Institute for Cultural Policy Studies.

McFadden, M. 1993. Youth Subcultures and Resistance: Desparately Seeking Solutions. In R. White (ed.), *Youth Subcultures: Theory, History and the Australian Experience.* Hobart: National Clearinghouse for Youth Studies.

McMahon, K. 1990. The *Cosmopolitan* Ideology and the Management of Desire. *The Journal of Sex Research.* 27(3):381–396.

McIntyre, S. 1991. *A Colonial Liberalism*. Melbourne: Oxford University Press.

McRobbie, A. 1980. Settling Accounts with Sub-cultures: A Feminist Critique. *Screen Education*. (Spring):37–50.

McRobbie, A. 1982. *Jackie*: An Ideology of Adolescent Femininity. In B. Waites, T. Bennett and G. Martin (eds.), *Popular Culture: Past and Present*. London: Croom Helm and Open University Press.

Mears, A. 1973. *Dialogue With Youth*. London: Fontana.

Meredyth, D. 1993. Twenty nimutes for the Heart: Pacing the Exercise of Critique. In D. Bennett (ed.) *Cultural Studies: Pluralism and Theory*. Melbourne: Melbourne University Literary and Culrual Studies.

Miller, P. and M. Fowlkes. 1987. Social and Behavioural Constructions of Female Sexuality. In S. Harding and J. O'Barr (eds.), *Sex and Scientific Inquiry*. Chicago: University of Chicago Press.

Miller, P. and N. Rose. 1990. Governing Economic Life. *Economy and Society*. 19(1):1–31.

Mort, F. 1987. *Dangerous Sexualities: Medico-Moral Politics in England Since 1830*. London: Routledge and Kegan Paul.

Moysey, S. 1993. Marxism and Subculture. In R. White (ed.), *Youth Subculture: Theory, History and the Australian Experience*. Hobart: National Clearinghouse for Youth Studies.

Muncie, J. 1984. *The Trouble with Kids Today: Youth and Crime in Post-War Britain*. London: Hutchinson.

Mungham, J. and G. Pearson (eds.). 1976. *Working Class Youth Culture*. London: Routledge and Kegan Paul.

Murdock, G. and R. McCron. 1976. Youth and Class: The Career of Confusion. In J. Mungham. and Pearson, G. (eds.), *Working Class Youth Culture*. London: Routledge and Kegan Paul.

Mussell, K. 1983. But Why Do They Read Those Things? The Female Audience and the Gothic Novel. In J. Fleenor (ed.), *The Female Gothic*. Montreal: Eden.

Nardini, M. and R. Antes. 1991. An At-Risk Assessment: Teachers Rate Their Students on Academic Skills and Behaviour. *The Clearing House*. (65):56–62.

National Clearinghouse for Youth Studies. 1989. *Responses to Burdekin: Selected Responses to "Our Homeless Youth."* Hobart: NCYS.

Neil, A. 1968. *Summerhill*. Harmondsworth: Penguin.

Neuman, P. and P. Halvorson. 1983. *Anorexia Nervosa and Bulimia: A Handbook for Counselors and Therapists.* New York: Van Nostrand Reinhold.

Nordquist, B. 1991. Punks. In P. Cunningham and S. Voso Lab (eds.), *Dress and Popular Culture.* Ohio: Bowling Green State University Popular Press.

O'Brien, M. 1990. Reaching the Unreachable. In P. Crane, G. Embelton, S. Harris and M. Stokes (eds.), *Participants Manual.* Queensland: Youth Sector Training Program, Division of Youth, 9.5.

O'Connor, I. 1989. *Our Homeless Youth: Their Experiences.* Report to the National Inquiry into Homeless Children by the Human Rights and Equal Opportunities Commission. Canberra: AGPS.

O'Farrell, C. 1990. *Foucault: Historian or Philosopher?* London: MacMillan.

Ogden, E. and V. Germinario. 1988. *The At-Risk Student: Answers for Educators.* Lancaster: Technomic.

O'Hagan, K. 1989. *Working With Child Sexual Abuse: A Post-Cleveland Guide to Effective Principles and Practice.* Milton Keynes: University Press.

Ong, W. 1982. *Orality and Literacy: The Technologizing of The Word.* New York: Methuen.

Orbach, S. 1978. *Fat Is a Feminist Issue.* London: Paddington Press.

Orren, K. 1991. *Belated Feudalism: Labor, The Law and Liberal Development in the USA.* Cambridge: Cambridge University Press.

Palazzoli, S. 1974. *Self Starvation: From the Intrapsychic to the Transpersonal Approach to Anorexia Nervosa.* London: Human Context Books.

Palmo, A. and D. Palmo. 1989. The Harmful Effects of Dysfunctional Family Dynamics. In D. Capuzzi and D. Gross (eds.), *Youth at Risk: A Resource for Counselors, Teachers and Parents.* Alexandria: American Association for Counseling and Development.

Parker, L. and J. Offer. 1987. Girls, Boys and Lower Secondary School Achievement: The Shifting Scene 1972–1986. *Unicorn.* 13(3):148–154.

Pearson, G. 1983. *Hooligan: A History of Respectable Fears.* London: MacMillan.

Pearson, K. 1979. *Surfing Subcultures.* St Lucia: University of Queensland Press.

Peirce, K. 1990. A Feminist Theoretical Perspective on the Socialisation of Teenage Girls Through *Seventeen* Magazine. *Sex Roles.* 23(9/10):491–500.

Petrie, S. 1986. *Child Abuse and Neglect: Guidelines For School Personnel*, Brisbane: Brisbane College of Advanced Education.

Philips, D. 1980. "A New Engine of Power and Authority": The Institutionalisation of Law Enforcement in England, 1780–1830. In V. Gatrell (ed.), *Crime and the Law.* London: Europa Publications.

Phillips, E. 1973. *Greek Medicine.* London: Thames and Hudson.

Pilkington, N. and L. Sara. 1991. Youth and the Language of AIDS. *Youth Studies.* 10(1):26–31.

Polanyi, K. 1944. *The Great Transformation.* Boston: Beacon.

Polk, K. 1993. Reflections on Youth Subcultures. In R. White (ed.), *Youth Subcultures: Theory, History and the Australian Experience.* Hobart: National Clearinghouse for Youth Studies.

Poster, M. 1984. *Foucault, Marxism and History: Mode of Production Versus Mode of Information.* Cambridge: Polity Press.

Potter, S. and H. Smith. 1976. Sex Education as Viewed by Unwed Mothers. *Intellect.* (104):515–516.

Potterat, J. 1985. On Becoming a Prostitute: An Exploratory Case-Comparison Study. *Journal of Sex Research.* 21(3):329–335.

Powell, J. 1978. *Why Am I Afraid to Tell You Who I Am?* Miles: Argus.

Powles, M. 1992. In Like Finn: Access to TAFE in the Context of the Finn Review. *Unicorn.* 18(1):56–61.

Queensland Department of Education. 1988. *Human Relationships Education for Queensland State Schools: Interim Policy and Guidelines Statement.* Queensland.

Rea, J. 1986. Girls Talk: 100 Girls at Risk. *Youth Studies.* (5:3):7–11.

Reiger, K. 1985. *The Disenchantment of the Home: Modernising the Australian Family.* Melbourne: Oxford University Press.

Restuccia, F. 1986. Female Gothic Writing: Under Cover with Alice. *Genre.* (18):245–266.

Rhodes, T. and R. Hartnoll. 1991. Reaching the Hard to Reach: Models of HIV Outreach Health Education. In P. Aggleton, G. Hart and P. Davies (eds.), *AIDS: Responses, Interventions and Care.* London: Falmer.

Robinson, S. 1989. Why Say No?: substance abuse among teenagers. In D. Capuzzi and D. Gross (eds.), *Youth at Risk: A Resource for Counselors,*

Teachers and Parents, American Association for Counseling and Development: Alexandria.

Roberts-Yates, C. 1990. Developing a Project to Improve Employability for Secondary Students with Special Education Needs. *Australian Journal of Special Education.* 14(1):38–42.

Rowse, T. 1992. Perspectives on the Cultures of Sexuality among Central Australian Aboriginal People. Paper presented to the History of the Present Group, Melbourne.

Rose, N. 1985. *The Psychological Complex: Psychology, Politics and Society in England 1869–1939.* London: Routledge and Kegan Paul.

Rose, N. 1988. Calculable Minds and Manageable Individuals. *History of the Human Sciences.* 1(2):179–199.

Rose, N. 1990. *Governing the Soul: The Shaping of the Private Self.* London: Routledge.

Rose, N. and P. Miller. 1992. Political Power Beyond the State: Problematics of Government. *British Journal of Sociology.* 43(2):173–205.

Rose, N. 1993. Government, Authority and Expertise in Advanced Liberalism, *Economy and Society.* 22(3):283–299.

Ruggiero, J. and L. Western. 1977. Sex-Role Characterisation of Women in "Modern Gothic" Novels. *Pacific Sociological Review.* 20(2):279–300.

Sandberg, D. 1989. *The Child Abuse-Delinquency Connection.* Lexington: Lexington Books.

Schwartz, B., J. Horowitz and A. Cardarelli. 1990. *Child Sexual Abuse: The Initial Effects.* London: Sage.

Schwartz, V. 1987. Does Jill Come Tumbling After? Let's Look at Girls in Education. *Unicorn.* 13(3):132–138.

Select Committe on HIV, Illegal Drugs and Prostitution, 1991. *Prostitution in the ACT—Interim Report.* Legislative Assembly for the Australian Capital Territory.

Senate Standing Committee on Social Welfare. 1982. *Report on Homeless Youth.* Parliamentary Paper No. 231/1982.

Seventeen. 1992. Pucker Up: How to Get You and Your Lips Ready For Action. (February):20.

Seventeen. 1993. Making the First Move? (October):130–134.

Shaw, C. and H. McKay. 1929. *Juvenile Delinquency and Urban Areas.* Chicago: University of Chicago Press.

Sheridan, A. 1980. *Michel Foucault: The Will to Truth*. London: Tavistock.
Shuker, R. 1989. From Bodgies to Gothics: Pop Culture and Moral Panic in New Zealand. *New Zealand Sociology*. 4(1):1–17.
Silbert, M. and A. Pines. 1982. Entrance into Prostitution, *Youth and Society*. 13(4):471–500.
Simoons, F. 1961. *Eat Not This Flesh: Food Avoidances in the Old World*. Madison: University of Wisconsin Press.
Smart, B. 1986. The Politics of Truth and the Problems of Hegemony. In D. Hoy (ed.), *Foucault: A Critical Reader*. Oxford: Blackwell.
Smith, B. 1989. Discipline: From the Classroom to the Community. Griffith University: Occasional Paper.
Smith, P. and D. Mumford. 1985. *Adolescent Reproductive Health*. New York: Gardner Press.
Sobski, J. 1992. Pathways to Finn. *Unicorn*. 18(1):49–55.
Solomos, J. 1988. *Black Youth, Racism and the State: The Politics of Ideology and Policy*. Cambridge: Cambridge University Press.
Sommerville, J. 1982. *The Rise and Fall of Childhood*. Beverly Hills: Sage.
Stow, D. 1850. *The Training System of Education*. London: Longman, Green, Longman and Roberts.
Stratton, J. 1985. Youth Subcultures and Their Cultural Contexts. *Australian and New Zealand Journal of Sociology*. 21(2):194–218.
Stratton, J. 1993. Bodgies and Widgies: Just Working Class Kids Doing Working-Class Things. In R. White (ed.), *Youth Subcultures: Theory, History and the Australian Experience*. Hobart: National Clearinghouse for Youth Studies.
Strober, M. 1986. Anorexia Nervosa: History and Psychological Concepts. In K. Brownell and J. Foreyt (eds.), *Handbook of Eating Disorders: Physiology, Psychology and Treatment of Obesity, Anorexia, and Bulimia*. New York: Basic Books.
Sugar, M. 1990. *Atypical Adolescence and Sexuality*. New York: Norton. New York.
Sullivan, G. and P. O'Connor. 1988. Women's Role Portrayals in Magazine Advertising: 1958–1983. *Sex Roles*. (18):181–188.
Swanson, M. 1991. *At-Risk Students in Elementary Education: Effective Schools for Disadvantaged Learners*. Illinois: Thomas Books.

Sweet, R. 1982. *Some Indicators of Teenage Girls' Disadvantaged Labour Market Status.* New South Wales: Department of Technical and Further Education.

Sweet, R. 1987. *The Youth Labour Market: A Twenty Year Perspective.* Canberra: Curriculum Development Centre.

Tagg, J. 1981. Power and Photography—A Means of Surveillance: The Photograph as Evidence in Law. In T. Bennett et. al. (eds.), *Culture, Ideology and the Social Process.* London: Batsford.

Teen. 1993. Ten Guy Goof-Up You Gotta Avoid: Find Out What Really Turns Them Off. (March):12–14.

Teen. 1993. I Had Sex with Him and Now I'm Sorry. (November):42–43.

Thrasher, F. 1927. *The Gang.* Chicago: University of Chicago Press.

Tomlinson, S. 1982. *A Sociology of Special Education.* London: Routledge and Kegan Paul.

Toumey, C. 1992. The Moral Character of Mad Scientists: A Cultural Critique of Science. *Science, Technology and Human Values.* 17(4):411–437.

Turley, P. 1988. Homeless Young People: A Psychological Study. *Youth Studies.* 7(3):23–27.

Turner, B. 1982a. The Government of the Body: Medical Regimens and the Rationalisation of Diet. *The British Journal of Sociology.* 32(2):254–269.

Turner, B. 1982b. The Discourse of Diet. *Theory, Culture and Society.* (1):23–32.

Tyler, D. 1992. "Going Like a Boy": Making Up Girls in the 1930s Kindergarten. Paper presented at the Australian Sociological Association Conference, Flinders University, December.

Tyler, D. 1993. Making Better Children. In D. Meredyth and D. Tyler (eds.), *Child and Citizen: Genealogies of Schooling and Subjectivity.* Griffith University: Institute For Cultural Policy Studies.

Vandereycken, W. and R. Meermann. 1984. *Anorexia Nervosa: A Clinician's Guide to Treatment.* Berlin: Walter de Gruyter.

Van Reyk, P. 1985. Shelter or the Streets: Young People and the Housing Crisis. *Impact.* 15(2):21–30.

Walker, J. 1985. Rebels with Our Applause? A Critique of Resistance Theory in Willis' Ethnography of Schooling. *The Journal of Schooling.* 167(2):63–83.

Walker, J. 1986. Romanticising Resistance, Romanticising Culture: A Critique of Willis' Theory of Cultural Production. *The British Journal of Sociology.* 7(1):59–80.

Walker, J. 1988. *Louts and Legends: Male Youth Culture in an Inner City School.* Sydney: Allen and Unwin.

Walker, L. 1993. Girls, Schooling and Subcultures of Resistance. In R. White (ed.), *Youth Subcultures: Theory, History and the Australian Experience.* Hobart: National Clearinghouse for Youth Studies.

Wallace, C. and M. Cross. 1990. *Youth in Transition: The Sociology of Youth and Youth Policy.* London: Falmer.

Ward, J. 1988. Increased Retention to the Senior Years of High School: Some Considerations. *Youth Studies.* 7(3): 8–10.

Watt, I. 1990. Identification of a Child in Difficulty. In P. Crane, G. Embelton, S. Harris, and M. Stokes (eds.), *Participants Manual.* Queensland: Youth Sector Training Program, Division of Youth.

Weeks, J. 1981. *Sex, Politics and Society: The Regulation of Sexuality Since 1880.* London: Longman.

Weeks, J. 1986. *Sexuality and Its Discontents.* New York: Routledge.

Weinstein, D. and R. Bell. 1982. *Saints and Society: The Two Worlds of Western Christendom, 1000–1700.* Chicago: The University of Chicago Press.

Welbourne, J. and J. Purgold. 1986. *The Eating Sickness: Anorexia, Bulimia and the Myth of Suicide by Slimming.* Brighton: Harvester Press.

Wellings, K. 1986. *First Love, First Sex: A Practical Guide to Relationships.* London: Greenhouse.

Wellings, K. 1988. Perceptions of Risk: Media Treatments of AIDS. In P. Aggleton and H. Homans (eds.), *Social Aspects of AIDS.* London: Falmer.

Went, D. 1985. *Sex Education: Some Guidelines for Teachers.* Bell and Hyman: London.

Western, L. and J. Ruggerio. 1978. Male-Female Relationships in Best-Selling Modern Gothic Novels. *Sex Roles.* 4(5):647–655.

White, R. 1993. *Youth Subcultures: Theory, History and the Australian Experience.* Hobart: National Clearinghouse for Youth Studies.

Wickham, G. 1990. Sport and the Formation of Manners. Paper presented at the Australian Sociological Association Conference at the University of Queensland, St. Lucia, Brisbane.

Wickham, G. 1993. Citizenship, Governance and the Consumption of Sport. Paper presented at the Australian Sociological Association Conference at MacQuarrie University, December, Sydney.

Widdicombe, S. and R. Wooffitt. 1990. Being Versus Doing Punk: On Achieving Authenticity as a Member. *Journal of Language and Social Psychology.* 9(4):257–277.

Willis, P. 1977. *Learning to Labour: How Working Class Kids Get Working Class Jobs.* Farnborough: Saxon House.

Willis, P. 1978. *Profane Culture.* London: Routledge and Kegan Paul.

Willis, P. 1990. *Common Culture: Report of the Gulbenkien Inquiry.* Milton Keynes: Open University Press. (Abridged as *Moving Culture).*

Wilson, P. 1982. *Runaway Behaviour and its Consequences.* Report to the Criminal Research Council.

Wilson, P. and J. Arnold. 1986. *Street Kids: Australia's Alienated Young.* Victoria: Collins Dove.

Wilson, S. 1981. The Image of Women in Canadian Magazines. In E. Katz and T. Szecsko (eds.), *Mass Media and Social Change.* London: Sage.

Wilton, T. and P. Aggleton. 1991. Condoms, Coercion and Control: Heterosexuality and the Limits to HIV/AIDS Education. In P. Aggleton, G. Hart and P. Davies (eds.), *AIDS: Responses, Interventions and Care.* London: Falmer.

Windschuttle, K. 1984. *The Media.* Harmondsworth: Penguin.

Winick, C. and P. Kinsie. 1971. *The Lively Commerce: Prostitution in the United States.* Chicago: Quadrangle Books.

Wolf, N. 1990. *The Beauty Myth,* London: Chatto and Windus.

Wolfe, L. 1981. *The Cosmo Report.* New York: Arbor House.

Wolfman, B. and J. Money. 1980. *Handbook of Human Sexuality.* New Jersey: Prentice-Hall.

Women's Coordination Unit, Premier's Department. 1986. *Girls at Risk.* Sydney: Report to Premier of NSW.

Wynn, J. and R. White. 1997. *Rethinking Youth.* Sydney: Allen and Unwin.

Young, K. and L. Craig. 1997. Beyond White Pride: Identity, Meaning and Contradiction in the Canadian Skinhead Culture. *Canadian Review of Sociology and Anthropology.* (34):175–206.

INDEX

A

adolescence, 7, 11, 48, 55, 72, 79, 84–90, 100, 103, 145, 147, 151, 155, 162, 167, 204, 209
anorexia aervosa, 10, 11, 136, 171–202
Aries, Phillipe, 79, 80, 221

B

Bennett, Tony, 36, 37, 165,
Bruch, Hilde, 173, 179, 186, 199
Brumberg, Joan, 185–188, 194–198
Burdekin Report, 51–54, 91, 92, 205
Bynum, Caroline, 177, 181–185

C

Carrington, Kerry, 94, 95, 216
Castel, Robert, 114–121, 224
Centre for Contemporary Cultural Studies (CCCS), 1, 13–36, 39, 40, 43–50, 53, 54, 56, 140
child, the, 7, 11, 46, 54, 55, 71, 78–89, 94, 99, 100, 103, 107, 131, 143, 145, 159, 194, 196, 205
childhood, 47, 52, 53, 59, 69–73, 78–86, 89, 94, 107, 110, 112, 118, 122, 128, 131, 132, 143, 145, 146, 150, 156, 192, 217,
Christianity, 3, 7, 10, 55, 73, 75, 100, 143, 150, 153, 171, 173, 176, 177, 180–182, 186, 204
Cleo, 146, 151, 157, 163,
consciousness, 5, 13, 18, 25–28, 32–34, 37–45, 50, 51, 54, 139, 142, 144, 209
consciousness, generational, 6, 15, 17, 18, 39, 54, 218
Cosmopolitan, 146, 149, 151–158, 161, 163, 167
counterhegemonic struggle, 17, 45

D

delinquency, 5, 6, 11, 13, 21, 22, 47, 48, 54, 55, 79, 86, 88, 89, 91, 94, 100, 107, 111–113, 116, 120, 121, 123, 130, 204, 205, 216
dietary Regimen, 83, 163, 171, 175–178, 189, 190, 200
discipline, 2, 7, 46, 61, 62,

83, 86, 87, 109, 111, 112, 119, 164, 166
Donzelot, Jacques, 69, 80, 94, 132

E

Ewald, Francois, 113, 114, 119, 227
expertise, 6–8, 11, 45, 64, 66, 68–73, 79, 85, 91, 93, 99, 100, 116, 120–122, 125, 134, 143, 154, 155, 157, 159, 161, 169, 195, 196, 198, 204

F

family, the, 4, 6, 8, 11, 52–53, 60, 61, 69–73, 79-96, 99–101, 106–112, 115–118, 121, 129–134, 140, 148, 159, 169, 192–198, 203, 208, 215, 217
fasting, 10, 11, 171, 172, 173, 176–187, 191, 193–200
femininity, 5, 10, 97, 147, 148, 163, 165, 168–171, 179, 180, 185, 199
Finn Report, 8, 101–105, 108, 122–131
Foucault, Michel, 3, 7, 9, 26, 27, 30–40, 46, 49, 54, 57–65, 73–82, 86, 87, 133, 141, 144–153, 166, 169, 174–176, 180, 188, 189, 191–193, 203, 205

G

Goths, 209–217
government at a distance, 64, 68–71, 95, 131
government, the limits of, 55, 65, 96, 98
governmentality, 5–7, 11, 26, 30, 55, 59, 61–65, 73, 86, 99, 132, 142, 203, 206

H

habitus, 3, 4, 9–11, 97, 133, 144–146, 149, 160, 162, 164–169, 183, 200, 205, 218
Hebdige, Dick, 5, 14, 15, 19, 20, 22, 29, 33, 40, 41, 44, 46, 47, 165
hegemony, critiques of, 5, 13, 15, 26, 27, 35–39, 44, 54, 140, 209
HIV/AIDS, 55, 96, 97, 204,
Hunter, Ian, 34, 41–43, 68, 83, 142
hysteria, 193–195

I

ideology, critiques of, 5, 16, 22, 24–35, 38–45, 147, 149, 205
imitatio Christi, 10, 171, 183, 186
individuation/normalization, 7, 70, 85, 87, 142, 192, 215

L

liberalism, 65–68, 95

Index

M

Mauss, Marcell, 3, 9, 137, 138, 162, 173, 203
McCallum, David, 88, 111, 112, 129
McRobbie, Angela, 23, 147, 163, 218
Mods, 15, 19, 20, 23, 40, 210, 215, 217

N

neo-liberalism, 67–71, 95

P

piety, 11, 177, 180–186, 195, 200
population, the, 5, 7–9, 11, 13, 31, 54, 55, 61, 62, 65, 66, 73, 76, 77, 81–84, 87, 94, 99, 100, 107, 112–115, 119–123, 129, 134, 141, 142, 145, 152. 154, 157–160, 171, 180, 188–190, 192–195, 204, 207, 217, 219
power, 1–6, 11, 13–16, 24–39, 44–46, 49, 54–70, 74–78, 99, 119, 134, 140, 141, 147, 149, 160, 170, 188, 189, 203, 206, 207, 218
practices of the self, 8, 11, 132–134, 146, 149, 160, 162, 166, 171, 205
problem children, 84, 88, 89
psychology, 2, 11, 45, 47, 55, 66, 69–78, 85, 87–91, 93, 100, 111, 112, 118, 135, 137, 143, 145, 149, 153–162, 167, 172, 184, 187, 193, 197, 198, 204,
punk, 209–212,

R

Resistance through Rituals, 17, 210
risk, 8, 57, 84, 101, 103, 105–131, 158, 217
risk, at-risk youth, 7, 8, 53, 101, 104–106, 107, 109, 111–118, 121–125, 129–131, 206
risk, family, 109–111, 129, 131
risk, risk factors, 107, 108, 110, 116, 119, 121–125, 131
Rose, Nik, 3, 47, 58, 63–68, 72, 79, 87, 88, 94, 95, 112, 143, 154, 155, 166, 192, 193, 203, 212

S

schooling, 2, 72, 83, 84, 85, 86, 104, 106–109, 122, 125, 126
self, the, 3, 8, 9, 10, 34, 67, 112, 123, 132–153, 159–162, 165, 166, 168–180, 198, 199, 205, 207, 212
self-government, 3, 8, 10, 96, 132, 134, 141, 144, 146, 156–161, 164, 168, 174, 205
self-interrogation/confession, 9, 75, 100, 160–162, 166, 167, 205

sex, 1–10, 50, 54, 55, 72–89, 93, 95–101, 105, 126, 130–136, 140, 144–169, 175, 178, 180, 190, 198, 200, 203, 206, 212, 219,
sexuality, 7, 26, 73–76, 80, 100, 148–151, 204
sovereignty, 7, 55, 58–64, 99, 203
St. Catherine of Siena, 184, 186, 199
state, the, 7, 11, 24, 27–30, 37, 49, 55–71, 79, 85, 88, 92, 94, 99, 104, 130, 134, 139, 141, 144, 154, 167, 172, 174, 184, 204, 206, 207
style, 3, 13–15, 19–21, 29, 33, 40, 44, 54, 65, 140, 163–165, 211, 212, 218
subculture theory, 1–6, 12–54, 140, 165, 203–218
surveillance, 46, 78, 84, 85, 115, 118, 140, 206

T

Teddy Boys, 17, 40, 209
transition, 8, 61, 101–105, 108, 122–125, 127–130, 167, 168, 182
truth, 28–38, 49, 75, 77, 136, 142, 197
Tyler, Debbie, 84, 85

W

Willis, Paul, 14, 23, 165,

Y

young women's magazines, 4, 9, 133, 146–169, 219
youth homelessness, 49–51, 92, 218
youth prostitution, 91–93,
youth suicide, 90, 94, 217

 **ERUPTIONS**
New Thinking across the Disciplines

Erica McWilliam
General Editor

This is a series of red-hot women's writing after the "isms." It focuses on new cultural assemblages that are emerging from the de-formation, breakout, ebullience, and discomfort of postmodern feminism. The series brings together a post-foundational generation of women's writing that, while still respectful of the idea of situated knowledge, does not rely on neat disciplinary distinctions and stable political coalitions. This writing transcends some of the more awkward textual performances of a first generation of "feminism-meets-postmodernism" scholarship. It has come to terms with its own body of knowledge as shifty, inflammatory, and ungovernable.

The aim of the series is to make this cutting edge thinking more readily available to undergraduate and postgraduate students, researchers and new academics, and professional bodies and practitioners. Thus, we seek contributions from writers whose unruly scholastic projects are expressed in texts that are accessible and seductive to a wider academic readership.

Proposals and/or manuscripts are invited from the domains of: "post" humanities, human movement studies, sexualities, media studies, literary criticism, information technologies, history of ideas, performing arts, gay and lesbian studies, cultural studies, post-colonial studies, pedagogics, social psychology, and the philosophy of science. We are particularly interested in publishing research and scholarship with international appeal from Australia, New Zealand, and the United Kingdom.

For further information about the series and for the submission of manuscripts, please contact:

> Erica McWilliam
> Faculty of Education
> Queensland University of Technology
> Victoria Park Rd., Kelvin Grove Q 4059
> Australia

To order other books in this series, please contact our Customer Service Department at:

> (800) 770-LANG (within the U.S.)
> (212) 647-7706 (outside the U.S.)
> (212) 647-7707 FAX

Or browse online by series at:
> www.peterlang.com